# 2018 SUPPLEMENT TO
# AMERICAN CRIMINAL PROCEDURE
## CASES AND COMMENTARY

## Eleventh Edition

■ ■ ■

### Stephen A. Saltzburg
*Wallace and Beverley Woodbury University Professor,*
*The George Washington University School of Law*

### Daniel J. Capra
*Philip D. Reed Professor of Law,*
*Fordham University School of Law*

**AMERICAN CASEBOOK SERIES®**

*American Casebook Series* is a trademark registered in the U.S. Patent and Trademark Office.

© 2018 LEG, Inc. d/b/a West Academic
        444 Cedar Street, Suite 700
        St. Paul, MN 55101
        1-877-888-1330

West, West Academic Publishing, and West Academic are trademarks of West Publishing Corporation, used under license.

Printed in the United States of America

**ISBN:** 978-1-64020-833-9

# TABLE OF CONTENTS

# TABLE OF CASES

The principal cases are in bold type.

# TABLE OF AUTHORITIES

# 2018 SUPPLEMENT TO

# AMERICAN CRIMINAL PROCEDURE

## CASES AND COMMENTARY

## Eleventh Edition

# CHAPTER 2

## SEARCHES AND SEIZURES OF PERSONS AND THINGS

■ ■ ■

## II. THRESHOLD REQUIREMENTS FOR FOURTH AMENDMENT PROTECTIONS: WHAT IS A "SEARCH"? WHAT IS A "SEIZURE"?

### D. APPLICATIONS OF THE REASONABLE EXPECTATION OF PRIVACY ANALYSIS (WITH THE TRESPASS SUPPLEMENT)

3. Access by Members of the Public—The Third Party Doctrine

   d. *Cellphone Location, Subscriber Information, etc.*

**Page 75. The Text flags the Supreme Court's forthcoming decision in *Carpenter*. Here is that decision.**

### CARPENTER v. UNITED STATES
Supreme Court of the United States, 2018.
138 S. Ct. 2206.

**CHIEF JUSTICE ROBERTS delivered the opinion of the Court.**

This case presents the question whether the Government conducts a search under the Fourth Amendment when it accesses historical cell phone records that provide a comprehensive chronicle of the user's past movements.

### I

### A

There are 396 million cell phone service accounts in the United States—for a Nation of 326 million people. Cell phones perform their wide and growing variety of functions by connecting to a set of radio antennas called "cell sites." Although cell sites are usually mounted on a tower, they can also be found on light posts, flagpoles, church steeples, or the sides of buildings. Cell sites have several directional antennas that divide the covered area into sectors.

Cell phones continuously scan their environment looking for the best signal, which generally comes from the closest cell site. Most modern devices, such as smartphones, tap into the wireless network several times a minute whenever their signal is on, even if the owner is not using one of the phone's features. Each time the phone connects to a cell site, it generates a time-stamped record known as cell-site location information (CSLI). The precision of this information depends on the size of the geographic area covered by the cell site. The greater the concentration of cell sites, the smaller the coverage area. As data usage from cell phones has increased, wireless carriers have installed more cell sites to handle the traffic. That has led to increasingly compact coverage areas, especially in urban areas.

Wireless carriers collect and store CSLI for their own business purposes, including finding weak spots in their network and applying "roaming" charges when another carrier routes data through their cell sites. In addition, wireless carriers often sell aggregated location records to data brokers, without individual identifying information of the sort at issue here. While carriers have long retained CSLI for the start and end of incoming calls, in recent years phone companies have also collected location information from the transmission of text messages and routine data connections. Accordingly, modern cell phones generate increasingly vast amounts of increasingly precise CSLI.

## B

In 2011, police officers arrested four men suspected of robbing a series of Radio Shack and (ironically enough) T-Mobile stores in Detroit. One of the men confessed that, over the previous four months, the group (along with a rotating cast of getaway drivers and lookouts) had robbed nine different stores in Michigan and Ohio. The suspect identified 15 accomplices who had participated in the heists and gave the FBI some of their cell phone numbers; the FBI then reviewed his call records to identify additional numbers that he had called around the time of the robberies.

Based on that information, the prosecutors applied for court orders under the Stored Communications Act to obtain cell phone records for petitioner Timothy Carpenter and several other suspects. That statute, as amended in 1994, permits the Government to compel the disclosure of certain telecommunications records when it "offers specific and articulable facts showing that there are reasonable grounds to believe" that the records sought "are relevant and material to an ongoing criminal investigation." 18 U. S. C. § 2703(d). Federal Magistrate Judges issued two orders directing Carpenter's wireless carriers—MetroPCS and

Sprint—to disclose "cell/site sector [information] for [Carpenter's] telephone[ ] at call origination and at call termination for incoming and outgoing calls" during the four-month period when the string of robberies occurred. The first order sought 152 days of cell-site records from MetroPCS, which produced records spanning 127 days. The second order requested seven days of CSLI from Sprint, which produced two days of records covering the period when Carpenter's phone was "roaming" in northeastern Ohio. Altogether the Government obtained 12,898 location points cataloging Carpenter's movements—an average of 101 data points per day.

Carpenter was charged with six counts of robbery and an additional six counts of carrying a firearm during a federal crime of violence. See 18 U. S. C. §§ 924(c), 1951(a). Prior to trial, Carpenter moved to suppress the cell-site data provided by the wireless carriers. He argued that the Government's seizure of the records violated the Fourth Amendment because they had been obtained without a warrant supported by probable cause. The District Court denied the motion.

At trial, seven of Carpenter's confederates pegged him as the leader of the operation. In addition, FBI agent Christopher Hess offered expert testimony about the cell-site data. Hess explained that each time a cell phone taps into the wireless network, the carrier logs a time-stamped record of the cell site and particular sector that were used. With this information, Hess produced maps that placed Carpenter's phone near four of the charged robberies. In the Government's view, the location records clinched the case: They confirmed that Carpenter was "right where the . . . robbery was at the exact time of the robbery." Carpenter was convicted on all but one of the firearm counts and sentenced to more than 100 years in prison.

The Court of Appeals for the Sixth Circuit affirmed. The court held that Carpenter lacked a reasonable expectation of privacy in the location information collected by the FBI because he had shared that information with his wireless carriers. Given that cell phone users voluntarily convey cell-site data to their carriers as "a means of establishing communication," the court concluded that the resulting business records are not entitled to Fourth Amendment protection. (quoting Smith v. Maryland, 442 U. S. 735, 741 (1979)).

We granted certiorari.

## II

### A

[The Chief Justice wrote that the basic purpose of the Fourth Amendment "is to safeguard the privacy and security of individuals against arbitrary invasions by government officials." He described the historical emphasis on trespass and physical intrusion as the focus of Fourth Amendment cases before the Court recognized reasonable expectations of privacy in *Katz*.]

Although no single rubric definitively resolves which expectations of privacy are entitled to protection,[a] the analysis is informed by historical understandings "of what was deemed an unreasonable search and seizure when [the Fourth Amendment] was adopted." Carroll v. United States, 267 U. S. 132, 149 (1925). On this score, our cases have recognized some basic guideposts. First, that the Amendment seeks to secure "the privacies of life" against "arbitrary power." Boyd v. United States, 116 U. S. 616, 630 (1886). Second, and relatedly, that a central aim of the Framers was "to place obstacles in the way of a too permeating police surveillance." United States v. Di Re, 332 U. S. 581, 595 (1948).

We have kept this attention to Founding-era understandings in mind when applying the Fourth Amendment to innovations in surveillance tools. As technology has enhanced the Government's capacity to encroach upon areas normally guarded from inquisitive eyes, this Court has sought to "assure[ ] preservation of that degree of privacy against government that existed when the Fourth Amendment was adopted." Kyllo v. United States, 533 U. S. 27, 34 (2001). For that reason, we rejected in *Kyllo* a "mechanical interpretation" of the Fourth Amendment and held that use of a thermal imager to detect heat radiating from the side of the defendant's home was a search. Because any other conclusion would leave homeowners "at the mercy of advancing technology," we determined that the Government—absent a warrant—could not capitalize on such new sense-enhancing technology to explore what was happening within the home.

Likewise in *Riley*, the Court recognized the "immense storage capacity" of modern cell phones in holding that police officers must generally obtain a warrant before searching the contents of a phone. We explained that while the general rule allowing warrantless searches incident to arrest "strikes the appropriate balance in the context of physical objects, neither of its rationales has much force with respect to" the vast store of sensitive information on a cell phone.

---

[a] JUSTICE KENNEDY believes that there is such a rubric—the "property-based concepts" that *Katz* purported to move beyond. But while property rights are often informative, our cases by no means suggest that such an interest is "fundamental" or "dispositive" in determining which expectations of privacy are legitimate. JUSTICE THOMAS (and to a large extent JUSTICE GORSUCH) would have us abandon *Katz* and return to an exclusively property-based approach. *Katz* of course "discredited" the "premise that property interests control," 389 U. S., at 353, and we have repeatedly emphasized that privacy interests do not rise or fall with property rights, see, *e.g., United States* v. *Jones*, 565 U. S. 400, 411 (2012) (refusing to "make trespass the exclusive test"); *Kyllo* v. *United States*, 533 U. S. 27, 32 (2001) ("We have since decoupled violation of a person's Fourth Amendment rights from trespassory violation of his property."). Neither party has asked the Court to reconsider *Katz* in this case.

B

The case before us involves the Government's acquisition of wireless carrier cell-site records revealing the location of Carpenter's cell phone whenever it made or received calls. This sort of digital data—personal location information maintained by a third party—does not fit neatly under existing precedents. Instead, requests for cell-site records lie at the intersection of two lines of cases, both of which inform our understanding of the privacy interests at stake.

The first set of cases addresses a person's expectation of privacy in his physical location and movements. In United States v. Knotts, 460 U. S. 276 (1983), we considered the Government's use of a "beeper" to aid in tracking a vehicle through traffic. Police officers in that case planted a beeper in a container of chloroform before it was purchased by one of Knotts's co-conspirators. The officers (with intermittent aerial assistance) then followed the automobile carrying the container from Minneapolis to Knotts's cabin in Wisconsin, relying on the beeper's signal to help keep the vehicle in view. The Court concluded that the "augment[ed]" visual surveillance did not constitute a search because "[a] person traveling in an automobile on public thoroughfares has no reasonable expectation of privacy in his movements from one place to another." Since the movements of the vehicle and its final destination had been "voluntarily conveyed to anyone who wanted to look," Knotts could not assert a privacy interest in the information obtained.

This Court in *Knotts*, however, was careful to distinguish between the rudimentary tracking facilitated by the beeper and more sweeping modes of surveillance. The Court emphasized the "limited use which the government made of the signals from this particular beeper" during a discrete "automotive journey." Significantly, the Court reserved the question whether "different constitutional principles may be applicable" if "twenty-four hour surveillance of any citizen of this country [were] possible."

Three decades later, the Court considered more sophisticated surveillance of the sort envisioned in *Knotts* and found that different principles did indeed apply. In *United States* v. *Jones*, FBI agents installed a GPS tracking device on Jones's vehicle and remotely monitored the vehicle's movements for 28 days. The Court decided the case based on the Government's physical trespass of the vehicle. At the same time, five Justices agreed that related privacy concerns would be raised by, for example, "surreptitiously activating a stolen vehicle detection system" in Jones's car to track Jones himself, or conducting GPS tracking of his cell phone. *Id.*, at 426, 428 (ALITO, J., concurring in judgment); *id.*, at 415 (SOTOMAYOR, J., concurring). Since GPS monitoring of a vehicle tracks "every movement" a person makes in that vehicle, the concurring Justices concluded that "longer term GPS monitoring in investigations of most offenses impinges on expectations of privacy"—regardless whether those movements were disclosed to the public at large. * * *[b]

In a second set of decisions, the Court has drawn a line between what a person keeps to himself and what he shares with others. We have previously held that "a person has no legitimate expectation of privacy in information he voluntarily turns over to third parties." *Smith,* 442 U. S., at 743–744. That remains true "even if the information is revealed on the assumption that it will be used only for a limited purpose." *United States v. Miller,* 425 U. S. 435, 443 (1976). As a result, the Government is typically free to obtain such information from the recipient without triggering Fourth Amendment protections.

This third-party doctrine largely traces its roots to *Miller.* While investigating Miller for tax evasion, the Government subpoenaed his banks, seeking several months of canceled checks, deposit slips, and monthly statements. The Court rejected a Fourth Amendment challenge to the records collection. For one, Miller could "assert neither ownership nor possession" of the documents; they were "business records of the banks." For another, the nature of those records confirmed Miller's limited expectation of privacy, because the checks were "not confidential communications but negotiable instruments to be used in commercial transactions," and the bank statements contained information "exposed to [bank] employees in the ordinary course of business." The Court thus concluded that Miller had "take[n] the risk, in revealing his affairs to another, that the information [would] be conveyed by that person to the Government."

Three years later, *Smith* applied the same principles in the context of information conveyed to a telephone company. The Court ruled that the Government's use of a pen register—a device that recorded the outgoing phone numbers dialed on a landline telephone—was not a search. Noting the pen register's "limited capabilities," the Court "doubt[ed] that people in general entertain any actual expectation of privacy in the numbers they dial." Telephone subscribers know, after all, that the numbers are used by the telephone company "for a variety of legitimate business purposes," including routing calls. And at any rate, the Court explained,

---

[b] JUSTICE KENNEDY argues that this case is in a different category from *Jones* and the dragnet-type practices posited in *Knotts* because the disclosure of the cell-site records was subject to "judicial authorization." That line of argument conflates the threshold question whether a "search" has occurred with the separate matter of whether the search was reasonable. The subpoena process set forth in the Stored Communications Act does not determine a target's expectation of privacy. And in any event, neither *Jones* nor *Knotts* purported to resolve the question of what authorization may be required to conduct such electronic surveillance techniques. But see *Jones,* 565 U. S., at 430 (ALITO, J., concurring in judgment) (indicating that longer term GPS tracking may require a warrant).

such an expectation "is not one that society is prepared to recognize as reasonable." When Smith placed a call, he "voluntarily conveyed" the dialed numbers to the phone company by "expos[ing] that information to its equipment in the ordinary course of business." Once again, we held that the defendant "assumed the risk" that the company's records "would be divulged to police."

### III

The question we confront today is how to apply the Fourth Amendment to a new phenomenon: the ability to chronicle a person's past movements through the record of his cell phone signals. Such tracking partakes of many of the qualities of the GPS monitoring we considered in *Jones*. Much like GPS tracking of a vehicle, cell phone location information is detailed, encyclopedic, and effortlessly compiled.

At the same time, the fact that the individual continuously reveals his location to his wireless carrier implicates the third-party principle of *Smith* and *Miller*. But while the third-party doctrine applies to telephone numbers and bank records, it is not clear whether its logic extends to the qualitatively different category of cell-site records. After all, when *Smith* was decided in 1979, few could have imagined a society in which a phone goes wherever its owner goes, conveying to the wireless carrier not just dialed digits, but a detailed and comprehensive record of the person's movements.

We decline to extend *Smith* and *Miller* to cover these novel circumstances. Given the unique nature of cell phone location records, the fact that the information is held by a third party does not by itself overcome the user's claim to Fourth Amendment protection. Whether the Government employs its own surveillance technology as in *Jones* or leverages the technology of a wireless carrier, we hold that an individual maintains a legitimate expectation of privacy in the record of his physical movements as captured through CSLI. The location information obtained from Carpenter's wireless carriers was the product of a search.[c]

### A

A person does not surrender all Fourth Amendment protection by venturing into the public sphere. To the contrary, "what [one] seeks to

---

[c] The parties suggest as an alternative to their primary submissions that the acquisition of CSLI becomes a search only if it extends beyond a limited period. See Reply Brief 12 (proposing a 24-hour cutoff); Brief for United States 55–56 (suggesting a seven-day cutoff). As part of its argument, the Government treats the seven days of CSLI requested from Sprint as the pertinent period, even though Sprint produced only two days of records. Brief for United States 56. Contrary to JUSTICE KENNEDY's assertion, we need not decide whether there is a limited period for which the Government may obtain an individual's historical CSLI free from Fourth Amendment scrutiny, and if so, how long that period might be. It is sufficient for our purposes today to hold that accessing seven days of CSLI constitutes a Fourth Amendment search.

preserve as private, even in an area accessible to the public, may be constitutionally protected." *Katz*, 389 U. S., at 351–352. A majority of this Court has already recognized that individuals have a reasonable expectation of privacy in the whole of their physical movements. *Jones*, 565 U. S., at 430 (ALITO, J., concurring in judgment); *id.*, at 415 (SOTOMAYOR, J., concurring). Prior to the digital age, law enforcement might have pursued a suspect for a brief stretch, but doing so "for any extended period of time was difficult and costly and therefore rarely undertaken." *Id.*, at 429 (opinion of ALITO, J.). For that reason, "society's expectation has been that law enforcement agents and others would not— and indeed, in the main, simply could not—secretly monitor and catalogue every single movement of an individual's car for a very long period."

Allowing government access to cell-site records contravenes that expectation. Although such records are generated for commercial purposes, that distinction does not negate Carpenter's anticipation of privacy in his physical location. Mapping a cell phone's location over the course of 127 days provides an all-encompassing record of the holder's whereabouts. As with GPS information, the time-stamped data provides an intimate window into a person's life, revealing not only his particular movements, but through them his "familial, political, professional, religious, and sexual associations." *Id.*, at 415 (opinion of SOTOMAYOR, J.). These location records "hold for many Americans the 'privacies of life.'" *Riley*, 573 U. S., at ___ (slip op., at 28). And like GPS monitoring, cell phone tracking is remarkably easy, cheap, and efficient compared to traditional investigative tools. With just the click of a button, the Government can access each carrier's deep repository of historical location information at practically no expense.

In fact, historical cell-site records present even greater privacy concerns than the GPS monitoring of a vehicle we considered in *Jones*. Unlike the bugged container in *Knotts* or the car in *Jones*, a cell phone— almost a "feature of human anatomy," *Riley*, 573 U. S., at ___ (slip op., at 9)—tracks nearly exactly the movements of its owner. While individuals regularly leave their vehicles, they compulsively carry cell phones with them all the time. A cell phone faithfully follows its owner beyond public thoroughfares and into private residences, doctor's offices, political headquarters, and other potentially revealing locales. See *id.*, at ___ (slip op., at 19) (noting that "nearly three-quarters of smart phone users report being within five feet of their phones most of the time, with 12% admitting that they even use their phones in the shower"); contrast Cardwell v. Lewis, 417 U. S. 583, 590 (1974) (plurality opinion) ("A car has little capacity for escaping public scrutiny."). Accordingly, when the Government tracks the location of a cell phone it achieves near perfect surveillance, as if it had attached an ankle monitor to the phone's user.

Moreover, the retrospective quality of the data here gives police access to a category of information otherwise unknowable. In the past, attempts to reconstruct a person's movements were limited by a dearth of records and the frailties of recollection. With access to CSLI, the Government can now travel back in time to retrace a person's whereabouts, subject only to the retention polices of the wireless carriers, which currently maintain records for up to five years. Critically, because location information is continually logged for all of the 400 million devices in the United States—not just those belonging to persons who might happen to come under investigation—this newfound tracking capacity runs against everyone. Unlike with the GPS device in *Jones*, police need not even know in advance whether they want to follow a particular individual, or when.

Whoever the suspect turns out to be, he has effectively been tailed every moment of every day for five years, and the police may—in the Government's view—call upon the results of that surveillance without regard to the constraints of the Fourth Amendment. Only the few without cell phones could escape this tireless and absolute surveillance.

The Government and JUSTICE KENNEDY contend, however, that the collection of CSLI should be permitted because the data is less precise than GPS information. Not to worry, they maintain, because the location records did "not on their own suffice to place [Carpenter] at the crime scene"; they placed him within a wedge-shaped sector ranging from one-eighth to four square miles. Yet the Court has already rejected the proposition that "inference insulates a search." *Kyllo*, 533 U. S., at 36. From the 127 days of location data it received, the Government could, in combination with other information, deduce a detailed log of Carpenter's movements, including when he was at the site of the robberies. And the Government thought the CSLI accurate enough to highlight it during the closing argument of his trial.

At any rate, the rule the Court adopts "must take account of more sophisticated systems that are already in use or in development." *Kyllo*, 533 U. S., at 36. While the records in this case reflect the state of technology at the start of the decade, the accuracy of CSLI is rapidly approaching GPS-level precision. As the number of cell sites has proliferated, the geographic area covered by each cell sector has shrunk, particularly in urban areas. In addition, with new technology measuring the time and angle of signals hitting their towers, wireless carriers already have the capability to pinpoint a phone's location within 50 meters.

Accordingly, when the Government accessed CSLI from the wireless carriers, it invaded Carpenter's reasonable expectation of privacy in the whole of his physical movements.

B

The Government's primary contention to the contrary is that the third-party doctrine governs this case. In its view, cell-site records are fair game because they are "business records" created and maintained by the wireless carriers. The Government (along with JUSTICE KENNEDY) recognizes that this case features new technology, but asserts that the legal question nonetheless turns on a garden-variety request for information from a third-party witness.

The Government's position fails to contend with the seismic shifts in digital technology that made possible the tracking of not only Carpenter's location but also everyone else's, not for a short period but for years and years. Sprint Corporation and its competitors are not your typical witnesses. Unlike the nosy neighbor who keeps an eye on comings and goings, they are ever alert, and their memory is nearly infallible. There is a world of difference between the limited types of personal information addressed in *Smith* and *Miller* and the exhaustive chronicle of location information casually collected by wireless carriers today. The Government thus is not asking for a straightforward application of the third-party doctrine, but instead a significant extension of it to a distinct category of information.

The third-party doctrine partly stems from the notion that an individual has a reduced expectation of privacy in information knowingly shared with another. But the fact of "diminished privacy interests does not mean that the Fourth Amendment falls out of the picture entirely." *Riley*, 573 U. S., at ___ (slip op., at 16). *Smith* and *Miller*, after all, did not rely solely on the act of sharing. Instead, they considered "the nature of the particular documents sought" to determine whether "there is a legitimate 'expectation of privacy' concerning their contents." *Miller*, 425 U. S., at 442. *Smith* pointed out the limited capabilities of a pen register; as explained in *Riley*, telephone call logs reveal little in the way of "identifying information." *Smith*, 442 U. S., at 742; *Riley*, 573 U. S., at ___ (slip op., at 24). *Miller* likewise noted that checks were "not confidential communications but negotiable instruments to be used in commercial transactions." 425 U. S., at 442. In mechanically applying the third-party doctrine to this case, the Government fails to appreciate that there are no comparable limitations on the revealing nature of CSLI.

The Court has in fact already shown special solicitude for location information in the third-party context. In *Knotts*, the Court relied on *Smith* to hold that an individual has no reasonable expectation of privacy in public movements that he "voluntarily conveyed to anyone who wanted to look." But when confronted with more pervasive tracking, five Justices agreed that longer term GPS monitoring of even a vehicle traveling on public streets constitutes a search. *Jones*, 565 U. S., at 430 (ALITO, J., concurring in judgment); *id.*, at 415 (SOTOMAYOR, J., concurring). JUSTICE GORSUCH wonders why "someone's location when using a phone" is sensitive, and JUSTICE KENNEDY assumes that a person's discrete movements "are not particularly private." Yet this case is not about "using a phone" or a person's movement at a particular time. It is about a detailed chronicle of a person's physical presence compiled every day, every moment, over several years. Such a chronicle implicates privacy concerns far beyond those considered in *Smith* and *Miller*.

Neither does the second rationale underlying the third-party doctrine—voluntary exposure—hold up when it comes to CSLI. Cell phone location information is not truly "shared" as one normally understands the term. In the first place, cell phones and the services they provide are "such a pervasive and insistent part of daily life" that carrying one is indispensable to participation in modern society. *Riley*, 573 U. S., at ___ (slip op., at 9). Second, a cell phone logs a cell-site record by dint of its operation, without any affirmative act on the part of the user beyond powering up. Virtually any activity on the phone generates CSLI, including incoming calls, texts, or e-mails and countless other data connections that a phone automatically makes when checking for news, weather, or social media updates. Apart from disconnecting the phone from the network, there is no way to avoid leaving behind a trail of location data. As a result, in no meaningful sense does the user voluntarily "assume the risk" of turning over a comprehensive dossier of his physical movements.

We therefore decline to extend *Smith* and *Miller* to the collection of CSLI. Given the unique nature of cell phone location information, the fact that the Government obtained the information from a third party does not overcome Carpenter's claim to Fourth Amendment protection. The Government's acquisition of the cell-site records was a search within the meaning of the Fourth Amendment.

\* \* \*

Our decision today is a narrow one. We do not express a view on matters not before us: real-time CSLI or "tower dumps" (a download of information on all the devices that connected to a particular cell site during a particular interval). We do not disturb the application of *Smith* and *Miller* or call into question conventional surveillance techniques and tools, such as security cameras. Nor do we address other business records that might incidentally reveal location information. Further, our opinion does not consider other collection techniques involving foreign affairs or national security. As Justice Frankfurter noted when considering new innovations in airplanes and radios, the Court must tread carefully in such cases, to ensure that we do not "embarrass the future." Northwest Airlines, Inc. v. Minnesota, 322 U. S. 292, 300 (1944).[d]

## IV

Having found that the acquisition of Carpenter's CSLI was a search, we also conclude that the Government must generally obtain a warrant supported by probable cause before acquiring such records. * * * Thus, "[i]n the absence of a warrant, a search is reasonable only if it falls within a specific exception to the warrant requirement." *Riley*, 573 U. S., at ___ (slip op., at 5).

The Government acquired the cell-site records pursuant to a court order issued under the Stored Communications Act, which required the Government to show "reasonable grounds" for believing that the records were "relevant and material to an ongoing investigation." 18 U. S. C. § 2703(d). That showing falls well short of the probable cause required for a warrant. The Court usually requires "some quantum of individualized suspicion" before a search or seizure may take place. United States v. Martinez-Fuerte, 428 U. S. 543, 560–561 (1976). Under the standard in the Stored Communications Act, however, law enforcement need only show that the cell-site evidence might be pertinent to an ongoing investigation—a "gigantic" departure from the probable cause rule, as the Government explained below. Consequently, an order issued under Section 2703(d) of the Act is not a permissible mechanism for accessing historical cell-site records. Before compelling a wireless carrier to turn over a subscriber's CSLI, the Government's obligation is a familiar one—get a warrant.

JUSTICE ALITO contends that the warrant requirement simply does not apply when the Government acquires records using compulsory process. Unlike an actual search, he says, subpoenas for documents do not involve the direct taking of evidence; they are at most a "constructive search" conducted by the target of the subpoena. Given this lesser intrusion on personal privacy, JUSTICE ALITO argues that the compulsory production of records is not held to the same probable cause standard. In his view, this Court's precedents set forth a categorical rule—separate and distinct from the third-party doctrine—subjecting subpoenas to lenient scrutiny without regard to the suspect's expectation of privacy in the records.

But this Court has never held that the Government may subpoena third parties for records in which the suspect has a reasonable expectation of privacy. Almost all of the examples JUSTICE ALITO cites

---

[d] JUSTICE GORSUCH faults us for not promulgating a complete code addressing the manifold situations that may be presented by this new technology—under a constitutional provision turning on what is "reasonable," no less. Like JUSTICE GORSUCH, we "do not begin to claim all the answers today," and therefore decide no more than the case before us.

contemplated requests for evidence implicating diminished privacy interests or for a corporation's own books.[e] The lone exception, of course, is *Miller*, where the Court's analysis of the third-party subpoena merged with the application of the third-party doctrine. 425 U. S., at 444 (concluding that Miller lacked the necessary privacy interest to contest the issuance of a subpoena to his bank).

JUSTICE ALITO overlooks the critical issue. At some point, the dissent should recognize that CSLI is an entirely different species of business record—something that implicates basic Fourth Amendment concerns about arbitrary government power much more directly than corporate tax or payroll ledgers. When confronting new concerns wrought by digital technology, this Court has been careful not to uncritically extend existing precedents.

If the choice to proceed by subpoena provided a categorical limitation on Fourth Amendment protection, no type of record would ever be protected by the warrant requirement. Under JUSTICE ALITO's view, private letters, digital contents of a cell phone—any personal information reduced to document form, in fact—may be collected by subpoena for no reason other than "official curiosity." JUSTICE KENNEDY declines to adopt the radical implications of this theory, leaving open the question whether the warrant requirement applies "when the Government obtains the modern-day equivalents of an individual's own 'papers' or 'effects,' even when those papers or effects are held by a third party." That would be a sensible exception, because it would prevent the subpoena doctrine from overcoming any reasonable expectation of privacy. If the third-party doctrine does not apply to the "modern-day equivalents of an individual's own 'papers' or 'effects,' " then the clear implication is that the documents should receive full Fourth Amendment protection. We simply think that such protection should extend as well to a detailed log of a person's movements over several years.

This is certainly not to say that all orders compelling the production of documents will require a showing of probable cause. The Government will be able to use subpoenas to acquire records in the overwhelming majority of investigations. We hold only that a warrant is required in the

---

[e] See *United States* v. *Dionisio*, 410 U. S. 1, 14 (1973) ("No person can have a reasonable expectation that others will not know the sound of his voice"); *Donovan* v. *Lone Steer, Inc.*, 464 U. S. 408, 411, 415 (1984) (payroll and sales records); *California Bankers Assn.* v. *Shultz*, 416 U. S. 21, 67 (1974) (Bank Secrecy Act reporting requirements); *See* v. *Seattle*, 387 U. S. 541, 544 (1967) (financial books and records); *United States* v. *Powell*, 379 U. S. 48, 49, 57 (1964) (corporate tax records); *McPhaul* v. *United States*, 364 U. S. 372, 374, 382 (1960) (books and records of an organization); *United States* v. *Morton Salt Co.*, 338 U. S. 632, 634, 651–653 (1950) (Federal Trade Commission reporting requirement); *Oklahoma Press Publishing Co.* v. *Walling*, 327 U. S. 186, 189, 204–208 (1946) (payroll records); *Hale* v. *Henkel*, 201 U. S. 43, 45, 75 (1906) (corporate books and papers).

rare case where the suspect has a legitimate privacy interest in records held by a third party.

Further, even though the Government will generally need a warrant to access CSLI, case-specific exceptions may support a warrantless search of an individual's cellsite records under certain circumstances. "One well-recognized exception applies when "the exigencies of the situation" make the needs of law enforcement so compelling that [a] warrantless search is objectively reasonable under the Fourth Amendment." Kentucky v. King, 563 U. S. 452, 460 (2011). Such exigencies include the need to pursue a fleeing suspect, protect individuals who are threatened with imminent harm, or prevent the imminent destruction of evidence.

As a result, if law enforcement is confronted with an urgent situation, such fact-specific threats will likely justify the warrantless collection of CSLI. Lower courts, for instance, have approved warrantless searches related to bomb threats, active shootings, and child abductions. Our decision today does not call into doubt warrantless access to CSLI in such circumstances. While police must get a warrant when collecting CSLI to assist in the minerun criminal investigation, the rule we set forth does not limit their ability to respond to an ongoing emergency.

* * *

As Justice Brandeis explained in his famous dissent, the Court is obligated—as "[s]ubtler and more far-reaching means of invading privacy have become available to the Government"—to ensure that the "progress of science" does not erode Fourth Amendment protections. Olmstead v. United States, 277 U. S. 438, 473–474 (1928). Here the progress of science has afforded law enforcement a powerful new tool to carry out its important responsibilities. At the same time, this tool risks Government encroachment of the sort the Framers, "after consulting the lessons of history," drafted the Fourth Amendment to prevent.

We decline to grant the state unrestricted access to a wireless carrier's database of physical location information. In light of the deeply revealing nature of CSLI, its depth, breadth, and comprehensive reach, and the inescapable and automatic nature of its collection, the fact that such information is gathered by a third party does not make it any less deserving of Fourth Amendment protection. The Government's acquisition of the cell-site records here was a search under that Amendment.

**JUSTICE KENNEDY, with whom JUSTICE THOMAS and JUSTICE ALITO join, dissenting.**

This case involves new technology, but the Court's stark departure from relevant Fourth Amendment precedents and principles is, in my submission, unnecessary and incorrect, requiring this respectful dissent.

The new rule the Court seems to formulate puts needed, reasonable, accepted, lawful, and congressionally authorized criminal investigations at serious risk in serious cases, often when law enforcement seeks to prevent the threat of violent crimes. And it places undue restrictions on the lawful and necessary enforcement powers exercised not only by the Federal Government, but also by law enforcement in every State and locality throughout the Nation. Adherence to this Court's longstanding precedents and analytic framework would have been the proper and prudent way to resolve this case.

The Court has twice held that individuals have no Fourth Amendment interests in business records which are possessed, owned, and controlled by a third party. United States v. Miller, 425 U. S. 435 (1976); Smith v. Maryland, 442 U. S. 735 (1979). This is true even when the records contain personal and sensitive information. So when the Government uses a subpoena to obtain, for example, bank records, telephone records, and credit card statements from the businesses that create and keep these records, the Government does not engage in a search of the business's customers within the meaning of the Fourth Amendment.

\* \* \*

Cell-site records \* \* \* are no different from the many other kinds of business records the Government has a lawful right to obtain by compulsory process. Customers like petitioner do not own, possess, control, or use the records, and for that reason have no reasonable expectation that they cannot be disclosed pursuant to lawful compulsory process.

The Court today disagrees. It holds for the first time that by using compulsory process to obtain records of a business entity, the Government has not just engaged in an impermissible action, but has conducted a search of the business's customer. The Court further concludes that the search in this case was unreasonable and the Government needed to get a warrant to obtain more than six days of cell-site records.

In concluding that the Government engaged in a search, the Court unhinges Fourth Amendment doctrine from the property-based concepts that have long grounded the analytic framework that pertains in these cases. In doing so it draws an unprincipled and unworkable line between cell-site records on the one hand and financial and telephonic records on the other. According to today's majority opinion, the Government can acquire a record of every credit card purchase and phone call a person makes over months or years without upsetting a legitimate expectation of privacy. But, in the Court's view, the Government crosses a constitutional line when it obtains a court's approval to issue a subpoena for more than six days of cell-site records in order to determine whether a person was within several hundred city blocks of a crime scene. That distinction is illogical and will frustrate principled application of the Fourth Amendment in many routine yet vital law enforcement operations.

It is true that the Cyber Age has vast potential both to expand and restrict individual freedoms in dimensions not contemplated in earlier times. For the reasons that follow, however, there is simply no basis here for concluding that the Government interfered with information that the cell phone customer, either from a legal or commonsense standpoint, should have thought the law would deem owned or controlled by him.

## I

Before evaluating the question presented it is helpful to understand the nature of cell-site records, how they are commonly used by cell phone service providers, and their proper use by law enforcement.

When a cell phone user makes a call, sends a text message or e-mail, or gains access to the Internet, the cell phone establishes a radio connection to an antenna at a nearby cell site. The typical cell site covers a more-or-less circular geographic area around the site. It has three (or sometimes six) separate antennas pointing in different directions. Each provides cell service for a different 120-degree (or 60-degree) sector of the cell site's circular coverage area. So a cell phone activated on the north side of a cell site will connect to a different antenna than a cell phone on the south side. * * *

The location information revealed by cell-site records is imprecise, because an individual cell-site sector usually covers a large geographic area. The FBI agent who offered expert testimony about the cell-site records at issue here testified that a cell site in a city reaches between a half mile and two miles in all directions. That means a 60-degree sector covers between approximately one-eighth and two square miles (and a 120-degree sector twice that area). To put that in perspective, in urban areas cell-site records often would reveal the location of a cell phone user within an area covering between around a dozen and several hundred city blocks. In rural areas cell-site records can be up to 40 times more imprecise. By contrast, a Global Positioning System (GPS) can reveal an individual's location within around 15 feet.

Major cell phone service providers keep cell-site records for long periods of time. There is no law requiring them to do so. * * *

Cell-site records also can serve an important investigative function, as the facts of this case demonstrate. Petitioner, Timothy Carpenter, along with a rotating group of accomplices, robbed at least six RadioShack and T-Mobile stores at gunpoint over a 2-year period. Five of those robberies occurred in the Detroit area, each crime at least four miles from the last. The sixth took place in Warren, Ohio, over 200 miles from Detroit.

The Government, of course, did not know all of these details in 2011 when it began investigating Carpenter. In April of that year police arrested four of Carpenter's coconspirators. One of them confessed to committing nine robberies in Michigan and Ohio between December 2010 and March 2011. He identified 15 accomplices who had participated in at least one of those robberies; named Carpenter as one of the accomplices; and provided Carpenter's cell phone number to the authorities. The suspect also warned that the other members of the conspiracy planned to commit more armed robberies in the immediate future.

The Government at this point faced a daunting task. Even if it could identify and apprehend the suspects, still it had to link each suspect in this changing criminal gang to specific robberies in order to bring charges and convict. And, of course, it was urgent that the Government take all necessary steps to stop the ongoing and dangerous crime spree.

Cell-site records were uniquely suited to this task. The geographic dispersion of the robberies meant that, if Carpenter's cell phone were within even a dozen to several hundred city blocks of one or more of the stores when the different robberies occurred, there would be powerful circumstantial evidence of his participation; and this would be especially so if his cell phone usually was not located in the sectors near the stores except during the robbery times.

[Justice Kennedy explains the records obtained by the government and that they confirmed Carpenter's cell phone was in the general vicinity of four of the nine robberies at the time they occurred.]

## II

\* \* \*

Here the only question necessary to decide is whether the Government searched anything of Carpenter's when it used compulsory process to obtain cell-site records from Carpenter's cell phone service providers. This Court's decisions in *Miller* and *Smith* dictate that the answer is no, as every Court of Appeals to have considered the question has recognized. \* \* \*

### A

*Miller* and *Smith* hold that individuals lack any protected Fourth Amendment interests in records that are possessed, owned, and controlled only by a third party. \* \* \*

*Miller* and *Smith* have been criticized as being based on too narrow a view of reasonable expectations of privacy. Those criticisms, however, are unwarranted. The principle established in *Miller* and *Smith* is correct for two reasons, the first relating to a defendant's attenuated interest in property owned by another, and the second relating to the safeguards inherent in the use of compulsory process.

First, *Miller* and *Smith* placed necessary limits on the ability of individuals to assert Fourth Amendment interests in property to which they lack a "requisite connection." * * *

* * *

*Miller* and *Smith* set forth an important and necessary limitation on the *Katz* framework. They rest upon the commonsense principle that the absence of property law analogues can be dispositive of privacy expectations. The defendants in those cases could expect that the third-party businesses could use the records the companies collected, stored, and classified as their own for any number of business and commercial purposes. The businesses were not bailees or custodians of the records, with a duty to hold the records for the defendants' use. The defendants could make no argument that the records were their own papers or effects. * * *

The second principle supporting *Miller* and *Smith* is the longstanding rule that the Government may use compulsory process to compel persons to disclose documents and other evidence within their possession and control. A subpoena is different from a warrant in its force and intrusive power. While a warrant allows the Government to enter and seize and make the examination itself, a subpoena simply requires the person to whom it is directed to make the disclosure. A subpoena, moreover, provides the recipient the "opportunity to present objections" before complying, which further mitigates the intrusion. Oklahoma Press Publishing Co. v. Walling, 327 U. S. 186, 195 (1946).

For those reasons this Court has held that a subpoena for records, although a "constructive" search subject to Fourth Amendment constraints, need not comply with the procedures applicable to warrants—even when challenged by the person to whom the records belong. Rather, a subpoena complies with the Fourth Amendment's reasonableness requirement so long as it is "sufficiently limited in scope, relevant in purpose, and specific in directive so that compliance will not be unreasonably burdensome." Donovan v. Lone Steer, Inc., 464 U. S. 408, 415 (1984). Persons with no meaningful interests in the records sought by a subpoena, like the defendants in *Miller* and *Smith*, have no rights to object to the records' disclosure—much less to assert that the Government must obtain a warrant to compel disclosure of the records.

Based on *Miller* and *Smith* and the principles underlying those cases, it is well established that subpoenas may be used to obtain a wide variety of records held by businesses, even when the records contain private information. * * *

And law enforcement officers are not alone in their reliance on subpoenas to obtain business records for legitimate investigations. Subpoenas also are used for investigatory purposes by state and federal grand juries, see United States v. Dionisio, 410 U. S. 1 (1973), state and federal administrative agencies, see *Oklahoma Press, supra*, and state and federal legislative bodies, see McPhaul v. United States, 364 U. S. 372 (1960).

B

Carpenter does not question these traditional investigative practices. And he does not ask the Court to reconsider *Miller* and *Smith*. Carpenter argues only that, under *Miller* and *Smith*, the Government may not use compulsory process to acquire cell-site records from cell phone service providers.

There is no merit in this argument. Cell-site records, like all the examples just discussed, are created, kept, classified, owned, and controlled by cell phone service providers, which aggregate and sell this information to third parties. As in *Miller*, Carpenter can "assert neither ownership nor possession" of the records and has no control over them.

Carpenter argues that he has Fourth Amendment interests in the cell-site records because they are in essence his personal papers by operation of 47 U. S. C. § 222. That statute imposes certain restrictions on how providers may use "customer proprietary network information"—a term that encompasses cell-site records. §§ 222(c), (h)(1)(A). The statute in general prohibits providers from disclosing personally identifiable cell-site records to private third parties. § 222(c)(1). And it allows customers to request cell-site records from the provider. § 222(c)(2).

Carpenter's argument is unpersuasive, however, for § 222 does not grant cell phone customers any meaningful interest in cell-site records. The statute's confidentiality protections may be overridden by the interests of the providers or the Government. The providers may disclose the records "to protect the[ir] rights or property" or to "initiate, render, bill, and collect for telecommunications services." §§ 222(d)(1), (2). They also may disclose the records "as required by law"—which, of course, is how they were disclosed in this case. § 222(c)(1). Nor does the statute provide customers any practical control over the records. Customers do not create the records; they have no say in whether or for how long the records are stored; and they cannot require the records to be modified or destroyed. Even their right to request access to the records is limited, for the statute "does not preclude a carrier from being reimbursed by the customers . . . for the costs associated with making such disclosures." H. R. Rep. No. 104–204, pt. 1, p. 90 (1995). So in every legal and practical sense the "network information" regulated by § 222 is, under that statute, "proprietary" to the service providers, not Carpenter. The Court does not argue otherwise.

Because Carpenter lacks a requisite connection to the cell-site records, he also may not claim a reasonable expectation of privacy in them. He could expect that a third party—the cell phone service provider—could use the information it collected, stored, and classified as its own for a variety of business and commercial purposes.

All this is not to say that *Miller* and *Smith* are without limits. *Miller* and *Smith* may not apply when the Government obtains the modern-day equivalents of an individual's own "papers" or "effects," even when those papers or effects are held by a third party. As already discussed, however, this case does not involve property or a bailment of that sort. Here the Government's acquisition of cell-site records falls within the heartland of *Miller* and *Smith*.

In fact, Carpenter's Fourth Amendment objection is even weaker than those of the defendants in *Miller* and *Smith*. Here the Government did not use a mere subpoena to obtain the cell-site records. It acquired the records only after it proved to a Magistrate Judge reasonable grounds to believe that the records were relevant and material to an ongoing criminal investigation. See 18 U. S. C. § 2703(d). So even if § 222 gave Carpenter some attenuated interest in the records, the Government's conduct here would be reasonable under the standards governing subpoenas. See *Donovan*, 464 U. S., at 415.

Under *Miller* and *Smith*, then, a search of the sort that requires a warrant simply did not occur when the Government used court-approved compulsory process, based on a finding of reasonable necessity, to compel a cell phone service provider, as owner, to disclose cell-site records.

### III

The Court rejects a straightforward application of *Miller* and *Smith*. It concludes instead that applying those cases to cell-site records would work a "significant extension" of the principles underlying them, and holds that the acquisition of more than six days of cell-site records constitutes a search.

In my respectful view the majority opinion misreads this Court's precedents, old and recent, and transforms *Miller* and *Smith* into an unprincipled and unworkable doctrine. The Court's newly conceived constitutional standard will cause confusion; will undermine traditional and important law enforcement practices; and will allow the cell phone to become a protected medium that dangerous persons will use to commit serious crimes.

A

The Court errs at the outset by attempting to sidestep *Miller* and *Smith*. The Court frames this case as following instead from United States v. Knotts, 460 U. S. 276 (1983), and United States v. Jones, 565 U. S. 400 (2012). Those cases, the Court suggests, establish that "individuals have a reasonable expectation of privacy in the whole of their physical movements." *Knotts* held just the opposite: "A person traveling in an automobile on public thoroughfares has no reasonable expectation of privacy in his movements from one place to another." True, the Court in *Knotts* also suggested that "different constitutional principles may be applicable" to "dragnet-type law enforcement practices." But by dragnet practices the Court was referring to "twenty-four hour surveillance of any citizen of this country . . . without judicial knowledge or supervision."

Those "different constitutional principles" mentioned in *Knotts*, whatever they may be, do not apply in this case. Here the Stored Communications Act requires a neutral judicial officer to confirm in each case that the Government has "reasonable grounds to believe" the cell-site records "are relevant and material to an ongoing criminal investigation." 18 U. S. C. § 2703(d). This judicial check mitigates the Court's concerns about "a too permeating police surveillance." * * *

The Court's reliance on *Jones* fares no better. In *Jones* the Government installed a GPS tracking device on the defendant's automobile. The Court held the Government searched the automobile because it "physically occupied private property [of the defendant] for the purpose of obtaining information." So in *Jones* it was "not necessary to inquire about the target's expectation of privacy in his vehicle's movements."

Despite that clear delineation of the Court's holding in *Jones*, the Court today declares that *Jones* applied the "different constitutional principles" alluded to in *Knotts* to establish that an individual has an expectation of privacy in the sum of his whereabouts. For that proposition the majority relies on the two concurring opinions in *Jones*, one of which stated that "longer term GPS monitoring in investigations of most offenses impinges on expectations of privacy." 565 U. S., at 430 (ALITO, J., concurring). But *Jones* involved direct governmental surveillance of a defendant's automobile without judicial authorization—specifically, GPS surveillance accurate within 50 to 100 feet. Even assuming that the different constitutional principles mentioned in *Knotts* would apply in a case like *Jones*—a proposition the Court was careful not to announce in *Jones*—those principles are inapplicable here. Cases like this one, where the Government uses court-approved compulsory process to obtain records owned and controlled by a third party, are governed by the two majority opinions in *Miller* and *Smith*.

B

The Court continues its analysis by misinterpreting *Miller* and *Smith*, and then it reaches the wrong outcome on these facts even under its flawed standard.

The Court appears, in my respectful view, to read *Miller* and *Smith* to establish a balancing test. For each "qualitatively different category" of information, the Court suggests, the privacy interests at stake must be weighed against the fact that the information has been disclosed to a third party. When the privacy interests are weighty enough to "overcome" the third-party disclosure, the Fourth Amendment's protections apply.

That is an untenable reading of *Miller* and *Smith*. As already discussed, the fact that information was relinquished to a third party was the entire basis for concluding that the defendants in those cases lacked a reasonable expectation of privacy. *Miller* and *Smith* do not establish the kind of category-by-category balancing the Court today prescribes.

But suppose the Court were correct to say that *Miller* and *Smith* rest on so imprecise a foundation. Still the Court errs, in my submission, when it concludes that cellsite records implicate greater privacy interests—and thus deserve greater Fourth Amendment protection—than financial records and telephone records.

Indeed, the opposite is true. A person's movements are not particularly private. As the Court recognized in *Knotts*, when the defendant there "traveled over the public streets he voluntarily conveyed to anyone who wanted to look the fact that he was traveling over particular roads in a particular direction, the fact of whatever stops he made, and the fact of his final destination." Today expectations of privacy in one's location are, if anything, even less reasonable than when the Court decided *Knotts* over 30 years ago. Millions of Americans choose to share their location on a daily basis, whether by using a variety of location-based services on their phones, or by sharing their location with friends and the public at large via social media.

And cell-site records, as already discussed, disclose a person's location only in a general area. The records at issue here, for example, revealed Carpenter's location within an area covering between around a dozen and several hundred city blocks. "Areas of this scale might encompass bridal stores and Bass Pro Shops, gay bars and straight ones, a Methodist church and the local mosque." 819 F. 3d 880, 889 (CA6 2016). These records could not reveal where Carpenter lives and works, much less his " 'familial, political, professional, religious, and sexual associations. ' " *Ante*, at 12 (quoting *Jones, supra*, at 415 (SOTOMAYOR, J., concurring)).

By contrast, financial records and telephone records do "revea[l] . . . personal affairs, opinions, habits and associations." *Miller*, 425 U. S., at 451 (Brennan, J., dissenting). What persons purchase and to whom they talk might disclose how much money they make; the political and religious organizations to which they donate; whether they have visited a psychiatrist, plastic surgeon, abortion clinic, or AIDS treatment center; whether they go to gay bars or straight ones; and who are their closest friends and family members. The troves of intimate information the Government can and does obtain using financial records and telephone records dwarfs what can be gathered from cellsite records.

\* \* \*

Perhaps recognizing the difficulty of drawing the constitutional line between cell-site records and financial and telephonic records, the Court posits that the accuracy of cell-site records "is rapidly approaching GPS-level precision." That is certainly plausible in the era of cyber technology, yet the privacy interests associated with location information, which is often disclosed to the public at large, still would not outweigh the privacy interests implicated by financial and telephonic records.

Perhaps more important, those future developments are no basis upon which to resolve this case. In general, the Court "risks error by elaborating too fully on the Fourth Amendment implications of emerging technology before its role in society has become clear." Ontario v. Quon, 560 U. S. 746, 759 (2010). That judicial caution, prudent in most cases, is imperative in this one.

Technological changes involving cell phones have complex effects on crime and law enforcement. Cell phones make crimes easier to coordinate and conceal, while also providing the Government with new investigative tools that may have the potential to upset traditional privacy expectations. See Kerr, An Equilibrium-Adjustment Theory of the Fourth Amendment, 125 Harv. L. Rev 476, 512–517 (2011). How those competing effects balance against each other, and how property norms and expectations of privacy form around new technology, often will be difficult to determine during periods of rapid technological change. In those instances, and where the governing legal standard is one of reasonableness, it is wise to defer to legislative judgments like the one embodied in § 2703(d) of the Stored Communications Act. See *Jones*, 565 U. S., at 430 (ALITO, J., concurring). In § 2703(d) Congress weighed the privacy interests at stake and imposed a judicial check to prevent executive overreach. The Court should be wary of upsetting that legislative balance and erecting constitutional barriers that foreclose further legislative instructions. The last thing the Court should do is incorporate an arbitrary and outside limit—in this case six days' worth of cell-site records—and use it as the foundation for a new constitutional framework. The Court's decision runs roughshod over the mechanism Congress put in place to govern the acquisition of cell-site records and closes off further legislative debate on these issues.

C

The Court says its decision is a "narrow one." But its reinterpretation of *Miller* and *Smith* will have dramatic consequences for law enforcement, courts, and society as a whole.

Most immediately, the Court's holding that the Government must get a warrant to obtain more than six days of cell-site records limits the effectiveness of an important investigative tool for solving serious crimes. * * *

The Court's decision also will have ramifications that extend beyond cell-site records to other kinds of information held by third parties, yet the Court fails "to provide clear guidance to law enforcement" and courts on key issues raised by its reinterpretation of *Miller* and *Smith*.

*First*, the Court's holding is premised on cell-site records being a "distinct category of information" from other business records. But the Court does not explain what makes something a distinct category of information. Whether credit card records are distinct from bank records; whether payment records from digital wallet applications are distinct from either; whether the electronic bank records available today are distinct from the paper and microfilm records at issue in *Miller*; or whether cell-phone call records are distinct from the home-phone call records at issue in *Smith*, are just a few of the difficult questions that require answers under the Court's novel conception of *Miller* and *Smith*.

*Second*, the majority opinion gives courts and law enforcement officers no indication how to determine whether any particular category of information falls on the financial-records side or the cell-site-records side of its newly conceived constitutional line. The Court's multifactor analysis—considering intimacy, comprehensiveness, expense, retrospectivity, and voluntariness—puts the law on a new and unstable foundation.

*Third*, even if a distinct category of information is deemed to be more like cell-site records than financial records, courts and law enforcement officers will have to guess how much of that information can be requested before a warrant is required. The Court suggests that less than seven days of location information may not require a warrant. * * * But the Court does not explain why that is so, and nothing in its opinion even alludes to the considerations that should determine whether greater or lesser thresholds should apply to information like IP addresses or website browsing history.

*Fourth*, by invalidating the Government's use of court-approved compulsory process in this case, the Court calls into question the subpoena practices of federal and state grand juries, legislatures, and other investigative bodies, as JUSTICE ALITO's opinion explains. Yet the Court fails even to mention the serious consequences this will have for the proper administration of justice.

\* \* \*

This case should be resolved by interpreting accepted property principles as the baseline for reasonable expectations of privacy. Here the Government did not search anything over which Carpenter could assert ownership or control. Instead, it issued a court-authorized subpoena to a third party to disclose information it alone owned and controlled. That should suffice to resolve this case.

Having concluded, however, that the Government searched Carpenter when it obtained cell-site records from his cell phone service providers, the proper resolution of this case should have been to remand for the Court of Appeals to determine in the first instance whether the search was reasonable. Most courts of appeals, believing themselves bound by *Miller* and *Smith*, have not grappled with this question. And the Court's reflexive imposition of the warrant requirement obscures important and difficult issues, such as the scope of Congress' power to authorize the Government to collect new forms of information using processes that deviate from traditional warrant procedures, and how the Fourth Amendment's reasonableness requirement should apply when the Government uses compulsory process instead of engaging in an actual, physical search.

\* \* \*

### JUSTICE THOMAS, dissenting.

This case should not turn on "whether" a search occurred. It should turn, instead, on *whose* property was searched. \* \* \* By obtaining the cell-site records of MetroPCS and Sprint, the Government did not search Carpenter's property. He did not create the records, he does not maintain them, he cannot control them, and he cannot destroy them. Neither the terms of his contracts nor any provision of law makes the records his. The records belong to MetroPCS and Sprint.

The Court concludes that, although the records are not Carpenter's, the Government must get a warrant because Carpenter had a reasonable "expectation of privacy" in the location information that they reveal. I agree with JUSTICE KENNEDY, JUSTICE ALITO, JUSTICE GORSUCH, and every Court of Appeals to consider the question that this is not the best reading of our precedents.

The more fundamental problem with the Court's opinion, however, is its use of the "reasonable expectation of privacy" test, which was first articulated by Justice Harlan in *Katz* v. *United States*, 389 U. S. 347, 360–361 (1967) (concurring opinion). The *Katz* test has no basis in the text or history of the Fourth Amendment. And, it invites courts to make judgments about policy, not law. Until we confront the problems with this test, *Katz* will continue to distort Fourth Amendment jurisprudence.

I respectfully dissent.

## I

[Justice Thomas looks at the Court's early wiretap cases and moves to *Katz*. He argued that Justice Harlan's *Katz* opinion, not the majority's, "profoundly changed our Fourth Amendment Jurisprudence."]

## II

[In this section he argues that "the *Katz* test misconstrues virtually every one of" the words of the Fourth Amendment. He concludes that "[t]he *Katz* test distorts the original meaning of 'search'"; the word was not associated with a reasonable expectation of privacy before Justice Harlan's opinion; the *Katz* test mistakenly focuses on privacy; *Katz* reads "persons, houses, papers and effects" out of the text.; and makes short shrift of the word "their."

Justice Thomas applies the analysis and concludes that Carpenter cannot prevail unless he proves the cell-site records are his.

He concludes that the Founders would not recognize the Court's warrant requirement because a subpoena for third-party records was not a search.]

## III

[His final conclusion is that "[a]fter 50 years, it is still unclear what question the *Katz* test is even asking," and that "[b]ecause the *Katz* test is a failed experiment, this Court is dutybound to reconsider it."]

**JUSTICE ALITO, with whom JUSTICE THOMAS joins, dissenting.**

I share the Court's concern about the effect of new technology on personal privacy, but I fear that today's decision will do far more harm than good. The Court's reasoning fractures two fundamental pillars of Fourth Amendment law, and in doing so, it guarantees a blizzard of litigation while threatening many legitimate and valuable investigative practices upon which law enforcement has rightfully come to rely.

First, the Court ignores the basic distinction between an actual search (dispatching law enforcement officers to enter private premises and root through private papers and effects) and an order merely requiring a party to look through its own records and produce specified documents. The former, which intrudes on personal privacy far more deeply, requires probable cause; the latter does not. Treating an order to produce like an actual search, as today's decision does, is revolutionary. It violates both the original understanding of the Fourth Amendment and more than a century of Supreme Court precedent. Unless it is somehow restricted to the particular situation in the present case, the Court's move will cause upheaval. Must every grand jury subpoena *duces tecum* be supported by probable cause? If so, investigations of terrorism, political corruption, white-collar crime, and many other offenses will be stymied. And what about subpoenas and other document-production orders issued by administrative agencies?

Second, the Court allows a defendant to object to the search of a third party's property. This also is revolutionary. The Fourth Amendment protects "[t]he right of the people to be secure in *their* persons, houses, papers, and effects" (emphasis added), not the persons, houses, papers, and effects of others. Until today, we have been careful to heed this fundamental feature of the Amendment's text. This was true when the Fourth Amendment was tied to property law, and it remained true after *Katz* v. *United States*, 389 U. S. 347 (1967), broadened the Amendment's reach.

By departing dramatically from these fundamental principles, the Court destabilizes long-established Fourth Amendment doctrine. We will be making repairs—or picking up the pieces—for a long time to come.

I

[Justice Alito traces the history of subpoenas in England, their close association with grand juries in the colonies, and the distinction between "searches" and compulsory production of documents. He finds no evidence that the Founders intended the Fourth Amendment to regulate courts' use of compulsory process. His analysis of Hale v. Henkel, 201 US. 43 (1906), and Oklahoma Press Publishing Co. v. Walling, 327 U.S. 186 (1946), concludes that the Fourth Amendment regulated the compelled production of documents but set a different standard than for searches and seizures; when it came to compulsory process the protection guarded against too much indefiniteness or breath.

Justice Alito agreed with Justice Kennedy that no search or seizure of Carpenter or his property occurred and, even if the government had done a "constructive search," it would have satisfied the *Oklahoma Press* standard.

He questioned why a third party who actually has information could only rely on the *Oklahoma Press* standard in objecting to a subpoena while someone like Carpenter could claim greater protection in records he did not create or possess.]

## II

[Justice Alito argued that permitting a person to object to a search of a third person's property "cannot be defended under either a property-based interpretation of that Amendment or our decisions applying the reasonable-expectations-of-privacy test adopted in *Katz*." His analysis of the Telecommunications Act paralleled that of Justice Kennedy.]

Although the majority professes a desire not to "embarrass the future," we can guess where today's decision will lead.

One possibility is that the broad principles that the Court seems to embrace will be applied across the board. All subpoenas *duces tecum* and all other orders compelling the production of documents will require a demonstration of probable cause, and individuals will be able to claim a protected Fourth Amendment interest in any sensitive personal information about them that is collected and owned by third parties. Those would be revolutionary developments indeed.

The other possibility is that this Court will face the embarrassment of explaining in case after case that the principles on which today's decision rests are subject to all sorts of qualifications and limitations that have not yet been discovered. If we take this latter course, we will inevitably end up "making a crazy quilt of the Fourth Amendment."

All of this is unnecessary. In the Stored Communications Act, Congress addressed the specific problem at issue in this case. The Act restricts the misuse of cell-site records by cell service providers, something that the Fourth Amendment cannot do. The Act also goes beyond current Fourth Amendment case law in restricting access by law enforcement. It permits law enforcement officers to acquire cell-site records only if they meet a heightened standard and obtain a court order. If the American people now think that the Act is inadequate or needs updating, they can turn to their elected representatives to adopt more protective provisions. Because the collection and storage of cell-site records affects nearly every American, it is unlikely that the question whether the current law requires strengthening will escape Congress's notice.

Legislation is much preferable to the development of an entirely new body of Fourth Amendment caselaw for many reasons, including the enormous complexity of the subject, the need to respond to rapidly changing technology, and the Fourth Amendment's limited scope. The Fourth Amendment restricts the conduct of the Federal Government and the States; it does not apply to private actors. But today, some of the greatest threats to individual privacy may come from powerful private companies that collect and sometimes misuse vast quantities of data about the lives of ordinary Americans. If today's decision encourages the public to think that this Court can protect them from this looming threat to their privacy, the decision will mislead as well as disrupt. And if holding a provision of the Stored Communications Act to be unconstitutional dissuades Congress from further legislation in this field, the goal of protecting privacy will be greatly disserved.

The desire to make a statement about privacy in the digital age does not justify the consequences that today's decision is likely to produce.

### JUSTICE GORSUCH, dissenting.

In the late 1960s this Court suggested for the first time that a search triggering the Fourth Amendment occurs when the government violates an "expectation of privacy" that "society is prepared to recognize as 'reasonable.'" Katz v. United States, 389 U. S. 347, 361 (1967) (Harlan, J., concurring). Then, in a pair of decisions in the 1970s applying the Katz test, the Court held that a "reasonable expectation of privacy" doesn't attach to information shared with "third parties." See Smith v. Maryland, 442 U. S. 735, 743–744 (1979); United States v. Miller, 425 U. S. 435, 443 (1976). By these steps, the Court came to conclude, the Constitution does nothing to limit investigators from searching records you've entrusted to your bank, accountant, and maybe even your doctor.

What's left of the Fourth Amendment? Today we use the Internet to do most everything. Smartphones make it easy to keep a calendar, correspond with friends, make calls, conduct banking, and even watch the game. Countless Internet companies maintain records about us and, increasingly, *for* us. Even our most private documents—those that, in other eras, we would have locked safely in a desk drawer or destroyed— now reside on third party servers. *Smith* and *Miller* teach that the police can review all of this material, on the theory that no one reasonably expects any of it will be kept private. But no one believes that, if they ever did.

What to do? It seems to me we could respond in at least three ways. The first is to ignore the problem, maintain *Smith* and *Miller*, and live with the consequences. If the confluence of these decisions and modern technology means our Fourth Amendment rights are reduced to nearly nothing, so be it. The second choice is to set *Smith* and *Miller* aside and try again using the *Katz* "reasonable expectation of privacy" jurisprudence that produced them. The third is to look for answers elsewhere.

Start with the first option. * * * Today the Court suggests that *Smith* and *Miller* distinguish between *kinds* of information disclosed to third parties and require courts to decide whether to "extend" those decisions to particular classes of information, depending on their sensitivity. But as the Sixth Circuit recognized and JUSTICE KENNEDY explains, no balancing test of this kind can be found in *Smith* and *Miller*. Those cases announced a categorical rule: Once you disclose information to third parties, you forfeit any reasonable expectation of privacy you might have had in it. And even if *Smith* and *Miller* did permit courts to conduct a balancing contest of the kind the Court now suggests, it's still hard to see how that would help the petitioner in this case. Why is someone's location when using a phone so much more sensitive than who he was talking to (*Smith*) or what financial transactions he engaged in (*Miller*)? I do not know and the Court does not say.

The problem isn't with the Sixth Circuit's application of *Smith* and *Miller* but with the cases themselves. Can the government demand a copy of all your e-mails from Google or Microsoft without implicating your Fourth Amendment rights? Can it secure your DNA from 23andMe without a warrant or probable cause? *Smith* and *Miller* say yes it can—at least without running afoul of *Katz*. But that result strikes most lawyers and judges today—me included—as pretty unlikely. In the years since its adoption, countless scholars, too, have come to conclude that the "third-party doctrine is not only wrong, but horribly wrong." Kerr, The Case for the Third-Party Doctrine, 107 Mich. L. Rev. 561, 563, n. 5, 564 (2009) (collecting criticisms but defending the doctrine (footnotes omitted)). The reasons are obvious. "As an empirical statement about subjective expectations of privacy," the doctrine is "quite dubious." Baude & Stern, The Positive Law Model of the Fourth Amendment, 129 Harv. L. Rev. 1821, 1872 (2016). People often *do* reasonably expect that information they entrust to third parties, especially information subject to confidentiality agreements, will be kept private. Meanwhile, if the third party doctrine is supposed to represent a normative assessment of when a person should expect privacy, the notion that the answer might be "never" seems a pretty unattractive societal prescription.

What, then, is the explanation for our third party doctrine? The truth is, the Court has never offered a persuasive justification. The Court has said that by conveying information to a third party you " 'assum[e] the risk' " it will be revealed to the police and therefore lack a reasonable expectation of privacy in it. But assumption of risk doctrine developed in tort law. It generally applies when "by contract or otherwise [one] expressly agrees to accept a risk of harm" or impliedly does so by "manifest[ing] his willingness to accept" that risk and thereby "take[s] his chances as to harm which may result from it." Restatement (Second) of Torts §§ 496B, 496C(1), and Comment *b* (1965). That rationale has little play in this context. Suppose I entrust a friend with a letter and he promises to keep it secret until he delivers it to an intended recipient. In what sense have I agreed to bear the risk that he will turn around, break his promise, and spill its contents to someone else? More confusing still, what have I done to "manifest my willingness to accept" the risk that the government will pry the document from my friend and read it *without* his consent?

One possible answer concerns knowledge. I know that my friend *might* break his promise, or that the government *might* have some reason to search the papers in his possession. But knowing about a risk doesn't mean you assume responsibility for it. Whenever you walk down the sidewalk you know a car may negligently or recklessly veer off and hit you, but that hardly means you accept the consequences and absolve the driver of any damage he may do to you.

Some have suggested the third party doctrine is better understood to rest on consent than assumption of risk. "So long as a person knows that they are disclosing information to a third party," the argument goes, "their choice to do so is voluntary and the consent valid." Kerr, *supra,* at 588. I confess I still don't see it. Consenting to give a third party access to private papers that remain my property is not the same thing as consenting to a *search of those papers by the government.* Perhaps there are exceptions, like when the third party is an undercover government agent. But otherwise this conception of consent appears to be just assumption of risk relabeled—you've "consented" to whatever risks are foreseeable.

Another justification sometimes offered for the third party doctrine is clarity. You (and the police) know exactly how much protection you have in information confided to others: none. As rules go, "the king always wins" is admirably clear. But the opposite rule would be clear too: Third party disclosures *never* diminish Fourth Amendment protection (call it "the king always loses"). So clarity alone cannot justify the third party doctrine.

In the end, what do *Smith* and *Miller* add up to? A doubtful application of *Katz* that lets the government search almost whatever it wants whenever it wants. The Sixth Circuit had to follow that rule and faithfully did just that, but it's not clear why we should.

*

There's a second option. What if we dropped *Smith* and *Miller*'s third party doctrine and retreated to the root *Katz* question whether there is a "reasonable expectation of privacy" in data held by third parties? Rather than solve the problem with the third party doctrine, I worry this option only risks returning us to its source: After all, it was *Katz* that produced *Smith* and *Miller* in the first place.

*Katz's* problems start with the text and original understanding of the Fourth Amendment, as JUSTICE THOMAS thoughtfully explains today. The Amendment's protections do not depend on the breach of some abstract "expectation of privacy" whose contours are left to the judicial imagination. Much more concretely, it protects your "person," and your "houses, papers, and effects." Nor does your right to bring a Fourth Amendment claim depend on whether a judge happens to agree that your subjective expectation to privacy is a "reasonable" one. Under its plain terms, the Amendment grants you the right to invoke its guarantees whenever one of your protected things (your person, your house, your papers, or your effects) is unreasonably searched or seized. Period.

History too holds problems for *Katz*. Little like it can be found in the law that led to the adoption of the Fourth Amendment or in this Court's jurisprudence until the late 1960s. The Fourth Amendment came about in response to a trio of 18th century cases "well known to the men who wrote and ratified the Bill of Rights, [and] famous throughout the colonial population." Stuntz, The Substantive Origins of Criminal Procedure, 105 Yale L. J. 393, 397 (1995). The first two were English cases invalidating the Crown's use of general warrants to enter homes and search papers. Entick v. Carrington, 19 How. St. Tr. 1029 (K. B. 1765); Wilkes v. Wood, 19 How. St. Tr. 1153 (K. B. 1763). The third was American: the Boston Writs of Assistance Case, which sparked colonial outrage at the use of writs permitting government agents to enter houses and business, breaking open doors and chests along the way, to conduct searches and seizures—and to force third parties to help them. No doubt the colonial outrage engendered by these cases rested in part on the government's intrusion upon privacy. But the framers chose not to protect privacy in some ethereal way dependent on judicial intuitions. They chose instead to protect privacy in particular places and things—"persons, houses, papers, and effects"—and against particular threats—"unreasonable" governmental "searches and seizures."

Even taken on its own terms, *Katz* has never been sufficiently justified. In fact, we still don't even know what its "reasonable expectation of privacy" test *is*. Is it supposed to pose an empirical question (what privacy expectations do people *actually* have) or a normative one (what expectations *should* they have)? Either way brings problems. If the test is supposed to be an empirical one, it's unclear why judges rather than legislators should conduct it. Legislators are responsive to their constituents and have institutional resources designed to help them discern and enact majoritarian preferences. Politically insulated judges come armed with only the attorneys' briefs, a few law clerks, and their own idiosyncratic experiences. They are hardly the representative group you'd expect (or want) to be making empirical judgments for hundreds of millions of people. Unsurprisingly, too, judicial judgments often fail to reflect public views. Consider just one example. Our cases insist that the seriousness of the offense being investigated does *not* reduce Fourth Amendment protection. Mincey v. Arizona, 437 U. S. 385, 393–394 (1978). Yet scholars suggest that most people *are* more tolerant of police intrusions when they investigate more serious crimes. See Blumenthal, Adya, & Mogle, The Multiple Dimensions of Privacy: Testing Lay "Expectations of Privacy," 11 U. Pa. J. Const. L. 331, 352–353

(2009). And I very much doubt that this Court would be willing to adjust its *Katz* cases to reflect these findings even if it believed them.

Maybe, then, the *Katz* test should be conceived as a normative question. But if that's the case, why (again) do judges, rather than legislators, get to determine whether society *should be* prepared to recognize an expectation of privacy as legitimate? Deciding what privacy interests *should be* recognized often calls for a pure policy choice, many times between incommensurable goods—between the value of privacy in a particular setting and society's interest in combating crime. Answering questions like that calls for the exercise of raw political will belonging to legislatures, not the legal judgment proper to courts. See The Federalist No. 78, p. 465 (C. Rossiter ed. 1961) (A. Hamilton). When judges abandon legal judgment for political will we not only risk decisions where "reasonable expectations of privacy" come to bear "an uncanny resemblance to those expectations of privacy" shared by Members of this Court. Minnesota v. Carter, 525 U. S. 83, 97 (1998) (Scalia, J., concurring). We also risk undermining public confidence in the courts themselves.

My concerns about *Katz* come with a caveat. *Sometimes*, I accept, judges may be able to discern and describe existing societal norms. See, *e.g., Florida* v. *Jardines*, 569 U. S. 1, 8 (2013) (inferring a license to enter on private property from the "habits of the country" ). That is particularly true when the judge looks to positive law rather than intuition for guidance on social norms. See *Byrd* v. *United States,* 584 U. S. \_\_\_, \_\_\_– \_\_\_ (2018) (slip op., at 7–9) ("general property-based concept[s] guid[e] the resolution of this case"). So there may be *some* occasions where *Katz* is capable of principled application—though it may simply wind up approximating the more traditional option I will discuss in a moment. Sometimes it may also be possible to apply *Katz* by analogizing from precedent when the line between an existing case and a new fact pattern is short and direct. But so far this Court has declined to tie itself to any significant restraints like these. * * *

As a result, *Katz* has yielded an often unpredictable—and sometimes unbelievable—jurisprudence. *Smith* and *Miller* are only two examples; there are many others. Take Florida v. Riley, 488 U. S. 445 (1989), which says that a police helicopter hovering 400 feet above a person's property invades no reasonable expectation of privacy. Try that one out on your neighbors. Or California v. Greenwood, 486 U. S. 35 (1988), which holds that a person has no reasonable expectation of privacy in the garbage he puts out for collection. In that case, the Court said that the homeowners forfeited their privacy interests because "[i]t is common knowledge that plastic garbage bags left on or at the side of a public street are readily accessible to animals, children, scavengers, snoops, and other members of the public." But the habits of raccoons don't prove much about the habits of the country. I doubt, too, that most people spotting a neighbor rummaging through their garbage would think they lacked reasonable grounds to confront the rummager. Making the decision all the stranger, California state law expressly *protected* a homeowner's property rights in discarded trash. Yet rather than defer to that as evidence of the people's habits and reasonable expectations of privacy, the Court substituted its own curious judgment.

Resorting to *Katz* in data privacy cases threatens more of the same. Just consider. The Court today says that judges should use *Katz*'s reasonable expectation of privacy test to decide what Fourth Amendment rights people have in cell-site location information, explaining that "no single rubric definitively resolves which expectations of privacy are entitled to protection." But then it offers a twist. Lower courts should be sure to add two special principles to their *Katz* calculus: the need to avoid "arbitrary power" and the importance of "plac[ing] obstacles in the way of a too permeating police surveillance." While surely laudable, these principles don't offer lower courts much guidance. The Court does not tell us, for example, how far to carry either principle or how to weigh them against the legitimate needs of law enforcement. At what point does access to electronic data amount to "arbitrary" authority? When does police surveillance become "too permeating"? And what sort of "obstacles" should judges "place" in law enforcement's path when it does? We simply do not know.

The Court's application of these principles supplies little more direction. The Court declines to say whether there is any sufficiently limited period of time "for which the Government may obtain an individual's historical [location information] free from Fourth Amendment scrutiny." But then it tells us that access to seven days' worth of information *does* trigger Fourth Amendment scrutiny—even though here the carrier "produced only two days of records." Why is the relevant fact the seven days of information the government *asked for* instead of the two days of information the government *actually saw*? Why seven days instead of ten or three or one? And in what possible sense did the government "search" five days' worth of location information it was never even sent? We do not know.

Later still, the Court adds that it can't say whether the Fourth Amendment is triggered when the government collects "real-time CSLI or 'tower dumps' (a download of information on all the devices that connected to a particular cell site during a particular interval)." But what distinguishes historical data from real-time data, or seven days of a single person's data from a down-load of *everyone*'s data over some indefinite period of time? Why isn't a tower dump the *paradigmatic* example of "too permeating police surveillance" and a dangerous tool of "arbitrary" authority—the touchstones of the majority's modified *Katz* analysis? On what possible basis could such mass data collection survive the Court's test while collecting a single person's data does not? Here again we are left to guess. At the same time, though, the Court offers some firm assurances. It tells us its decision does *not* "call into question conventional surveillance techniques and tools, such as security cameras." That, however, just raises more questions for lower courts to sort out about what techniques qualify as "conventional" and why those techniques would be okay *even if* they lead to "permeating police surveillance" or "arbitrary police power."

Nor is this the end of it. After finding a reasonable expectation of privacy, the Court says there's still more work to do. Courts must determine whether to "extend" *Smith* and *Miller* to the circumstances before them. So apparently *Smith* and *Miller* aren't quite left for dead; they just no longer have the clear reach they once did. How do we measure their new reach? The Court says courts now must conduct a *second Katz*-like balancing inquiry, asking whether the fact of disclosure to a third party outweighs privacy interests in the "category of information" so disclosed. But how are lower courts supposed to weigh these radically different interests? Or assign values to different categories of information? All we know is that historical cell-site location information (for seven days, anyway) escapes *Smith* and *Miller*'s shorn grasp, while a lifetime of bank or phone records does not. As to any other kind of information, lower courts will have to stay tuned.

In the end, our lower court colleagues are left with two amorphous balancing tests, a series of weighty and incommensurable principles to consider in them, and a few illustrative examples that seem little more than the product of judicial intuition. In the Court's defense, though, we have arrived at this strange place not because the Court has misunderstood *Katz*. Far from it. We have arrived here because this is where *Katz* inevitably leads.

*

There is another way. From the founding until the 1960s, the right to assert a Fourth Amendment claim didn't depend on your ability to appeal to a judge's personal sensibilities about the "reasonableness" of your expectations or privacy. It was tied to the law. *Jardines*, 569 U. S., at 11; United States v. Jones, 565 U. S. 400, 405 (2012). The Fourth Amendment protects "the right of the people to be secure in their persons, houses, papers and effects, against unreasonable searches and seizures." True to those words and their original understanding, the traditional approach asked if a house, paper or effect was *yours* under law. No more was needed to trigger the Fourth Amendment. Though now often lost in *Katz*'s shadow, this traditional understanding persists. *Katz* only "supplements, rather than displaces the traditional property-based understanding of the Fourth Amendment."

Beyond its provenance in the text and original understanding of the Amendment, this traditional approach comes with other advantages. Judges are supposed to decide cases based on "democratically legitimate sources of law"—like positive law or analogies to items protected by the enacted Constitution—rather than "their own biases or personal policy preferences." Pettys, Judicial Discretion in Constitutional Cases, 26 J. L. & Pol. 123, 127 (2011). A Fourth Amendment model based on positive legal rights carves out significant room for legislative participation in the Fourth Amendment context, too, by asking judges to consult what the people's representatives have to say about their rights. Nor is this approach hobbled by *Smith* and *Miller*, for those cases are just *limitations* on *Katz*, addressing only the question whether individuals have a reasonable expectation of privacy in materials they share with third parties. Under this more traditional approach, Fourth Amendment protections for your papers and effects do not automatically disappear just because you share them with third parties.

Given the prominence *Katz* has claimed in our doctrine, American courts are pretty rusty at applying the traditional approach to the Fourth Amendment. We know that if a house, paper, or effect is yours, you have a Fourth Amendment interest in its protection. But what kind of legal interest is sufficient to make something *yours*? And what source of law determines that? Current positive law? The common law at 1791, extended by analogy to modern times? Both? Much work is needed to revitalize this area and answer these questions. I do not begin to claim all the answers today, but (unlike with *Katz*) at least I have a pretty good idea what the questions *are*. And it seems to me a few things can be said.

*First*, the fact that a third party has access to or possession of your papers and effects does not necessarily eliminate your interest in them. Ever hand a private document to a friend to be returned? Toss your keys to a valet at a restaurant? Ask your neighbor to look after your dog while you travel? You would not expect the friend to share the document with others; the valet to lend your car to his buddy; or the neighbor to put Fido up for adoption. Entrusting your stuff to others is a *bailment*. A bailment is the "delivery of personal property by one person (the *bailor*) to another (the *bailee*) who holds the property for a certain purpose." * * * A bailee normally owes a legal duty to keep the item safe, according to the terms of the parties' contract if they have one, and according to the "implication[s] from their conduct" if they don't. A bailee who uses the item in a different way than he's supposed to, or against the bailor's instructions, is liable for conversion. This approach is quite different from *Smith* and *Miller*'s (counter)-intuitive approach to reasonable expectations of privacy; where those cases extinguish Fourth Amendment interests once records are given to a third party, property law may preserve them.

Our Fourth Amendment jurisprudence already reflects this truth. In Ex parte Jackson, 96 U. S. 727 (1878), this Court held that sealed letters placed in the mail are "as fully guarded from examination and inspection, except as to their outward form and weight, as if they were retained by the parties forwarding them in their own domiciles." The reason, drawn from the Fourth Amendment's text, was that "[t]he constitutional guaranty of the right of the people to be secure in their papers against unreasonable searches and seizures extends to *their papers*, thus closed against inspection, *wherever they may be*." It did not matter that letters were bailed to a third party (the government, no less). The sender enjoyed the same Fourth Amendment protection as he does "when papers are subjected to search in one's own household."

These ancient principles may help us address modern data cases too. Just because you entrust your data—in some cases, your modern-day papers and effects—to a third party may not mean you lose any Fourth Amendment interest in its contents. Whatever may be left of *Smith* and *Miller*, few doubt that e-mail should be treated much like the traditional mail it has largely supplanted—as a bailment in which the owner retains a vital and protected legal interest. * * *

*Second*, I doubt that complete ownership or exclusive control of property is always a necessary condition to the assertion of a Fourth Amendment right. Where houses are concerned, for example, individuals can enjoy Fourth Amendment protection without fee simple title. Both the text of the Amendment and the common law rule support that conclusion. * * * That is why tenants and resident family members— though they have no legal title—have standing to complain about searches of the houses in which they live.

Another point seems equally true: just because you *have* to entrust a third party with your data doesn't necessarily mean you should lose all Fourth Amendment protections in it. Not infrequently one person comes into possession of someone else's property without the owner's consent. Think of the finder of lost goods or the policeman who impounds a car. The law recognizes that the goods and the car still belong to their true owners, for "where a person comes into lawful possession of the personal property of another, even though there is no formal agreement between the property's owner and its possessor, the possessor will become a constructive bailee when justice so requires." At least some of this Court's decisions have already suggested that use of technology is functionally compelled by the demands of modern life, and in that way the fact that we store data with third parties may amount to a sort of involuntary bailment too. See *Riley* v. *California*, 573 U. S. ___, ___ (2014) (slip op., at 9).

*Third*, positive law may help provide detailed guidance on evolving technologies without resort to judicial intuition. State (or sometimes federal) law often creates rights in both tangible and intangible things. In the context of the Takings Clause we often ask whether those state-created rights are sufficient to make something someone's property for constitutional purposes. A similar inquiry may be appropriate for the Fourth Amendment. Both the States and federal government are actively legislating in the area of third party data storage and the rights users enjoy. See, *e.g.,* Stored Communications Act, 18 U. S. C. § 2701 *et seq.*; Tex. Prop. Code Ann. § 111.004(12) (West 2017) (defining "[p]roperty" to include "property held in any digital or electronic medium"). State courts are busy expounding common law property principles in this area as well. *E.g.,* Ajemian v. Yahoo!, Inc., 478 Mass. 169, 170, 84 N. E. 3d 766, 768 (2017) (e-mail account is a "form of property often referred to as a 'digital asset' "); Eysoldt v. ProScan Imaging, 194 Ohio App. 3d 630, 638, 2011–Ohio–2359, 957 N. E. 2d 780, 786 (2011) (permitting action for conversion of web account as intangible property). If state legislators or state courts say that a digital record has the attributes that normally make something property, that may supply a sounder basis for judicial decisionmaking than judicial guesswork about societal expectations.

*Fourth*, while positive law may help establish a person's Fourth Amendment interest there may be some circumstances where positive law cannot be used to defeat it. *Ex parte Jackson* reflects that understanding. There this Court said that "[n]o law of Congress" could authorize letter carriers "to invade the secrecy of letters." So the post office couldn't impose a regulation dictating that those mailing letters surrender all legal interests in them once they're deposited in a mailbox. If that is right, *Jackson* suggests the existence of a constitutional floor below which Fourth Amendment rights may not descend. Legislatures cannot pass laws declaring your house or papers to be your property except to the extent the police wish to search them without cause. As the Court has previously explained, "we must assur[e] preservation of that degree of privacy against government that existed when the Fourth Amendment was adopted." *Jones*, 565 U. S., at 406 ). Nor does this mean protecting only the specific rights known at the founding; it means protecting their modern analogues too. So, for example, while thermal imaging was unknown in 1791, this Court has recognized that using that technology to look inside a home constitutes a Fourth Amendment "search" of that "home" no less than a physical inspection might.

*Fifth*, this constitutional floor may, in some instances, bar efforts to circumvent the Fourth Amendment's protection through the use of subpoenas. No one thinks the government can evade *Jackson*'s prohibition on opening sealed letters without a warrant simply by issuing a subpoena to a postmaster for "all letters sent by John Smith" or, worse, "all letters sent by John Smith concerning a particular transaction." So the question courts will confront will be this: What other kinds of records are sufficiently similar to letters in the mail that the same rule should apply?

It may be that, as an original matter, a subpoena requiring the recipient to produce records wasn't thought of as a "search or seizure" by the government implicating the Fourth Amendment, but instead as an act of compelled self-incrimination implicating the Fifth Amendment. But the common law of searches and seizures does not appear to have confronted a case where private documents equivalent to a mailed letter were entrusted to a bailee and then subpoenaed. As a result, "[t]he common-law rule regarding subpoenas for documents held by third parties entrusted with information from the target is . . . unknown and perhaps unknowable." Given that (perhaps insoluble) uncertainty, I am content to adhere to *Jackson* and its implications for now.

\* \* \*

What does all this mean for the case before us? To start, I cannot fault the Sixth Circuit for holding that *Smith* and *Miller* extinguish any *Katz*-based Fourth Amendment interest in third party cell-site data. That is the plain effect of their categorical holdings. Nor can I fault the Court today for its implicit but unmistakable conclusion that the rationale of *Smith* and *Miller* is wrong; indeed, I agree with that. The Sixth Circuit was powerless to say so, but this Court can and should. At the same time, I do not agree with the Court's decision today to keep *Smith* and *Miller* on life support and supplement them with a new and multilayered inquiry that seems to be only *Katz*-squared. Returning there, I worry, promises more trouble than help. Instead, I would look to a more traditional Fourth Amendment approach. \* \* \* Neglecting more traditional approaches may mean failing to vindicate the full protections of the Fourth Amendment.

Our case offers a cautionary example. It seems to me entirely possible a person's cell-site data could qualify as *his* papers or effects under existing law. Yes, the telephone carrier holds the information. But 47 U. S. C. § 222 designates a customer's cell-site location information as "customer proprietary network information" (CPNI), § 222(h)(1)(A), and gives customers certain rights to control use of and access to CPNI about themselves. The statute generally forbids a carrier to "use, disclose, or permit access to individually identifiable" CPNI without the customer's consent, except as needed to provide the customer's telecommunications services. § 222(c)(1). It also requires the carrier to disclose CPNI "upon affirmative written request by the customer, to any person designated by the customer." § 222(c)(2). Congress even afforded customers a private cause of action for damages against carriers who violate the Act's terms. § 207. Plainly, customers have substantial legal interests in this information, including at least some right to include, exclude, and control its use. Those interests might even rise to the level of a property right.

The problem is that we do not know anything more. Before the district court and court of appeals, Mr. Carpenter pursued only a *Katz* "reasonable expectations" argument. He did not invoke the law of property or any analogies to the common law, either there or in his petition for certiorari. Even in his merits brief before this Court, Mr. Carpenter's discussion of his positive law rights in cell-site data was cursory. He offered no analysis, for example, of what rights state law might provide him in addition to those supplied by § 222. In these circumstances, I cannot help but conclude—reluctantly—that Mr. Carpenter forfeited perhaps his most promising line of argument.

Unfortunately, too, this case marks the second time this Term that individuals have forfeited Fourth Amendment arguments based on positive law by failing to preserve them. See *Byrd*, 584 U. S., at ___ (slip op., at 7). Litigants have had fair notice since at least *United States v. Jones (2012) and Florida v. Jardines* (2013) that arguments like these may vindicate Fourth Amendment interests even where *Katz* arguments do not. Yet the arguments have gone unmade, leaving courts to the usual *Katz* handwaving. These omissions do not serve the development of a sound or fully protective Fourth Amendment jurisprudence.

# IV.  OBTAINING A SEARCH WARRANT: CONSTITUTIONAL PREREQUISITES

## A.  DEMONSTRATING PROBABLE CAUSE

### 5.  Quantity of Information Required for Probable Cause

### Page 141. Add at the end of the section on Probable Cause to Arrest:

In District of Columbia v. Wesby, 138 S. Ct. 577 (2018), Justice Thomas wrote for the Court as it held that police officers had probable cause to arrest 21 individuals who were partying in a house with the permission of a woman with whom the owner of the house had been trying to negotiate a lease. The police arrived at the house in response to a complaint about loud music and illegal activities. They found the house to be in disarray, smelled marijuana and saw beer bottles and liquor cups on the floor, discovered a "makeshift strip club" in the living room and "more debauchery upstairs." An officer was told by two "women working the party" that a woman named "Peaches" or "Tasty" was renting the house and had given them permission to be there. One of the woman called Peaches at the officer's request, and Peaches said she had just gone to the store. A sergeant spoke with her, and she claimed to be renting the house from the owner who was fixing it up for her. In a subsequent call, she admitted she did not have permission to use the house. After the officers contacted the owner and he confirmed that he had not given Peaches or anyone else permission to be in house, the officers made the arrests.

16 of the 21 partygoers sued the District. The district court awarded them partial summary judgment and held that the officers lacked probable cause to arrest because nothing they learned suggested that the partygoers knew or should have known that they were in the house against the owner's will. A jury awarded damages. A divided panel of the court of appeals affirmed, and the court denied rehearing en banc over four dissents.

Justice Thomas's opinion found that the officers reasonably could have concluded that they had probable cause to arrest and, even assuming that there was no probable cause, they had qualified immunity.

## B. PROBABLE CAUSE, SPECIFICITY AND REASONABLENESS

**Page 173. Add the following section at the end of the material on obtaining a search warrant:**

### 11. Warrants for Information Stored Abroad

In United States v. Microsoft Corp., 138 S. Ct. 1186 (2018) (per curiam), the Court dismissed as moot a case in which the government obtained a warrant pursuant to 18 U.S.C. § 2703 (the Stored Communications Act) compelling Microsoft to disclose all e-mails and other information associated with the account of one of its customers. Microsoft determined that all of the e-mail contents were stored in a data center in Dublin and moved to quash the warrant as beyond the territorial coverage of the Stored Communications Act. The district court denied Microsoft's motion and, acting on a stipulation jointly submitted by the parties, held Microsoft in civil contempt. But, the Second Circuit reversed the decision, vacated the civil contempt finding, and held that requiring Microsoft to disclose the electronic communications in question would be an unauthorized extraterritorial application of § 2703, While the case was pending before the Supreme Court, Congress enacted and the President signed into law the Clarifying Lawful Overseas Use of Data Act (CLOUD Act), as part of the Consolidated Appropriations Act, 2018, Pub. L. 115–141. The Court held that the enactment of the Act mooted the case.

The CLOUD Act amends the Stored Communications Act, 18 U. S. C. § 2701 et seq., by adding the following provision:

> A [service provider] shall comply with the obligations of this chapter to preserve, backup, or disclose the contents of a wire or electronic communication and any record or other information pertaining to a customer or subscriber within such provider's possession, custody, or control, regardless of whether such communication, record, or other information is located within or outside of the United States.

Litigation over the accessibility of records stored in foreign countries is not likely to end because the CLOUD Act is now law. The Act permits companies to challenge law enforcement data requests if an order would pose international conflict of law issues. Companies can challenge warrants for data if there is a bilateral law enforcement pact between the United States and a "qualifying foreign government," and also if the warrant would cause a conflict of law issue with other countries absent a law enforcement sharing agreement.

# V.   TO APPLY OR NOT APPLY THE WARRANT CLAUSE

## A.  ARRESTS IN PUBLIC AND IN THE HOME

### 3.   The Constitutional Rule: Arrests in Public

### Page 199. Add after the second full paragraph:

#### *Qualified Immunity: Kisela v. Hughes*

In Kisela v Hughes, 138 S. Ct. 1148 (2018) (per curiam), the Court summarily reversed the Ninth Circuit's holding that a police officer who shot a knife-wielding suspect was not entitled to qualified immunity. The Court did not decide whether the officer violated the Fourth Amendment, and held only that this was far from an obvious case in which any competent officer would have known that the shooting constituted excessive force under the Fourth Amendment.

Justice Sotomayor, joined by Justice Ginsburg, dissented, and argued that the Ninth Circuit was correct and the case should not have been summarily decided. She ended her opinion by pointing out the Court's willingness to intervene when lower courts deny officers qualified immunity and its unwillingness to intervene when the courts grant officers qualified immunity. She wrote that the Court's signal to law enforcement officers was "they can shoot first and think later."

## D.  PRETEXTUAL STOPS AND ARRESTS

**Page 381. Add after second full paragraph:**

### *First Amendment Issues*

In Lozman v. City of Riviera Beach, 138 S. Ct. 975 (2018), Justice Kennedy wrote for eight Justices as the Court held that Lozman could proceed with his claim that his arrest was in retaliation for protected speech despite the fact that he conceded that there was probable cause for the arrest.

Lozman owned a floating home which he towed into a marina owned by the City. He became a fierce critic of the City's plan to use its eminent domain authority to seize waterfront homes for private development, often made critical comments about officials during public-comment periods at city council meetings, and brought a lawsuit alleging that the council's agreement with developers violated Florida's open-meetings law. During one public comment session, Lozman began to speak about the arrests of officials from other jurisdictions and refused a councilmember's request to stop speaking. The councilmember told a police officer to "carry him out," and the officer handcuffed Lozman and removed him.

The City claimed that the arrest occurred because Lozman violated the council's rules of procedure by discussing issues unrelated to the city and then refusing to leave the podium. Lozman alleged that five months before his arrest the council had held a closed-door session to discuss his open-meetings suit and devised an official plan to intimidate him, and that the arrest was retaliation for his filing the suit and his prior criticisms of officials. The state's attorney determined that there was probable cause to arrest Lozman for disorderly conduct and resisting arrest without violence, but decided to dismiss the charges. In the Supreme Court Lozman conceded that there was probable cause for his arrest.

Justice Kennedy explained that the Court's earlier decisions in Mt. Healthy City Bd. of Ed. v. Doyle, 429 U. S. 274 (1977), and Hartman v. Moore, 547 U. S. 250 (2006), were important precedents in this new case. In *Mt. Healthy,* the Court held that, even if the decision not to rehire an untenured teacher was based in substantial part on a desire to retaliate because of protected speech, there was no liability unless the alleged constitutional violation was a but-for cause of the employment termination. In *Hartman,* the Court held that a plaintiff alleging a retaliatory prosecution must show the absence of probable cause for the underlying criminal charge, and that the case ends if there was probable cause.

Justice Kennedy explained *Hartman* as recognizing that prosecutors have absolute immunity for their prosecutorial decisions so that any retaliation claim must be made against other people or entities, which means that it often can be difficult to determine whether the decision to prosecute was influenced by the others as opposed to being simply a prosecutorial judgment. In response to the City's heavy reliance on *Hartman*, he observed that "[t]here is undoubted force in the City's position." He explained the "force" in the City's argument by pointing out that there are on average about 29,000 arrests per day in this country; police officers often make split-second judgments, and the content of a suspect's speech might be a consideration in circumstances where the officer must decide whether the suspect is ready to cooperate or presents a continuing threat; and retaliatory arrest claims, much like retaliatory prosecution claims, can make it difficult to determine what connection, if any, exists between a defendant's alleged animus and the arrest.

In the end, the Court did not choose between *Mt. Healthy* and *Hartman* in the typical case:

> The parties' arguments raise difficult questions about the scope of First Amendment protections when speech is made in connection with, or contemporaneously to, criminal activity. But whether in a retaliatory arrest case the *Hartman* approach should apply, thus barring a suit where probable cause exists, or, on the other hand, the inquiry should be governed only by *Mt. Healthy* is a determination that must await a different case. For Lozman's claim is far afield from the typical retaliatory arrest claim, and the difficulties that might arise if *Mt. Healthy* is applied to the mine run of arrests made by police officers are not present here.

> Here Lozman does not sue the officer who made the arrest. Indeed, Lozman likely could not have maintained a retaliation claim against the arresting officer in these circumstances, because the officer appears to have acted in good faith, and there is no showing that the officer had any knowledge of Lozman's prior speech or any motive to arrest him for his earlier expressive activities.

> Instead Lozman alleges more governmental action than simply an arrest. His claim is that the City itself retaliated against him pursuant to an "official municipal policy" of intimidation. In particular, he alleges that the City, through its legislators, formed a premeditated plan to intimidate him in retaliation for his criticisms of city officials and his open-meetings lawsuit. * * *

The fact that Lozman must prove the existence and enforcement of an official policy motivated by retaliation separates Lozman's claim from the typical retaliatory arrest claim. An official retaliatory policy is a particularly troubling and potent form of retaliation, for a policy can be long term and pervasive, unlike an ad hoc, on-the-spot decision by an individual officer. An official policy also can be difficult to dislodge. A citizen who suffers retaliation by an individual officer can seek to have the officer disciplined or removed from service, but there may be little practical recourse when the government itself orchestrates the retaliation. For these reasons, when retaliation against protected speech is elevated to the level of official policy, there is a compelling need for adequate avenues of redress.

In addition, Lozman's allegations, if proved, alleviate the problems that the City says will result from applying *Mt. Healthy* in retaliatory arrest cases. The causation problem in arrest cases is not of the same difficulty where, as is alleged here, the official policy is retaliation for prior, protected speech bearing little relation to the criminal offense for which the arrest is made. In determining whether there was probable cause to arrest Lozman for disrupting a public assembly, it is difficult to see why a city official could have legitimately considered that Lozman had, months earlier, criticized city officials or filed a lawsuit against the City. * * *

Justice Thomas was the sole dissenter. He noted that the Court granted certiorari to decide "whether the existence of probable cause defeats a First Amendment claim for retaliatory arrest under [42 U. S. C.] § 1983," observed that the Court creates a special rule for a "unique class of retaliatory arrest claims," and wrote that "[i]Instead of dreaming up our own rule, I would have answered the question presented and held that plaintiffs must plead and prove a lack of probable cause as an element of a First Amendment retaliatory-arrest claim."

## F.  AUTOMOBILES AND OTHER MOVABLE OBJECTS

### 2.   The Progeny of *Carroll*

**Page 398. Add at the end of the section:**

#### *Vehicles on Private Property: Collins v. Virginia*

### COLLINS V. VIRGINIA
Supreme Court of the United States, 2018.
138 S. Ct. 1663.

**JUTICE SOTOMAYOR delivered the opinion of the Court.**

This case presents the question whether the automobile exception to the Fourth Amendment permits a police officer, uninvited and without a warrant, to enter the curtilage of a home in order to search a vehicle parked therein. It does not.

I

Officer Matthew McCall of the Albemarle County Police Department in Virginia saw the driver of an orange and black motorcycle with an extended frame commit a traffic infraction. The driver eluded Officer McCall's attempt to stop the motorcycle. A few weeks later, Officer David Rhodes of the same department saw an orange and black motorcycle traveling well over the speed limit, but the driver got away from him, too. The officers compared notes and concluded that the two incidents involved the same motorcyclist.

Upon further investigation, the officers learned that the motorcycle likely was stolen and in the possession of petitioner Ryan Collins. After discovering photographs on Collins' Facebook profile that featured an orange and black motorcycle parked at the top of the driveway of a house, Officer Rhodes tracked down the address of the house, drove there, and parked on the street. It was later established that Collins' girlfriend lived in the house and that Collins stayed there a few nights per week.

From his parked position on the street, Officer Rhodes saw what appeared to be a motorcycle with an extended frame covered with a white tarp, parked at the same angle and in the same location on the driveway as in the Facebook photograph. Officer Rhodes, who did not have a warrant, exited his car and walked toward the house. He stopped to take a photograph of the covered motorcycle from the sidewalk, and then walked onto the residential property and up to the top of the driveway to where the motorcycle was parked. In order "to investigate further," Officer Rhodes pulled off the tarp, revealing a motorcycle that looked like the one from the speeding incident. He then ran a search of the license plate and vehicle identification numbers, which confirmed that the motorcycle was stolen. After gathering this information, Officer Rhodes took a photograph of the uncovered motorcycle, put the tarp back on, left the property, and returned to his car to wait for Collins.

Shortly thereafter, Collins returned home. Officer Rhodes walked up to the front door of the house and knocked. Collins answered, agreed to speak with Officer Rhodes, and admitted that the motorcycle was his and that he had bought it without title. Officer Rhodes then arrested Collins.

Collins was indicted by a Virginia grand jury for receiving stolen property. He filed a pretrial motion to suppress the evidence that Officer Rhodes had obtained as a result of the warrantless search of the motorcycle. Collins argued that Officer Rhodes had trespassed on the curtilage of the house to conduct an investigation in violation of the Fourth Amendment. The trial court denied the motion and Collins was convicted.

The Court of Appeals of Virginia affirmed. It assumed that the motorcycle was parked in the curtilage of the home and held that Officer Rhodes had probable cause to believe that the motorcycle under the tarp was the same motorcycle that had evaded him in the past. It further concluded that Officer Rhodes' actions were lawful under the Fourth Amendment even absent a warrant because "numerous exigencies justified both his entry onto the property and his moving the tarp to view the motorcycle and record its identification number."

The Supreme Court of Virginia affirmed on different reasoning. It explained that the case was most properly resolved with reference to the Fourth Amendment's automobile exception. Under that framework, it held that Officer Rhodes had probable cause to believe that the motorcycle was contraband, and that the warrantless search therefore was justified.

We granted certiorari, and now reverse.

## II

The Fourth Amendment provides in relevant part that the "right of the people to be secure in their persons, houses, papers, and effects, against unreasonable searches and seizures, shall not be violated." This case arises at the intersection of two components of the Court's Fourth Amendment jurisprudence: the automobile exception to the warrant requirement and the protection extended to the curtilage of a home.

### A

#### 1

The Court has held that the search of an automobile can be reasonable without a warrant. The Court first articulated the so-called automobile exception in Carroll v. United States, 267 U. S. 132 (1925). In that case, law enforcement officers had probable cause to believe that a car they observed traveling on the road contained illegal liquor. They stopped and searched the car, discovered and seized the illegal liquor, and arrested the occupants. The Court upheld the warrantless search and seizure, explaining that a "necessary difference" exists between searching "a store, dwelling house or other structure" and searching "a ship, motor boat, wagon or automobile" because a "vehicle can be quickly moved out of the locality or jurisdiction in which the warrant must be sought."

The "ready mobility" of vehicles served as the core justification for the automobile exception for many years. California v. Carney, 471 U. S. 386, 390 (1985) (citing, e.g., Cooper v. California, 386 U. S. 58, 59 (1967); Chambers v. Maroney, 399 U. S. 42, 51–52 (1970)). Later cases then introduced an additional rationale based on "the pervasive regulation of vehicles capable of traveling on the public highways." *Carney,* 471 U. S., at 392.

In announcing each of these two justifications, the Court took care to emphasize that the rationales applied only to automobiles and not to houses, and therefore supported "treating automobiles differently from houses" as a constitutional matter. Cady v. Dombrowski, 413 U. S. 433, 441 (1973).

When these justifications for the automobile exception "come into play," officers may search an automobile without having obtained a warrant so long as they have probable cause to do so. *Carney*, 471 U. S., at 392–393.

2

Like the automobile exception, the Fourth Amendment's protection of curtilage has long been black letter law. "[W]hen it comes to the Fourth Amendment, the home is first among equals." Florida v. Jardines, 569 U. S. 1, 6 (2013). "At the Amendment's 'very core' stands 'the right of a man to retreat into his own home and there be free from unreasonable governmental intrusion.'" *Ibid.* To give full practical effect to that right, the Court considers curtilage—"the area immediately surrounding and associated with the home"—to be "part of the home itself for Fourth Amendment purposes." *Jardines*, 569 U. S., at 6. "The protection afforded the curtilage is essentially a protection of families and personal privacy in an area intimately linked to the home, both physically and psychologically, where privacy expectations are most heightened." California v. Ciraolo, 476 U. S. 207, 212–213 (1986).

When a law enforcement officer physically intrudes on the curtilage to gather evidence, a search within the meaning of the Fourth Amendment has occurred. *Jardines*, 569 U. S., at 11. Such conduct thus is presumptively unreasonable absent a warrant.

B

1

With this background in mind, we turn to the application of these doctrines in the instant case. As an initial matter, we decide whether the part of the driveway where Collins' motorcycle was parked and subsequently searched is curtilage.

According to photographs in the record, the driveway runs alongside the front lawn and up a few yards past the front perimeter of the house. The top portion of the driveway that sits behind the front perimeter of the house is enclosed on two sides by a brick wall about the height of a car and on a third side by the house. A side door provides direct access between this partially enclosed section of the driveway and the house. A visitor endeavoring to reach the front door of the house would have to walk partway up the driveway, but would turn off before entering the enclosure and instead proceed up a set of steps leading to the front porch. When Officer Rhodes searched the motorcycle, it was parked inside this partially enclosed top portion of the driveway that abuts the house.

The "conception defining the curtilage is . . . familiar enough that it is 'easily understood from our daily experience." *Jardines*, 569 U. S., at 7 . Just like the front porch, side garden, or area "outside the front window," *Jardines,* 569 U. S., at 6, the driveway enclosure where Officer Rhodes searched the motorcycle constitutes "an area adjacent to the home and to which the activity of home life extends," and so is properly considered curtilage, *id.,* at 7.

2

In physically intruding on the curtilage of Collins' home to search the motorcycle, Officer Rhodes not only invaded Collins' Fourth Amendment interest in the item searched, *i.e.,* the motorcycle, but also invaded Collins' Fourth Amendment interest in the curtilage of his home. The question before the Court is whether the automobile exception justifies the invasion of the curtilage. The answer is no.

Applying the relevant legal principles to a slightly different factual scenario confirms that this is an easy case. Imagine a motorcycle parked inside the living room of a house, visible through a window to a passerby on the street. Imagine further that an officer has probable cause to believe that the motorcycle was involved in a traffic infraction. Can the officer, acting without a warrant, enter the house to search the motorcycle and confirm whether it is the right one? Surely not.

The reason is that the scope of the automobile exception extends no further than the automobile itself. See, e.g., Pennsylvania v. Labron, 518 U. S. 938, 940 (1996) (*per curiam*) (explaining that the automobile exception "permits police to search the vehicle"); Wyoming v. Houghton,

526 U. S. 295, 300 (1999) ("[T]he Framers would have regarded as reasonable (if there was probable cause) the warrantless search of containers *within* an automobile"). Virginia asks the Court to expand the scope of the automobile exception to permit police to invade any space outside an automobile even if the Fourth Amendment protects that space. Nothing in our case law, however, suggests that the automobile exception gives an officer the right to enter a home or its curtilage to access a vehicle without a warrant. Expanding the scope of the automobile exception in this way would both undervalue the core Fourth Amendment protection afforded to the home and its curtilage and untether the automobile exception from the justifications underlying it.

The Court already has declined to expand the scope of other exceptions to the warrant requirement to permit warrantless entry into the home. The reasoning behind those decisions applies equally well in this context. For instance, under the plain-view doctrine, "any valid warrantless seizure of incriminating evidence" requires that the officer "have a lawful right of access to the object itself." Horton v. California, 496 U. S. 128, 136–137 (1990); see also id., at 137, n. 7 ("[E]ven where the object is contraband, this Court has repeatedly stated and enforced the basic rule that the police may not enter and make a warrantless seizure"); G. M. Leasing Corp. v. United States, 429 U. S. 338, 354 (1977) ("It is one thing to seize without a warrant property resting in an open area . . . , and it is quite another thing to effect a warrantless seizure of property . . . situated on private premises to which access is not otherwise available for the seizing officer"). A plain-view seizure thus cannot be justified if it is effectuated by unlawful trespass. Soldal v. Cook County, 506 U. S. 56, 66 (1992). Had Officer Rhodes seen illegal drugs through the window of Collins' house, for example, assuming no other warrant exception applied, he could not have entered the house to seize them without first obtaining a warrant.

Similarly, it is a settled rule that warrantless arrests in public places are valid, but, absent another exception such as exigent circumstances, officers may not enter a home to make an arrest without a warrant, even when they have probable cause. Payton v. New York, 445 U. S. 573, 587–590 (1980). That is because being "arrested in the home involves not only the invasion attendant to all arrests but also an invasion of the sanctity of the home." *Id.*, at 588–589. Likewise, searching a vehicle parked in the curtilage involves not only the invasion of the Fourth Amendment interest in the vehicle but also an invasion of the sanctity of the curtilage.

Just as an officer must have a lawful right of access to any contraband he discovers in plain view in order to seize it without a warrant, and just as an officer must have a lawful right of access in order to arrest a person in his home, so, too, an officer must have a lawful right of access to a vehicle in order to search it pursuant to the automobile exception. The automobile exception does not afford the necessary lawful right of access to search a vehicle parked within a home or its curtilage because it does not justify an intrusion on a person's separate and substantial Fourth Amendment interest in his home and curtilage.

As noted, the rationales underlying the automobile exception are specific to the nature of a vehicle and the ways in which it is distinct from a house. The rationales thus take account only of the balance between the intrusion on an individual's Fourth Amendment interest in his vehicle and the governmental interests in an expedient search of that vehicle; they do not account for the distinct privacy interest in one's home or curtilage. To allow an officer to rely on the automobile exception to gain entry into a house or its curtilage for the purpose of conducting a vehicle search would unmoor the exception from its justifications, render hollow the core Fourth Amendment protection the Constitution extends to the house and its curtilage, and transform what was meant to be an exception into a tool with far broader application. Indeed, its name alone should make all this clear enough: It is, after all, an exception for automobiles.[a]

Given the centrality of the Fourth Amendment interest in the home and its curtilage and the disconnect between that interest and the justifications behind the automobile exception, we decline Virginia's

---

[a]   The dissent concedes that "the degree of the intrusion on privacy" is relevant in determining whether a warrant is required to search a motor vehicle "located on private property." *Post*, at 5–6 (opinion of ALITO, J.). Yet it puzzlingly asserts that the "privacy interests at stake" here are no greater than when a motor vehicle is searched "on public streets." "An ordinary person of common sense," however, clearly would understand that the privacy interests at stake in one's private residential property are far greater than on a public street. Contrary to the dissent's suggestion, it is of no significance that the motorcycle was parked just a "short walk up the driveway." The driveway was private, not public, property, and the motorcycle was parked in the portion of the driveway beyond where a neighbor would venture, in an area "intimately linked to the home, ... where privacy expectations are most heightened." California v. Ciraolo, 476 U. S. 207, 213 (1986). Nor does it matter that Officer Rhodes "did not damage any property," for an officer's care in conducting a search does not change the character of the place being searched. And, as we explain, it is not dispositive that Officer Rhodes did not "observe anything along the way" to the motorcycle "that he could not have seen from the street." Law enforcement officers need not "shield their eyes when passing by a home on public thoroughfares," Ciraolo, 476 U. S., at 213, but the ability visually to observe an area protected by the Fourth Amendment does not give officers the green light physically to intrude on it. It certainly does not permit an officer physically to intrude on curtilage, remove a tarp to reveal license plate and vehicle identification numbers, and use those numbers to confirm that the defendant committed a crime.

The dissent also mistakenly relies on a law enacted by the First Congress and mentioned in Carroll v. United States, 267 U. S. 32, 150–151 (1925), that authorized the warrantless search of vessels. The dissent thinks it implicit in that statute that "officers could cross private property such as wharves in order to reach and board those vessels." Even if it were so that a police officer could have entered a private wharf to search a vessel, that would not prove he could enter the curtilage of a home to do so. To the contrary, whereas the statute relied upon in *Carroll* authorized warrantless searches of vessels, it expressly required warrants to search houses. See 267 U. S., at 150–157; Act of July 31, 1789, §24, 1 Stat. 43. Here, Officer Rhodes did not invade a private wharf to undertake a search; he invaded the curtilage of a home.

invitation to extend the automobile exception to permit a warrantless intrusion on a home or its curtilage.

## III

### A

Virginia argues that this Court's precedent indicates that the automobile exception is a categorical one that permits the warrantless search of a vehicle anytime, anywhere, including in a home or curtilage. Specifically, Virginia points to two decisions that it contends resolve this case in its favor. Neither is dispositive or persuasive.

First, Virginia invokes Scher v. United States, 305 U. S. 251 (1938). In that case, federal officers received a confidential tip that a particular car would be transporting bootleg liquor at a specified time and place. The officers identified and followed the car until the driver "turned into a garage a few feet back of his residence and within the curtilage." As the driver exited his car, an officer approached and stated that he had been informed that the car was carrying contraband. The driver acknowledged that there was liquor in the trunk, and the officer proceeded to open the trunk, find the liquor, arrest the driver, and seize both the car and the liquor. Although the officer did not have a search warrant, the Court upheld the officer's actions as reasonable.

*Scher* is inapposite. Whereas Collins' motorcycle was parked and unattended when Officer Rhodes intruded on the curtilage to search it, the officers in *Scher* first encountered the vehicle when it was being driven on public streets, approached the curtilage of the home only when the driver turned into the garage, and searched the vehicle only after the driver admitted that it contained contraband. *Scher* by no means established a general rule that the automobile exception permits officers to enter a home or its curtilage absent a warrant. The Court's brief analysis referenced *Carroll*, but only in the context of observing that, consistent with that case, the "officers properly could have stopped" and searched the car "just before [petitioner] entered the garage," a proposition the petitioner did "not seriously controvert." The Court then explained that the officers did not lose their ability to stop and search the car when it entered "the open garage closely followed by the observing officer" because "[n]o search was made of the garage." It emphasized that "[e]xamination of the automobile accompanied an arrest, without objection and upon admission of probable guilt," and cited two search-incident-to-arrest cases. *Scher*'s reasoning thus was both case specific and imprecise, sounding in multiple doctrines, particularly, and perhaps most appropriately, hot pursuit. The decision is best regarded as a factbound one, and it certainly does not control this case.

Second, Virginia points to *Labron*, 518 U. S. 938, where the Court upheld under the automobile exception the warrantless search of an individual's pickup truck that was parked in the driveway of his father-in-law's farmhouse. But *Labron* provides scant support for Virginia's position. Unlike in this case, there was no indication that the individual who owned the truck in *Labron* had any Fourth Amendment interest in the farmhouse or its driveway, nor was there a determination that the driveway was curtilage.

B

Alternatively, Virginia urges the Court to adopt a more limited rule regarding the intersection of the automobile exception and the protection afforded to curtilage. Virginia would prefer that the Court draw a bright line and hold that the automobile exception does not permit warrantless entry into "the physical threshold of a house or a similar fixed, enclosed structure inside the curtilage like a garage." Requiring officers to make "case-by-case curtilage determinations," Virginia reasons, unnecessarily complicates matters and "raises the potential for confusion and . . . error."

The Court, though, has long been clear that curtilage is afforded constitutional protection. See *Oliver*, 466 U. S., at 180. As a result, officers regularly assess whether an area is curtilage before executing a search. Virginia provides no reason to conclude that this practice has proved to be unadministrable, either generally or in this context. Moreover, creating a carveout to the general rule that curtilage receives Fourth Amendment protection, such that certain types of curtilage would receive Fourth Amendment protection only for some purposes but not for others, seems far more likely to create confusion than does uniform application of the Court's doctrine.

In addition, Virginia's proposed rule rests on a mistaken premise about the constitutional significance of visibility. The ability to observe inside curtilage from a lawful vantage point is not the same as the right to enter curtilage without a warrant for the purpose of conducting a search to obtain information not otherwise accessible. Cf. *Ciraolo*, 476 U. S., at 213–214 (holding that "physically nonintrusive" warrantless aerial observation of the curtilage of a home did not violate the Fourth Amendment, and could form the basis for probable cause to support a warrant to search the curtilage). So long as it is curtilage, a parking patio or carport into which an officer can see from the street is no less entitled to protection from trespass and a warrantless search than a fully enclosed garage.

Finally, Virginia's proposed bright-line rule automatically would grant constitutional rights to those persons with the financial means to afford residences with garages in which to store their vehicles but deprive those persons without such resources of any individualized consideration as to whether the areas in which they store their vehicles qualify as curtilage. See *United States* v. *Ross*, 456 U. S. 798, 822 (1982) ("[T]he most frail cottage in the kingdom is absolutely entitled to the same guarantees of privacy as the most majestic mansion").

## IV

For the foregoing reasons, we conclude that the automobile exception does not permit an officer without a warrant to enter a home or its curtilage in order to search a vehicle therein. We leave for resolution on remand whether Officer Rhodes' warrantless intrusion on the curtilage of Collins' house may have been reasonable on a different basis, such as the exigent circumstances exception to the warrant requirement. The judgment of the Supreme Court of Virginia is therefore reversed, and the case is remanded for further proceedings not inconsistent with this opinion.

### JUSTICE THOMAS, concurring.

I join the Court's opinion because it correctly resolves the Fourth Amendment question in this case. Notably, the only reason that Collins asked us to review this question is because, if he can prove a violation of the Fourth Amendment, our precedents require the Virginia courts to apply the exclusionary rule and potentially suppress the incriminating evidence against him. I write separately because I have serious doubts about this Court's authority to impose that rule on the States. The assumption that state courts must apply the federal exclusionary rule is legally dubious, and many jurists have complained that it encourages "distort[ions]" in substantive Fourth Amendment law, Rakas v. Illinois, 439 U. S. 128, 157 (1978) (White, J., dissenting); see also Coolidge v. New Hampshire, 403 U. S. 443, 490 (1971) (Harlan, J., concurring); Calabresi, The Exclusionary Rule, 26 Harv. J. L. & Pub. Pol'y 111, 112 (2003).

\* \* \*

While those who ratified the Fourth and Fourteenth Amendments would agree that a constitutional violation occurred here, they would be deeply confused about the posture of this case and the remedy that Collins is seeking. Historically, the only remedies for unconstitutional searches and seizures were "tort suits" and "self-help."

The exclusionary rule—the practice of deterring illegal searches and seizures by suppressing evidence at criminal trials—did not exist. No such rule existed in "Roman Law, Napoleonic Law or even the Common Law of England." Burger, Who Will Watch the Watchman? 14 Am. U. L. Rev. 1 (1964). And this Court did not adopt the federal exclusionary rule until the 20th century. See Weeks v. United States, 232 U. S. 383 (1914). As late as 1949, nearly two-thirds of the States did not have an exclusionary rule. See Wolf v. Colorado, 338 U. S. 25, 29 (1949). Those States, as then-Judge Cardozo famously explained, did not understand the logic of a rule that allowed "[t]he criminal . . . to go free because the constable has blundered." People v. Defore, 242 N. Y. 13, 21, 150 N. E. 585, 587 (1926).

The Founders would not have understood the logic of the exclusionary rule either. Historically, if evidence was relevant and reliable, its admissibility did not "depend upon the lawfulness or unlawfulness of the mode, by which it [was] obtained." * * * And the common law sometimes reflected the inverse of the exclusionary rule: The fact that someone turned out to be guilty could *justify* an illegal seizure. See Gelston v. Hoyt, 3 Wheat. 246, 310 (1818) (Story, J.) ("At common law, any person may at his peril, seize for a forfeiture to the government; and if the government adopt his seizure, and the property is condemned, he will be completely justified"); 2 W. Hawkins, Pleas of the Crown 77 (1721) ("And where a Man arrests another, who is actually guilty of the Crime for which he is arrested, . . . he needs not in justifying it, set forth any special Cause of his Suspicion").

Despite this history, the Court concluded in Mapp v. Ohio, 367 U. S. 643 (1961), that the States must apply the federal exclusionary rule in their own courts. *Mapp* suggested that the exclusionary rule was required by the Constitution itself. * * * But that suggestion could not withstand even the slightest scrutiny. The exclusionary rule appears nowhere in the Constitution, postdates the founding by more than a century, and contradicts several longstanding principles of the common law. * * *

Recognizing this, the Court has since rejected *Mapp*'s "[e]xpansive dicta" and clarified that the exclusionary rule is not required by the Constitution. Davis v. United States, 564 U. S. 229, 237 (2011) (quoting Hudson v. Michigan, 547 U. S. 586, 591 (2006)). Suppression, this Court has explained, is not "a personal constitutional right." United States v. Calandra, 414 U. S. 338, 348 (1974); accord, Stone v. Powell, 428 U. S. 465, 486 (1976). The Fourth Amendment "says nothing about suppressing evidence," *Davis, supra,* at 236, and a prosecutor's "use of fruits of a past unlawful search or seizure works no new Fourth Amendment wrong," United States v. Leon, 468 U. S. 897, 906 (1984). Instead, the exclusionary rule is a "judicially created" doctrine that is "prudential rather than constitutionally mandated." Pennsylvania Bd. of Probation and Parole v. Scott, 524 U. S. 357, 363 (1998); accord, Herring v. United States, 555 U. S. 135, 139 (2009); Arizona v. Evans, 514 U. S. 1, 10 (1995); United States v. Janis, 428 U. S. 433, 459–460 (1976).

Although the exclusionary rule is not part of the Constitution, this Court has continued to describe it as "federal law" and assume that it applies to the States. Yet the Court has never attempted to justify this assumption. If the exclusionary rule is federal law, but is not grounded in the Constitution or a federal statute, then it must be federal common law.

As federal common law, however, the exclusionary rule cannot bind the States.

* * *b

In sum, I am skeptical of this Court's authority to impose the exclusionary rule on the States. We have not yet revisited that question in light of our modern precedents, which reject *Mapp*'s essential premise that the exclusionary rule is required by the Constitution. We should do so.

### JUSTICE ALITO, dissenting.

The Fourth Amendment prohibits "unreasonable" searches. What the police did in this case was entirely reasonable. The Court's decision is not.

On the day in question, Officer David Rhodes was standing at the curb of a house where petitioner, Ryan Austin Collins, stayed a couple of nights a week with his girlfriend. From his vantage point on the street, Rhodes saw an object covered with a tarp in the driveway, just a car's length or two from the curb. It is undisputed that Rhodes had probable cause to believe that the object under the tarp was a motorcycle that had been involved a few months earlier in a dangerous highway chase, eluding the police at speeds in excess of 140 mph. Rhodes also had probable cause to believe that petitioner had been operating the motorcycle and that a search of the motorcycle would provide evidence that the motorcycle had been stolen.

If the motorcycle had been parked at the curb, instead of in the driveway, it is undisputed that Rhodes could have searched it without obtaining a warrant. Nearly a century ago, this Court held that officers with probable cause may search a motor vehicle without obtaining a warrant. Carroll v. United States, 267 U. S. 132, 153, 155–156 (1925). The principal rationale for this so-called automobile or motor-vehicle exception to the warrant requirement is the risk that the vehicle will be moved during the time it takes to obtain a warrant. *Id.*, at 153; California v. Carney, 471 U. S. 386, 390–391 (1985). We have also observed that the owner of an automobile has a diminished expectation of privacy in its contents.

So why does the Court come to the conclusion that Officer Rhodes needed a warrant in this case? Because, in order to reach the motorcycle, he had to walk 30 feet or so up the driveway of the house rented by petitioner's girlfriend, and by doing that, Rhodes invaded the home's "curtilage." The Court does not dispute that the motorcycle, when parked

---

b     Of course, the States are free to adopt their own exclusionary rules as a matter of state law. But nothing in the Federal Constitution requires them to do so. Even assuming the Constitution requires particular state-law remedies for federal constitutional violations, it does not require the exclusionary rule.

in the driveway, was just as mobile as it would have been had it been parked at the curb. Nor does the Court claim that Officer Rhodes's short walk up the driveway did petitioner or his girlfriend any harm. Rhodes did not damage any property or observe anything along the way that he could not have seen from the street. But, the Court insists, Rhodes could not enter the driveway without a warrant, and therefore his search of the motorcycle was unreasonable and the evidence obtained in that search must be suppressed.

An ordinary person of common sense would react to the Court's decision the way Mr. Bumble famously responded when told about a legal rule that did not comport with the reality of everyday life. If that is the law, he exclaimed, "the law is a ass—a idiot." C. Dickens, Oliver Twist 277 (1867).

The Fourth Amendment is neither an "ass" nor an "idiot." Its hallmark is reasonableness, and the Court's strikingly unreasonable decision is based on a misunderstanding of Fourth Amendment basics.

* * * Ascertaining the boundaries of the curtilage thus determines only whether a search is governed by the Fourth Amendment. The concept plays no other role in Fourth Amendment analysis.

In this case, there is no dispute that the search of the motorcycle was governed by the Fourth Amendment, and therefore whether or not it occurred within the curtilage is not of any direct importance. The question before us is not whether there was a Fourth Amendment search but whether the search was reasonable. And the only possible argument as to why it might not be reasonable concerns the need for a warrant. For nearly a century, however, it has been well established that officers do not need a warrant to search a motor vehicle on public streets so long as they have probable cause. * * * Thus, the issue here is whether there is any good reason why this same rule should not apply when the vehicle is parked in plain view in a driveway just a few feet from the street.

In considering that question, we should ask whether the reasons for the "automobile exception" are any less valid in this new situation. Is the vehicle parked in the driveway any less mobile? Are any greater privacy interests at stake? If the answer to those questions is "no," then the automobile exception should apply. And here, the answer to each question is emphatically "no." The tarp-covered motorcycle parked in the driveway could have been uncovered and ridden away in a matter of seconds. And Officer Rhodes's brief walk up the driveway impaired no real privacy interests.

In this case, the Court uses the curtilage concept in a way that is contrary to our decisions regarding other, exigency-based exceptions to the warrant requirement. Take, for example, the "emergency aid" exception. See Brigham City v. Stuart, 547 U. S. 398 (2006). When officers reasonably believe that a person inside a dwelling has urgent need of assistance, they may cross the curtilage and enter the building without first obtaining a warrant. The same is true when officers reasonably believe that a person in a dwelling is destroying evidence. See Kentucky v. King, 563 U. S. 452, 460 (2011). In both of those situations, we ask whether "the exigencies of the situation make the needs of law enforcement so compelling that the warrantless search is objectively reasonable." *Brigham City, supra*, at 403. We have not held that the need to cross the curtilage independently necessitates a warrant, and there is no good reason to apply a different rule here.[c]

It is no answer to this argument that the emergency-aid and destruction-of-evidence exceptions require an inquiry into the practicality of obtaining a warrant in the particular circumstances of the case. Our precedents firmly establish that the motor-vehicle exception, unlike these other exceptions, "has no separate exigency requirement." Maryland v. Dyson, 527 U. S. 465, 466–467 (1999) (*per curiam*). It is settled that the mobility of a motor vehicle categorically obviates any need to engage in such a case-specific inquiry. Requiring such an inquiry here would mark a substantial alteration of settled Fourth Amendment law.

This does not mean, however, that a warrant is never needed when officers have probable cause to search a motor vehicle, no matter where the vehicle is located. While a case-specific inquiry regarding *exigency* would be inconsistent with the rationale of the motor-vehicle exception, a case-specific inquiry regarding *the degree of intrusion on privacy* is entirely appropriate when the motor vehicle to be searched is located on private property. After all, the ultimate inquiry under the Fourth Amendment is whether a search is reasonable, and that inquiry often turns on the degree of the intrusion on privacy. Thus, contrary to the opinion of the Court, an affirmance in this case would not mean that officers could perform a warrantless search if a motorcycle were located inside a house. In that situation, the intrusion on privacy would be far greater than in the present case, where the real effect, if any, is negligible.

I would affirm the decision below.

---

[c] Indeed, I believe that the First Congress implicitly made the same judgment in enacting the statute on which *Carroll* v. *United States*, 267 U. S. 132 (1925), relied when the motor-vehicle exception was first recognized. Since the First Congress sent the Bill of Rights to the States for ratification, we have often looked to laws enacted by that Congress as evidence of the original understanding of the meaning of those Amendments. * * * *Carroll* itself noted that the First Congress enacted a law authorizing officers to search vessels without a warrant. Although this statute did not expressly state that these officers could cross private property such as wharves in order to reach and board those vessels, I think that was implicit. Otherwise, the statute would very often have been ineffective. And when Congress later enacted similar laws, it made this authorization express. See, *e.g.*, An Act Further to Prevent Smuggling and for Other Purposes, §5, 14 Stat. 179. For this reason, Officer Rhodes's conduct in this case is consistent with the original understanding of the Fourth Amendment, as explicated in *Carroll*.

# VI.  ELECTRONIC SURVEILLANCE AND UNDERCOVER ACTIVITY

## C.  STATUTORY REGULATION OF DOMESTIC ELECTRONIC SURVEILLANCE

**Page 555. Add as Factor 13:** *Territorial Reach*:

In Dahda v. United States, 138 S. Ct. 1491 (2018), the Court addressed the scope of a federal judge's power to order an interception of communications. Under federal law, a judge normally may issue a wiretap order permitting the interception of communications only "within the territorial jurisdiction of the court in which the judge is sitting." 18 U. S. C. § 2518(3). But, in this case a Kansas federal judge authorized nine wiretap orders as part of a Government investigation of a suspected drug distribution ring in that state. The Government intercepted most of the communications from a listening post within Kansas, but also relied on a sentence in each order purporting to authorize interceptions outside Kansas to intercept communications from a listening post in Missouri. Two defendants indicted as drug conspirators moved to suppress the evidence because the judge had no authority to authorize interceptions outside Kansas, and this meant the orders were insufficient on their face so that suppression of all intercepted communications was required. The government agreed it would not use evidence obtained from the Missouri listening post, but the defendants argued that this did not cure the facial defect in the orders.

The statute, § 2518(10)(a), provides for the suppression of "the contents of any wire or oral communication" that a wiretap "intercept[s]" along with any "evidence derived therefrom" if

(i)  the communication was unlawfully intercepted;

(ii)  the order of . . . approval under which it was intercepted is insufficient on its face; or

(iii)  the interception was not made in conformity

with the order of authorization or approval.

Justice Breyer wrote for the Court as it rejected the defendant's argument that the orders were "insufficient" on their face. He described what a federal judge must find pursuant to § 2518(4)(a)-(e) before issuing an interception order:

[T]he Government must submit an application that describes the particular offense being investigated as well as the type of communications it seeks to intercept; that sets forth the basis for an appropriate finding of "probable cause"; that explains why other less intrusive methods are inadequate, have failed, or are too dangerous to try; and that meets other requirements, showing, for example, authorization by a specified governmental official. § 2518(1). If the judge accepts the application, finds probable cause, and issues an authorizing order, that order must itself contain specified information, including, for example, the identity of the "person" whose "communications are to be intercepted"; the "nature and location of the [relevant] communications facilities"; a "particular description of the type of communication sought to be intercepted"; a statement of the "particular offense" to which the intercept "relates"; the "identity of the agency authorized to intercept"; the identity of the "person authorizing the application"; and "the period of time during which" the "interception is authorized." §§ 2518(4)(a)–(e).

The Tenth Circuit had agreed with the government's position that subdivision (ii) focused on the core concerns of the statute which were protecting the privacy of wire and oral communications, and (2) delineating on a uniform basis the circumstances and conditions under which the interception of wire and oral communications may be authorized "—and concluded that neither applies to the statute's territorial limitation. Justice Breyer found that this approach was too narrow.

Instead, Justice Breyer concluded that

> subparagraph (ii) does not cover each and every error that appears in an otherwise sufficient order. It is clear that subparagraph (ii) covers at least an order's failure to include information that § 2518(4) specifically requires the order to contain. See §§ 2518(4)(a)–(e) * * *. An order lacking that information would deviate from the uniform authorizing requirements that Congress explicitly set forth, while also falling literally within the phrase "insufficient on its face."

He explicitly rejected the defendants' argument that that any defect that may appear on an order's face would render it insufficient and recognized that the nine orders contained a defect:

> The Orders do contain a defect, namely, the sentence authorizing interception outside Kansas, which we set forth above. But not every defect results in an insufficiency. In that sentence, the District Court "further" ordered that interception may take place "outside the territorial jurisdiction of the court." The sentence is without legal effect because, as the parties agree, the Orders could not legally authorize a wiretap outside the District Court's "territorial jurisdiction." But, more importantly, the sentence itself is surplus. Its presence is not connected to any

other relevant part of the Orders. Were we to remove the sentence from the Orders, they would then properly authorize wiretaps within the authorizing court's territorial jurisdiction. As we discussed above, a listening post within the court's territorial jurisdiction could lawfully intercept communications to or from telephones located within Kansas or outside Kansas. Consequently, every wiretap that produced evidence introduced at the Dahdas' trial was properly authorized under the statute.

Justice Gorsuch did not participate in the case.

# VII.  REMEDIES FOR FOURTH AMENDMENT VIOLATIONS

## E.  LIMITATIONS ON EXCLUSION

### 3.  Establishing a Violation of a Personal Fourth Amendment Right

### Page 621. In the Section on Rental Cars, add the following case:

### BYRD V. UNITED STATES
Supreme Court of the United States, 2018.
138 S. Ct. 1518.

**JUSTICE KENNEDY delivered the opinion of the Court.**

In September 2014, Pennsylvania State Troopers pulled over a car driven by petitioner Terrence Byrd. Byrd was the only person in the car. In the course of the traffic stop the troopers learned that the car was rented and that Byrd was not listed on the rental agreement as an authorized driver. For this reason, the troopers told Byrd they did not need his consent to search the car, including its trunk where he had stored personal effects. A search of the trunk uncovered body armor and 49 bricks of heroin.

The evidence was turned over to federal authorities, who charged Byrd with distribution and possession of heroin with the intent to distribute * ** and possession of body armor by a prohibited person * * * . Byrd moved to suppress the evidence as the fruit of an unlawful search. The United States District Court * * * denied the motion, and the Court of Appeals for the Third Circuit affirmed. Both courts concluded that, because Byrd was not listed on the rental agreement, he lacked a reasonable expectation of privacy in the car. Based on this conclusion, it appears that both the District Court and Court of Appeals deemed it unnecessary to consider whether the troopers had probable cause to search the car.

This Court granted certiorari to address the question whether a driver has a reasonable expectation of privacy in a rental car when he or she is not listed as an authorized driver on the rental agreement. The Court now holds that, as a general rule, someone in otherwise lawful possession and control of a rental car has a reasonable expectation of privacy in it even if the rental agreement does not list him or her as an authorized driver.

The Court concludes a remand is necessary to address in the first instance the Government's argument that this general rule is inapplicable because, in the circumstances here, Byrd had no greater expectation of privacy than a car thief. If that is so, our cases make clear he would lack a legitimate expectation of privacy. It is necessary to remand as well to determine whether, even if Byrd had a right to object to the search, probable cause justified it in any event.

I

On September 17, 2014, petitioner Terrence Byrd and Latasha Reed drove in Byrd's Honda Accord to a Budget car-rental facility in Wayne, New Jersey. Byrd stayed in the parking lot in the Honda while Reed went to the Budget desk and rented a Ford Fusion. The agreement Reed signed required her to certify that she had a valid driver's license and had not committed certain vehicle-related offenses within the previous three years. An addendum to the agreement, which Reed initialed, provides the following restriction on who may drive the rental car:

> "I understand that the only ones permitted to drive the vehicle other than the renter are the renter's spouse, the renter's co-employee (with the renter's permission, while on company business), or a person who appears at the time of the rental and signs an Additional Driver Form. These other drivers must also be at least 25 years old and validly licensed.

> "PERMITTING AN UNAUTHORIZED DRIVER TO OPERATE THE VEHICLE IS A VIOLATION OF THE RENTAL AGREEMENT. THIS MAY RESULT IN ANY AND ALL COVERAGE OTHERWISE PROVIDED BY THE RENTAL AGREEMENT BEING VOID AND MY BEING FULLY RESPONSIBLE FOR ALL LOSS OR DAMAGE, INCLUDING LIABILITY TO THIRD PARTIES."

In filling out the paperwork for the rental agreement, Reed did not list an additional driver.

With the rental keys in hand, Reed returned to the parking lot and gave them to Byrd. The two then left the facility in separate cars—she in his Honda, he in the rental car. Byrd returned to his home in Patterson, New Jersey, and put his personal belongings in the trunk of the rental car. Later that afternoon, he departed in the car alone and headed toward Pittsburgh, Pennsylvania.

After driving nearly three hours, or roughly half the distance to Pittsburgh, Byrd passed State Trooper David Long, who was parked in the median of Interstate 81 near Harrisburg, Pennsylvania. Long was suspicious of Byrd because he was driving with his hands at the "10 and 2" position on the steering wheel, sitting far back from the steering wheel, and driving a rental car. Long knew the Ford Fusion was a rental car because one of its windows contained a barcode. Based on these observations, he decided to follow Byrd and, a short time later, stopped him for a possible traffic infraction.

When Long approached the passenger window of Byrd's car to explain the basis for the stop and to ask for identification, Byrd was "visibly nervous" and "was shaking and had a hard time obtaining his driver's license." He handed an interim license and the rental agreement to Long, stating that a friend had rented the car. Long returned to his vehicle to verify Byrd's license and noticed Byrd was not listed as an additional driver on the rental agreement. Around this time another trooper, Travis Martin, arrived at the scene. While Long processed Byrd's license, Martin conversed with Byrd, who again stated that a friend had rented the vehicle. After Martin walked back to Long's patrol car, Long commented to Martin that Byrd was "not on the renter agreement," to which Martin replied, "yeah, he has no expectation of privacy."

A computer search based on Byrd's identification returned two different names. Further inquiry suggested the other name might be an alias and also revealed that Byrd had prior convictions for weapons and drug charges as well as an outstanding warrant in New Jersey for a probation violation. After learning that New Jersey did not want Byrd arrested for extradition, the troopers asked Byrd to step out of the vehicle and patted him down.

Long asked Byrd if he had anything illegal in the car. When Byrd said he did not, the troopers asked for his consent to search the car. At that point Byrd said he had a "blunt" in the car and offered to retrieve it for them. The officers understood "blunt" to mean a marijuana cigarette. They declined to let him retrieve it and continued to seek his consent to search the car, though they stated they did not need consent because he was not listed on the rental agreement. The troopers then opened the passenger and driver doors and began a thorough search of the passenger compartment.

Martin proceeded from there to search the car's trunk, including by opening up and taking things out of a large cardboard box, where he found a laundry bag containing body armor. At this point, the troopers decided to detain Byrd. As Martin walked toward Byrd and said he would be placing him in handcuffs, Byrd began to run away. A third trooper who had arrived on the scene joined Long and Martin in pursuit. When the troopers caught up to Byrd, he surrendered and admitted there was heroin in the car. Back at the car, the troopers resumed their search of the laundry bag and found 49 bricks of heroin.

In pretrial proceedings Byrd moved to suppress the evidence found in the trunk of the rental car, arguing that the search violated his Fourth Amendment rights. Although Long contended at a suppression hearing that the troopers had probable cause to search the car after Byrd stated it contained marijuana, the District Court denied Byrd's motion on the ground that Byrd lacked "standing" to contest the search as an initial matter. Byrd later entered a conditional guilty plea, reserving the right to appeal the suppression ruling.

The Court of Appeals affirmed in a brief summary opinion. As relevant here, the Court of Appeals recognized that a "circuit split exists as to whether the sole occupant of a rental vehicle has a Fourth Amendment expectation of privacy when that occupant is not named in the rental agreement"; but it noted that Circuit precedent already had "spoken as to this issue . . . and determined such a person has no expectation of privacy and therefore no standing to challenge a search of the vehicle." The Court of Appeals did not reach the probable-cause question.

This Court granted Byrd's petition for a writ of certiorari to address the conflict among the Courts of Appeals over whether an unauthorized driver has a reasonable expectation of privacy in a rental car. * * *

## II

Few protections are as essential to individual liberty as the right to be free from unreasonable searches and seizures. The Framers made that right explicit in the Bill of Rights following their experience with the indignities and invasions of privacy wrought by "general warrants and warrantless searches that had so alienated the colonists and had helped speed the movement for independence." Chimel v. California, 395 U. S. 752, 761 (1969). Ever mindful of the Fourth Amendment and its history, the Court has viewed with disfavor practices that permit "police officers unbridled discretion to rummage at will among a person's private effects." Arizona v. Gant, 556 U. S. 332, 345 (2009).

This concern attends the search of an automobile. See Delaware v. Prouse, 440 U. S. 648, 662 (1979). The Court has acknowledged, however, that there is a diminished expectation of privacy in automobiles, which often permits officers to dispense with obtaining a warrant before conducting a lawful search. See, e.g., California v. Acevedo, 500 U. S. 565, 579 (1991).

Whether a warrant is required is a separate question from the one the Court addresses here, which is whether the person claiming a constitutional violation "has had his own Fourth Amendment rights infringed by the search and seizure which he seeks to challenge." Rakas v. Illinois, 439 U. S. 128, 133 (1978). Answering that question requires examination of whether the person claiming the constitutional violation had a "legitimate expectation of privacy in the premises" searched. "Expectations of privacy protected by the Fourth Amendment, of course, need not be based on a common-law interest in real or personal property, or on the invasion of such an interest." Still, "property concepts" are instructive in "determining the presence or absence of the privacy interests protected by that Amendment."

Indeed, more recent Fourth Amendment cases have clarified that the test most often associated with legitimate expectations of privacy, which was derived from the second Justice Harlan's concurrence in Katz v. United States, 389 U. S. 347 (1967), supplements, rather than displaces, "the traditional property-based understanding of the Fourth Amendment." Florida v. Jardines, 569 U. S. 1, 11 (2013). Perhaps in light of this clarification, Byrd now argues in the alternative that he had a common-law property interest in the rental car as a second bailee that would have provided him with a cognizable Fourth Amendment interest in the vehicle. But he did not raise this argument before the District Court or Court of Appeals, and those courts did not have occasion to address whether Byrd was a second bailee or what consequences might follow from that determination. In those courts he framed the question solely in terms of the *Katz* test noted above. Because this is "a court of review, not of first view," it is generally unwise to consider arguments in the first instance, and the Court declines to reach Byrd's contention that he was a second bailee.

Reference to property concepts, however, aids the Court in assessing the precise question here: Does a driver of a rental car have a reasonable expectation of privacy in the car when he or she is not listed as an authorized driver on the rental agreement?

### III

### A

One who owns and possesses a car, like one who owns and possesses a house, almost always has a reasonable expectation of privacy in it. More difficult to define and delineate are the legitimate expectations of privacy of others.

On the one hand, as noted above, it is by now well established that a person need not always have a recognized common-law property interest in the place searched to be able to claim a reasonable expectation of privacy in it. See Jones v. United States, 362 U. S. 257, 259 (1960); *Katz,* supra, at 352; Minnesota v. Olson, 495 U. S. 91, 98 (1990).

On the other hand, it is also clear that legitimate presence on the premises of the place searched, standing alone, is not enough to accord a reasonable expectation of privacy, because it "creates too broad a gauge for measurement of Fourth Amendment rights." *Rakas,* 439 U.S. at 142; see also *id.,* at 148 ("We would not wish to be understood as saying that legitimate presence on the premises is irrelevant to one's expectation of privacy, but it cannot be deemed controlling").

Although the Court has not set forth a single metric or exhaustive list of considerations to resolve the circumstances in which a person can be said to have a reasonable expectation of privacy, it has explained that "[l]egitimation of expectations of privacy by law must have a source outside of the Fourth Amendment, either by reference to concepts of real or personal property law or to understandings that are recognized and permitted by society." *Rakas,* 439 U. S., at 144, n. 12. The two concepts in cases like this one are often linked. "One of the main rights attaching to property is the right to exclude others," and, in the main, "one who owns or lawfully possesses or controls property will in all likelihood have a legitimate expectation of privacy by virtue of the right to exclude." This general property-based concept guides resolution of this case.

## B

Here, the Government contends that drivers who are not listed on rental agreements always lack an expectation of privacy in the automobile based on the rental company's lack of authorization alone. This per se rule rests on too restrictive a view of the Fourth Amendment's protections. Byrd, by contrast, contends that the sole occupant of a rental car always has an expectation of privacy in it based on mere possession and control. There is more to recommend Byrd's proposed rule than the Government's; but, without qualification, it would include within its ambit thieves and others who, not least because of their lack of any property-based justification, would not have a reasonable expectation of privacy.

## 1

Stripped to its essentials, the Government's position is that only authorized drivers of rental cars have expectations of privacy in those vehicles. This position is based on the following syllogism: Under *Rakas,* passengers do not have an expectation of privacy in an automobile glove compartment or like places; an unauthorized driver like Byrd would have been the passenger had the renter been driving; and the unauthorized driver cannot obtain greater protection when he takes the wheel and leaves the renter behind. The flaw in this syllogism is its major premise, for it is a misreading of *Rakas*.

The Court in *Rakas* did not hold that passengers cannot have an expectation of privacy in automobiles. To the contrary, the Court disclaimed any intent to hold "that a passenger lawfully in an automobile may not invoke the exclusionary rule and challenge a search of that vehicle unless he happens to own or have a possessory interest in it." The Court instead rejected the argument that legitimate presence alone was sufficient to assert a Fourth Amendment interest, which was fatal to the petitioners' case there because they had "claimed only that they were 'legitimately on [the] premises' and did not claim that they had any legitimate expectation of privacy in the areas of the car which were searched."

What is more, the Government's syllogism is beside the point, because this case does not involve a passenger at all but instead the driver and sole occupant of a rental car. As Justice Powell observed in his concurring opinion in *Rakas*, a "distinction . . . may be made in some circumstances between the Fourth Amendment rights of passengers and the rights of an individual who has exclusive control of an automobile or of its locked compartments." This situation would be similar to the defendant in *Jones*, *supra*, who, as *Rakas* notes, had a reasonable expectation of privacy in his friend's apartment because he "had complete dominion and control over the apartment and could exclude others from it." Justice Powell's observation was also consistent with the majority's explanation that "one who owns or lawfully possesses or controls property will in all likelihood have a legitimate expectation of privacy by virtue of [the] right to exclude," an explanation tied to the majority's discussion of Jones.

The Court sees no reason why the expectation of privacy that comes from lawful possession and control and the attendant right to exclude would differ depending on whether the car in question is rented or privately owned by someone other than the person in current possession of it, much as it did not seem to matter whether the friend of the defendant in Jones owned or leased the apartment he permitted the defendant to use in his absence. Both would have the expectation of privacy that comes with the right to exclude. Indeed, the Government conceded at oral argument that an unauthorized driver in sole possession of a rental car would be permitted to exclude third parties from it, such as a carjacker.

2

The Government further stresses that Byrd's driving the rental car violated the rental agreement that Reed signed, and it contends this violation meant Byrd could not have had any basis for claiming an expectation of privacy in the rental car at the time of the search. As anyone who has rented a car knows, car-rental agreements are filled with long lists of restrictions. Examples include prohibitions on driving the car on unpaved roads or driving while using a handheld cellphone. Few would contend that violating provisions like these has anything to do with a driver's reasonable expectation of privacy in the rental car—as even the Government agrees.

Despite this concession, the Government argues that permitting an unauthorized driver to take the wheel of a rental car is a breach different in kind from these others, so serious that the rental company would consider the agreement "void" the moment an unauthorized driver takes the wheel. To begin with, that is not what the contract says. It states: "Permitting an unauthorized driver to operate the vehicle is a violation of the rental agreement. This may result in any and all coverage otherwise provided by the rental agreement being void and my being fully responsible for all loss or damage, including liability to third parties."

Putting the Government's misreading of the contract aside, there may be countless innocuous reasons why an unauthorized driver might get behind the wheel of a rental car and drive it—perhaps the renter is drowsy or inebriated and the two think it safer for the friend to drive them to their destination. True, this constitutes a breach of the rental agreement, and perhaps a serious one, but the Government fails to explain what bearing this breach of contract, standing alone, has on expectations of privacy in the car. Stated in different terms, for Fourth Amendment purposes there is no meaningful difference between the authorized-driver provision and the other provisions the Government agrees do not eliminate an expectation of privacy, all of which concern risk allocation between private parties—violators might pay additional fees, lose insurance coverage, or assume liability for damage resulting from the breach. But that risk allocation has little to do with whether one would have a reasonable expectation of privacy in the rental car if, for example, he or she otherwise has lawful possession of and control over the car.

### 3

The central inquiry at this point turns on the concept of lawful possession, and this is where an important qualification of Byrd's proposed rule comes into play. *Rakas* makes clear that "wrongful presence at the scene of a search would not enable a defendant to object to the legality of the search." "A burglar plying his trade in a summer cabin during the off season," for example, "may have a thoroughly justified subjective expectation of privacy, but it is not one which the law recognizes as legitimate." Likewise, "a person present in a stolen automobile at the time of the search may [not] object to the lawfulness of the search of the automobile." No matter the degree of possession and control, the car thief would not have a reasonable expectation of privacy in a stolen car.

On this point, in its merits brief, the Government asserts that, on the facts here, Byrd should have no greater expectation of privacy than a car thief because he intentionally used a third party as a strawman in a calculated plan to mislead the rental company from the very outset, all to aid him in committing a crime. This argument is premised on the Government's inference that Byrd knew he would not have been able to rent the car on his own, because he would not have satisfied the rental company's requirements based on his criminal record, and that he used Reed, who had no intention of using the car for her own purposes, to procure the car for him to transport heroin to Pittsburgh.

It is unclear whether the Government's allegations, if true, would constitute a criminal offense in the acquisition of the rental car under applicable law. And it may be that there is no reason that the law should distinguish between one who obtains a vehicle through subterfuge of the type the Government alleges occurred here and one who steals the car outright.

The Government did not raise this argument in the District Court or the Court of Appeals, however. It relied instead on the sole fact that Byrd lacked authorization to drive the car. And it is unclear from the record whether the Government's inferences paint an accurate picture of what occurred. Because it was not addressed in the District Court or Court of Appeals, the Court declines to reach this question. The proper course is to remand for the argument and potentially further factual development to be considered in the first instance by the Court of Appeals or by the District Court.

IV

The Government argued in its brief in opposition to certiorari that, even if Byrd had a Fourth Amendment interest in the rental car, the troopers had probable cause to believe it contained evidence of a crime when they initiated their search. If that were true, the troopers may have been permitted to conduct a warrantless search of the car in line with the Court's cases concerning the automobile exception to the warrant requirement. The Court of Appeals did not reach this question because it concluded, as an initial matter, that Byrd lacked a reasonable expectation of privacy in the rental car.

It is worth noting that most courts analyzing the question presented in this case, including the Court of Appeals here, have described it as one of Fourth Amendment "standing," a concept the Court has explained is not distinct from the merits and "is more properly subsumed under substantive Fourth Amendment doctrine." *Rakas.*

The concept of standing in Fourth Amendment cases can be a useful shorthand for capturing the idea that a person must have a cognizable Fourth Amendment interest in the place searched before seeking relief for an unconstitutional search; but it should not be confused with Article III standing, which is jurisdictional and must be assessed before reaching the merits. * * * Because Fourth Amendment standing is subsumed under substantive Fourth Amendment doctrine, it is not a jurisdictional question and hence need not be addressed before addressing other aspects of the merits of a Fourth Amendment claim. On remand, then, the Court of Appeals is not required to assess Byrd's reasonable expectation of privacy in the rental car before, in its discretion, first addressing whether there was probable cause for the search, if it finds the latter argument has been preserved.

## V

Though new, the fact pattern here continues a well-traveled path in this Court's Fourth Amendment jurisprudence. Those cases support the proposition, and the Court now holds, that the mere fact that a driver in lawful possession or control of a rental car is not listed on the rental agreement will not defeat his or her otherwise reasonable expectation of privacy. The Court leaves for remand two of the Government's arguments: that one who intentionally uses a third party to procure a rental car by a fraudulent scheme for the purpose of committing a crime is no better situated than a car thief; and that probable cause justified the search in any event. The Court of Appeals has discretion as to the order in which these questions are best addressed.

\* \* \*

**JUSTICE THOMAS, with whom JUSTICE GORSUCH joins, concurring.**

Although I have serious doubts about the "reasonable expectation of privacy" test from *Katz v. United States*, 389 U. S. 347 (1967) (Harlan, J., concurring), I join the Court's opinion because it correctly navigates our precedents, which no party has asked us to reconsider. As the Court notes, Byrd also argued that he should prevail under the original meaning of the Fourth Amendment because the police interfered with a property interest that he had in the rental car. I agree with the Court's decision not to review this argument in the first instance. In my view, it would be especially "unwise" to reach that issue because the parties fail to adequately address several threshold questions.

\* \* \*

That issue seems to turn on at least three threshold questions. First, what kind of property interest do individuals need before something can be considered "their . . . effec[t]" under the original meaning of the Fourth Amendment? Second, what body of law determines whether that property interest is present—modern state law, the common law of 1791, or something else? Third, is the unauthorized use of a rental car illegal or otherwise wrongful under the relevant law, and, if so, does that illegality or wrongfulness affect the Fourth Amendment analysis?

The parties largely gloss over these questions, but the answers seem vitally important to assessing whether Byrd can claim that the rental car is his effect. In an appropriate case, I would welcome briefing and argument on these questions.

**JUSTICE ALITO, concurring.**

The Court holds that an unauthorized driver of a rental car is not always barred from contesting a search of the vehicle. Relevant questions bearing on the driver's ability to raise a Fourth Amendment claim may include: the terms of the particular rental agreement; the circumstances surrounding the rental; the reason why the driver took the wheel; any property right that the driver might have; and the legality of his conduct under the law of the State where the conduct occurred. On remand, the Court of Appeals is free to reexamine the question whether petitioner may assert a Fourth Amendment claim or to decide the appeal on another appropriate ground. On this understanding, I join the opinion of the Court.

# CHAPTER 3

# SELF-INCRIMINATION AND CONFESSIONS

■ ■ ■

## I. THE PRIVILEGE AGAINST COMPELLED SELF-INCRIMINATION

### B. SCOPE OF THE PRIVILEGE

**Page 679. Add as new section 5:**

### 5. Suppression Hearings

The Court in City of Hays v. Vogt, 138 S.Ct. 720 (2018), granted certiorari to decide whether the Fifth Amendment permitted compelled statements to be used in a probable cause hearing.

Vogt was employed as a police officer in city A and applied for a position with city B. During an interview with city B, he disclosed that he had kept a knife obtained while working at city A. The city B police chief offered Vogt employment provided that he reported his acquisition of the knife to city A and returned it. Vogt did this, and city A's police chief ordered Vogt to issue a statement regarding the knife along with a letter of resignation. Vogt complied, and city A's police chief began an informal investigation of Vogt and required him to issue a more detailed statement which let to additional evidence and a criminal investigation by the state Bureau of Investigation. City B then withdrew its employment offer. State A charged Vogt with two counts relating to his possession of the knife, but the state district court found probable cause lacking and dismissed the charges. Vogt sued in federal court and alleged that the use of his compelled statements at the probable cause hearing violated his Fifth Amendment rights. The district court dismissed all claims, but the Tenth Circuit found that one claim—the state's use of Vogt's statements during the probable cause hearing did violate the Fifth Amendment.

The Supreme Court dismissed the case as improvidently granted. 138 S. Ct. 1683 (2018).

# CHAPTER 10

# TRIAL AND TRIAL-RELATED RIGHTS

■ ■ ■

## VII. THE RIGHT TO EFFECTIVE ASSISTANCE OF COUNSEL

### A. INEFFECTIVENESS AND PREJUDICE

3. Assessing Counsel's Effectiveness

Page 1416. Add after Florida v. Nixon:

### *Conceding Guilt over a Defendant's Objection: McCoy v. Louisiana*

#### McCOY v. LOUISIANA
Supreme Court of the United States, 2018.
138 S. Ct. 1500.

**JUSTICE GINSBURG delivered the opinion of the Court.**

In Florida v. Nixon, 543 U. S. 175 (2004), this Court considered whether the Constitution bars defense counsel from conceding a capital defendant's guilt at trial "when [the] defendant, informed by counsel, neither consents nor objects." In that case, defense counsel had several times explained to the defendant a proposed guilt-phase concession strategy, but the defendant was unresponsive. We held that when counsel confers with the defendant and the defendant remains silent, neither approving nor protesting counsel's proposed concession strategy, "[no] blanket rule demand[s] the defendant's explicit consent" to implementation of that strategy.

In the case now before us, in contrast to *Nixon*, the defendant vociferously insisted that he did not engage in the charged acts and adamantly objected to any admission of guilt. Yet the trial court permitted counsel, at the guilt phase of a capital trial, to tell the jury the defendant "committed three murders.... [H]e's guilty." We hold that a defendant has the right to insist that counsel refrain from admitting guilt, even when counsel's experienced-based view is that confessing guilt offers the defendant the best chance to avoid the death penalty. Guaranteeing a defendant the right "to have the *Assistance* of Counsel for *his* defence," the Sixth Amendment so demands. With individual liberty—and, in capital cases, life—at stake, it is the defendant's prerogative, not counsel's, to decide on the objective of his defense: to admit guilt in the hope of gaining mercy at the sentencing stage, or to maintain his innocence, leaving it to the State to prove his guilt beyond a reasonable doubt.

I

On May 5, 2008, Christine and Willie Young and Gregory Colston were shot and killed in the Youngs' home in Bossier City, Louisiana. The three victims were the mother, stepfather, and son of Robert McCoy's estranged wife, Yolanda. Several days later, police arrested McCoy in Idaho. Extradited to Louisiana, McCoy was appointed counsel from the public defender's office. A Bossier Parish grand jury indicted McCoy on three counts of first-degree murder, and the prosecutor gave notice of intent to seek the death penalty. McCoy pleaded not guilty. Throughout the proceedings, he insistently maintained he was out of State at the time of the killings and that corrupt police killed the victims when a drug deal went wrong. At defense counsel's request, a court-appointed sanity commission examined McCoy and found him competent to stand trial.

In December 2009 and January 2010, McCoy told the court his relationship with assigned counsel had broken down irretrievably. He sought and gained leave to represent himself until his parents engaged new counsel for him. In March 2010, Larry English, engaged by McCoy's parents, enrolled as McCoy's counsel. English eventually concluded that the evidence against McCoy was overwhelming and that, absent a concession at the guilt stage that McCoy was the killer, a death sentence would be impossible to avoid at the penalty phase.[a] McCoy, English reported, was "furious" when told, two weeks before trial was scheduled to begin, that English would concede McCoy's commission of the triple murders.[b] McCoy told English "not to make that concession," and English knew of McCoy's complete opposition to English telling the jury that McCoy was guilty of killing the three victims; instead of any concession, McCoy pressed English to pursue acquittal.

---

[a] Part of English's strategy was to concede that McCoy committed the murders and to argue that he should be convicted only of second-degree murder, because his "mental incapacity prevented him from forming the requisite specific intent to commit first degree murder." But the second-degree strategy would have encountered a shoal, for Louisiana does not permit introduction of evidence of a defendant's diminished capacity absent the entry of a plea of not guilty by reason of insanity.

[b] The dissent states that English told McCoy his proposed trial strategy eight months before trial. English did encourage McCoy, "[a] couple of months before the trial," to plead guilty rather than proceed to trial. But English declared under oath that "the first time [he] told [McCoy] that [he] intended to concede to the jury that [McCoy] was the killer" was July 12, 2011, two weeks before trial commenced. Encouraging a guilty plea pretrial, of course, is not equivalent to imparting to a defendant counsel's strategic determination to concede guilt should trial occur.

At a July 26, 2011 hearing, McCoy sought to terminate English's representation, and English asked to be relieved if McCoy secured other counsel. With trial set to start two days later, the court refused to relieve English and directed that he remain as counsel of record. "[Y]ou are the attorney," the court told English when he expressed disagreement with McCoy's wish to put on a defense case, and "you have to make the trial decision of what you're going to proceed with."

At the beginning of his opening statement at the guilt phase of the trial, English told the jury there was "no way reasonably possible" that they could hear the prosecution's evidence and reach "any other conclusion than Robert McCoy was the cause of these individuals' death." McCoy protested; out of earshot of the jury, McCoy told the court that English was "selling [him] out" by maintaining that McCoy "murdered [his] family." The trial court reiterated that English was "representing" McCoy and told McCoy that the court would not permit "any other outbursts." Continuing his opening statement, English told the jury the evidence is "unambiguous," "my client committed three murders." McCoy testified in his own defense, maintaining his innocence and pressing an alibi difficult to fathom. In his closing argument, English reiterated that McCoy was the killer. On that issue, English told the jury that he "took [the] burden off of [the prosecutor]." The jury then returned a unanimous verdict of guilty of first-degree murder on all three counts. At the penalty phase, English again conceded "Robert McCoy committed these crimes," but urged mercy in view of McCoy's "serious mental and emotional issues." The jury returned three death verdicts.

Represented by new counsel, McCoy unsuccessfully moved for a new trial, arguing that the trial court violated his constitutional rights by allowing English to concede McCoy "committed three murders" over McCoy's objection. The Louisiana Supreme Court affirmed the trial court's ruling that defense counsel had authority so to concede guilt, despite the defendant's opposition to any admission of guilt. The concession was permissible, the court concluded, because counsel reasonably believed that admitting guilt afforded McCoy the best chance to avoid a death sentence.

We granted certiorari in view of a division of opinion among state courts of last resort on the question whether it is unconstitutional to allow defense counsel to concede guilt over the defendant's intransigent and unambiguous objection. * * *

II

A

The Sixth Amendment guarantees to each criminal defendant "the Assistance of Counsel for his defence." At common law, self-representation was the norm. See Faretta v. California, 422 U. S. 806,

823 (1975) (citing 1 F. Pollock & F. Maitland, The History of English Law 211 (2d ed. 1909)). As the laws of England and the American Colonies developed, providing for a right to counsel in criminal cases, self-representation remained common and the right to proceed without counsel was recognized. Even now, when most defendants choose to be represented by counsel, see, e.g., Goldschmidt & Stemen, Patterns and Trends in Federal Pro Se Defense, 1996–2011: An Exploratory Study, 8 Fed. Cts. L. Rev. 81, 91 (2015) (0.2% of federal felony defendants proceeded pro se), an accused may insist upon representing herself—however counterproductive that course may be. * * *

The choice is not all or nothing: To gain assistance, a defendant need not surrender control entirely to counsel. For the Sixth Amendment, in "grant[ing] to the accused personally the right to make his defense," speaks of the "assistance" of counsel, and an assistant, however expert, is still an assistant. * * * Trial management is the lawyer's province: Counsel provides his or her assistance by making decisions such as "what arguments to pursue, what evidentiary objections to raise, and what agreements to conclude regarding the admission of evidence." Gonzalez v. United States, 553 U. S. 242, 248, (2008). Some decisions, however, are reserved for the client—notably, whether to plead guilty, waive the right to a jury trial, testify in one's own behalf, and forgo an appeal. See Jones v. Barnes, 463 U. S. 745, 751 (1983).

Autonomy to decide that the objective of the defense is to assert innocence belongs in this latter category. Just as a defendant may steadfastly refuse to plead guilty in the face of overwhelming evidence against her, or reject the assistance of legal counsel despite the defendant's own inexperience and lack of professional qualifications, so may she insist on maintaining her innocence at the guilt phase of a capital trial. These are not strategic choices about how best to achieve a client's objectives; they are choices about what the client's objectives in fact are. * * *

Counsel may reasonably assess a concession of guilt as best suited to avoiding the death penalty, as English did in this case. But the client may not share that objective. He may wish to avoid, above all else, the opprobrium that comes with admitting he killed family members. Or he may hold life in prison not worth living and prefer to risk death for any hope, however small, of exoneration. * * * When a client expressly asserts that the objective of "his defence" is to maintain innocence of the charged criminal acts, his lawyer must abide by that objective and may not override it by conceding guilt. U. S. Const., Amdt. 6 (emphasis added); see ABA Model Rule of Professional Conduct 1.2(a) (2016) (a "lawyer shall abide by a client's decisions concerning the objectives of the representation").

Preserving for the defendant the ability to decide whether to maintain his innocence should not displace counsel's, or the court's, respective trial management roles. See *Gonzalez*, 553 U. S., at 249 ("[n]umerous choices affecting conduct of the trial" do not require client consent, including "the objections to make, the witnesses to call, and the arguments to advance"). Counsel, in any case, must still develop a trial strategy and discuss it with her client, see *Nixon*, 543 U. S., at 178, explaining why, in her view, conceding guilt would be the best option. In this case, the court had determined that McCoy was competent to stand trial, i.e., that McCoy had sufficient present ability to consult with his lawyer with a reasonable degree of rational understanding. If, after consultations with English concerning the management of the defense, McCoy disagreed with English's proposal to concede McCoy committed three murders, it was not open to English to override McCoy's objection. English could not interfere with McCoy's telling the jury "I was not the murderer," although counsel could, if consistent with providing effective assistance, focus his own collaboration on urging that McCoy's mental state weighed against conviction.

B

[The Court distinguished Florida v. Nixon on the ground that Nixon did not make his complaint about his lawyer's strategy until after trial. The Court also rejected both the Louisiana Supreme Court's conclusion that English's refusal to maintain McCoy's innocence was necessitated by Louisiana Rule of Professional Conduct 1.2(d) (2017), which provides that "[a] lawyer shall not counsel a client to engage, or assist a client, in conduct that the lawyer knows is criminal or fraudulent," and the suggestion that the case was similar to *Nix v. Whiteside,* 475 U. S. 157, 173–176 (1986) [Text, page 1470]). It found that Nix told his lawyer that he intended to commit perjury and that there was no such avowed perjury as to McCoy. The Court reasoned that English disbelieved McCoy but this did not warrant English to admit McCoy's guilt over his objection. The Court rejected the dissent's suggestion that the case presented rare facts that were unlikely to recur.]

III

Because a client's autonomy, not counsel's competence, is in issue, we do not apply our ineffective-assistance-of-counsel jurisprudence, Strickland v. Washington, 466 U. S. 668 (1984), or United States v. Cronic, 466 U. S. 648 (1984), to McCoy's claim. To gain redress for attorney error, a defendant ordinarily must show prejudice. Here, however, the violation of McCoy's protected autonomy right was complete when the court allowed counsel to usurp control of an issue within McCoy's sole prerogative.

Violation of a defendant's Sixth Amendment-secured autonomy ranks as error of the kind our decisions have called "structural"; when present, such an error is not subject to harmless-error review. * * *

* * *

[Justice Ginsburg's explanation of why the error was "structural" is found in Chapter 13 of this Supplement.]

----

Larry English was placed in a difficult position; he had an unruly client and faced a strong government case. He reasonably thought the objective of his representation should be avoidance of the death penalty. But McCoy insistently maintained: "I did not murder my family." Once he communicated that to court and counsel, strenuously objecting to English's proposed strategy, a concession of guilt should have been off the table. The trial court's allowance of English's admission of McCoy's guilt despite McCoy's insistent objections was incompatible with the Sixth Amendment. Because the error was structural, a new trial is the required corrective.

For the reasons stated, the judgment of the Louisiana Supreme Court is reversed, and the case is remanded for further proceedings not inconsistent with this opinion.

**JUSTICE ALITO, with whom JUSTICE THOMAS and JUSTICE GORSUCH join, dissenting.**

The Constitution gives us the authority to decide real cases and controversies; we do not have the right to simplify or otherwise change the facts of a case in order to make our work easier or to achieve a desired result. But that is exactly what the Court does in this case. The Court overturns petitioner's convictions for three counts of first-degree murder by attributing to his trial attorney, Larry English, something that English never did. The Court holds that English violated petitioner's constitutional rights by "admit[ting] h[is] client's guilt of a charged crime over the client's intransigent objection." But English did not admit that petitioner was guilty of first-degree murder. Instead, faced with overwhelming evidence that petitioner shot and killed the three victims, English admitted that petitioner committed one element of that offense, *i.e.*, that he killed the victims. But English strenuously argued that petitioner was not guilty of first-degree murder because he lacked the intent (the *mens rea*) required for the offense. So the Court's newly discovered fundamental right simply does not apply to the real facts of this case.

# I

The real case is far more complex. Indeed, the real situation English faced at the beginning of petitioner's trial was the result of a freakish confluence of factors that is unlikely to recur.

Retained by petitioner's family, English found himself in a predicament as the trial date approached. The evidence against his client was truly "overwhelming," as the Louisiana Supreme Court aptly noted. Among other things, the evidence showed the following. Before the killings took place, petitioner had abused and threatened to kill his wife, and she was therefore under police protection. On the night of the killings, petitioner's mother-in-law made a 911 call and was heard screaming petitioner's first name. She yelled: "'She ain't here, Robert . . . I don't know where she is. The detectives have her. Talk to the detectives. She ain't in there, Robert.' " Moments later, a gunshot was heard, and the 911 call was disconnected.

Officers were dispatched to the scene, and on arrival, they found three dead or dying victims—petitioner's mother-in-law, her husband, and the teenage son of petitioner's wife. The officers saw a man who fit petitioner's description fleeing in petitioner's car. They chased the suspect, but he abandoned the car along with critical evidence linking him to the crime: the cordless phone petitioner's mother-in-law had used to call 911 and a receipt for the type of ammunition used to kill the victims. Petitioner was eventually arrested while hitchhiking in Idaho, and a loaded gun found in his possession was identified as the one used to shoot the victims. In addition to all this, a witness testified that petitioner had asked to borrow money to purchase bullets shortly before the shootings, and surveillance footage showed petitioner purchasing the ammunition on the day of the killings. And two of petitioner's friends testified that he confessed to killing at least one person.

Despite all this evidence, petitioner, who had been found competent to stand trial and had refused to plead guilty by reason of insanity, insisted that he did not kill the victims. He claimed that the victims were killed by the local police and that he had been framed by a farflung conspiracy of state and federal officials, reaching from Louisiana to Idaho. Petitioner believed that even his attorney and the trial judge had joined the plot.

Unwilling to go along with this incredible and uncorroborated defense, English told petitioner "some eight months" before trial that the only viable strategy was to admit the killings and to concentrate on attempting to avoid a sentence of death. At that point—aware of English's strong views—petitioner could have discharged English and sought new counsel willing to pursue his conspiracy defense; under the Sixth Amendment, that was his right. See United States v. Gonzalez-Lopez, 548

U. S. 140, 144 (2006). But petitioner stated "several different times" that he was "confident with Mr. English."

The weekend before trial, however, petitioner changed his mind. He asked the trial court to replace English, and English asked for permission to withdraw. Petitioner stated that he had secured substitute counsel, but he was unable to provide the name of this new counsel, and no new attorney ever appeared. The court refused these requests and also denied petitioner's last-minute request to represent himself. (Petitioner does not challenge these decisions here.) So petitioner and English were stuck with each other, and petitioner availed himself of his right to take the stand to tell his wild story. Under those circumstances, what was English supposed to do?

The Louisiana Supreme Court held that English could not have put on petitioner's desired defense without violating state ethics rules, but this Court effectively overrules the state court on this issue of state law. However, even if it is assumed that the Court is correct on this ethics issue, the result of mounting petitioner's conspiracy defense almost certainly would have been disastrous. That approach stood no chance of winning an acquittal and would have severely damaged English's credibility in the eyes of the jury, thus undermining his ability to argue effectively against the imposition of a death sentence at the penalty phase of the trial. As English observed, taking that path would have only "help[ed] the District Attorney send [petitioner] to the death chamber." (In Florida v. Nixon, 543 U. S. 175, 191–192 (2004), this Court made essentially the same point.) So, again, what was English supposed to do?

When pressed at oral argument before this Court, petitioner's current counsel eventually provided an answer: English was not required to take any affirmative steps to support petitioner's bizarre defense, but instead of conceding that petitioner shot the victims, English should have ignored that element entirely. So the fundamental right supposedly violated in this case comes down to the difference between the two statements set out below.

Constitutional: "First-degree murder requires proof both that the accused killed the victim and that he acted with the intent to kill. I submit to you that my client did not have the intent required for conviction for that offense."

Unconstitutional: "First-degree murder requires proof both that the accused killed the victim and that he acted with the intent to kill. I admit that my client shot and killed the victims, but I submit to you that he did not have the intent required for conviction for that offense."

The practical difference between these two statements is negligible. If English had conspicuously refrained from endorsing petitioner's story and had based his defense solely on petitioner's dubious mental condition, the jury would surely have gotten the message that English was essentially conceding that petitioner killed the victims. But according to petitioner's current attorney, the difference is fundamental. The first formulation, he admits, is perfectly fine. The latter, on the other hand, is a violation so egregious that the defendant's conviction must be reversed even if there is no chance that the misstep caused any harm. It is no wonder that the Court declines to embrace this argument and instead turns to an issue that the case at hand does not actually present.

II

The constitutional right that the Court has now discovered—a criminal defendant's right to insist that his attorney contest his guilt with respect to all charged offenses—is like a rare plant that blooms every decade or so. Having made its first appearance today, the right is unlikely to figure in another case for many years to come. Why is this so?

First, it is hard to see how the right could come into play in any case other than a capital case in which the jury must decide both guilt and punishment. In all other cases, guilt is almost always the only issue for the jury, and therefore admitting guilt of all charged offenses will achieve nothing. It is hard to imagine a situation in which a competent attorney might take that approach. So the right that the Court has discovered is effectively confined to capital cases.

Second, few rational defendants facing a possible death sentence are likely to insist on contesting guilt where there is no real chance of acquittal and where admitting guilt may improve the chances of avoiding execution. Indeed, under such circumstances, the odds are that a rational defendant will plead guilty in exchange for a life sentence. By the same token, an attorney is unlikely to insist on admitting guilt over the defendant's objection unless the attorney believes that contesting guilt would be futile. So the right is most likely to arise in cases involving irrational capital defendants.[c]

Third, where a capital defendant and his retained attorney cannot agree on a basic trial strategy, the attorney and client will generally part ways unless, as in this case, the court is not apprised until the eve of trial. The client will then either search for another attorney or decide to represent himself. So the field of cases in which this right might arise is limited further still—to cases involving irrational capital defendants who disagree with their attorneys' proposed strategy yet continue to retain them.

---

[c]  The Court imagines cases in which a rational defendant prefers even a minuscule chance of acquittal over either the social opprobrium that would result from an admission of guilt or the sentence of imprisonment that would be imposed upon conviction. Such cases are likely to be rare, and in any event, as explained below, the defendant will almost always be able to get his way if he acts in time.

Fourth, if counsel is appointed, and unreasonably insists on admitting guilt over the defendant's objection, a capable trial judge will almost certainly grant a timely request to appoint substitute counsel. And if such a request is denied, the ruling may be vulnerable on appeal.

Finally, even if all the above conditions are met, the right that the Court now discovers will not come into play unless the defendant expressly protests counsel's strategy of admitting guilt. Where the defendant is advised of the strategy and says nothing, or is equivocal, the right is deemed to have been waived. See *Nixon*, 543 U. S., at 192.

In short, the right that the Court now discovers is likely to appear only rarely, and because the present case is so unique, it is hard to see how it meets our stated criteria for granting review. See this Court's Rules 10(b)–(c). Review would at least be understandable if the strategy that English pursued had worked an injustice, but the Court does not make that claim—and with good reason. Endorsing petitioner's bizarre defense would have been extraordinarily unwise, and dancing the fine line recommended by petitioner's current attorney would have done no good. It would have had no effect on the outcome of the trial, and it is hard to see how that approach would have respected petitioner's "autonomy," any more than the more straightforward approach that English took. If petitioner is retried, it will be interesting to see what petitioner's current counsel or any other attorney to whom the case is handed off will do. It is a safe bet that no attorney will put on petitioner's conspiracy defense.

## III

While the question that the Court decides is unlikely to make another appearance for quite some time, a related—and difficult—question may arise more frequently: When guilt is the sole issue for the jury, is it ever permissible for counsel to make the unilateral decision to concede an element of the offense charged? If today's decision were understood to address that question, it would have important implications.

Under current precedent, there are some decisions on which a criminal defendant has the final say. For example, a defendant cannot be forced to enter a plea against his wishes. See Brookhart v. Janis, 384 U. S. 1, 5–7 (1966). Similarly, no matter what counsel thinks best, a defendant has the right to insist on a jury trial and to take the stand and testify in his own defense. See Harris v. New York, 401 U. S. 222, 225 (1971). And if, as in this case, a defendant and retained counsel do not see eye to eye, the client can always attempt to find another attorney who will accede to his wishes. A defendant can also choose to dispense with counsel entirely and represent himself.

While these fundamental decisions must be made by a criminal defendant, most of the decisions that arise in criminal cases are the prerogative of counsel. (Our adversarial system would break down if defense counsel were required to obtain the client's approval for every important move made during the course of the case.) Among the decisions that counsel is free to make unilaterally are the following: choosing the basic line of defense, moving to suppress evidence, delivering an opening statement and deciding what to say in the opening, objecting to the admission of evidence, cross-examining witnesses, offering evidence and calling defense witnesses, and deciding what to say in summation. See, e.g., New York v. Hill, 528 U. S. 110, 114–115 (2000). On which side of the line does conceding some but not all elements of the charged offense fall?

Some criminal offenses contain elements that the prosecution can easily prove beyond any shadow of a doubt. A prior felony conviction is a good example. See 18 U. S. C. § 922(g) (possession of a firearm by a convicted felon). Suppose that the prosecution is willing to stipulate that the defendant has a prior felony conviction but is prepared, if necessary, to offer certified judgments of conviction for multiple prior violent felonies. If the defendant insists on contesting the convictions on frivolous grounds, must counsel go along? Does the same rule apply to all elements? If there are elements that may not be admitted over the defendant's objection, must counsel go further and actually contest those elements? Or is it permissible if counsel refrains from expressly conceding those elements but essentially admits them by walking the fine line recommended at argument by petitioner's current attorney?

What about conceding that a defendant is guilty, not of the offense charged, but of a lesser included offense? That is what English did in this case. He admitted that petitioner was guilty of the noncapital offense of second-degree murder in an effort to prevent a death sentence.[d] Is admitting guilt of a lesser included offense over the defendant's objection always unconstitutional? Where the evidence strongly supports conviction for first-degree murder, is it unconstitutional for defense counsel to make the decision to admit guilt of any lesser included form of homicide—even manslaughter? What about simple assault?

These are not easy questions, and the fact that they have not come up in this Court for more than two centuries suggests that they will arise infrequently in the future. I would leave those questions for another day and limit our decision to the particular (and highly unusual) situation in the actual case before us. And given the situation in which English found

---

[d]  The Court asserts that, under Louisiana law, English's "second-degree strategy would have encountered a shoal" and necessarily failed. But the final arbiter of Louisiana law—the Louisiana Supreme Court—disagreed. It held that "[t]he jury was left with several choices" after English's second-degree concession, "including returning a responsive verdict of second degree murder" and "not returning the death penalty."

himself when trial commenced, I would hold that he did not violate any fundamental right by expressly acknowledging that petitioner killed the victims instead of engaging in the barren exercise that petitioner's current counsel now recommends.

## IV

Having discovered a new right not at issue in the real case before us, the Court compounds its error by summarily concluding that a violation of this right "ranks as error of the kind our decisions have called 'structural.' "

The Court concedes that the Louisiana Supreme Court did not decide the structural-error question and that we "'did not grant certiorari to review' that question." We have stated time and again that we are "a court of review, not of first view" and, for that reason, have refused to decide issues not addressed below. * * *

In this case, however, the court-of-review maxim does not suit the majority's purposes, so it is happy to take the first view. And the majority does so without adversarial briefing on the question. * * *

The Court ignores the question actually presented by the case before us and instead decides this case on the basis of a newly discovered constitutional right that is not implicated by what really occurred at petitioner's trial. I would base our decision on what really took place, and under the highly unusual facts of this case, I would affirm the judgment below.

I therefore respectfully dissent.

# CHAPTER 11

## SENTENCING

■ ■ ■

## I. INTRODUCTION

### E. SENTENCING ALTERNATIVES OTHER THAN INCARCERATION

#### 3. Restitution

**Page 1548. Add at bottom of page:**

In Lagos v. United States, 138 S. Ct. 1684 (2018), Justice Breyer wrote for a unanimous Court as it rejected lower courts' analysis of the provision of the Mandatory Victims Restitution Act of 1996 requiring defendants to "reimburse the victim for lost income and necessary child care, transportation, and other expenses incurred during participation in the investigation or prosecution of the offense or attendance at proceedings related to the Offense." Lagos pled guilty to using a company he controlled to defraud a lender of tens of millions of dollars. When the lender became aware of the scheme and Lagos's company went bankrupt, the lender spent nearly $5 million dollars to conduct a private investigation and to participate as a party in the bankruptcy proceedings. The expenditures included legal, accounting and consulting fees. At sentencing the district court required Lagos to reimburse the lender for these expenditures, and the Fifth Circuit affirmed. Justice Breyer concluded that the words "investigation" and "proceedings" in the Act are limited to government investigations and criminal proceedings and do not include private investigations and civil or bankruptcy proceedings.

## II. GUIDELINES SENTENCING

## D. SUPREME COURT CONSTRUCTION OF THE FEDERAL SENTENCING GUIDELINES

### 2. Application of Advisory Guidelines After *Booker*

### Page 1589. Add at the end of the first partial paragraph:

### *Guideline Reductions and Sentence Modifications: The Required Explanation*

In Chavez-Meza v. United States, 138 S.Ct. 1959 (2018), the Court held that a district judge who originally sentenced the defendant to the bottom of his Guideline range (135–168 months) for possessing methamphetamine with intent to distribute adequately explained the reasons for imposing a revised sentence of 114 months after the Sentencing Commission lowered the relevant Guideline range to 108 to 135 months.

Justice Breyer wrote for the majority. He relied on Rita v. United States, 551 U. S. 338 (2007), in which the Court set forth the explanation requirement at sentencing, and concluded that "[a]t bottom, the sentencing judge need only set forth enough to satisfy the appellate court that he has considered the parties' arguments and has a reasoned basis for exercising his own legal decisionmaking authority." The government argued that this was a sentence modification and "this fact alone should secure it a virtually automatic victory." Justice Breyer found that it was unnecessary to go so far. He concluded that "[e]ven assuming (purely for argument's sake) district courts have equivalent duties when initially sentencing a defendant and when later modifying the sentence, what the District Court did here was sufficient."

Justice Breyer reasoned that "a judge's choice among points on a range will often simply reflect the judge's belief that the chosen sentence is the 'right' sentence (or as close as possible to the 'right' sentence) based on various factors, including those found in § 3553(a)," and because "that is so, it is unsurprising that changing the applicable range may lead a judge to choose a nonproportional point on the new range." He also found it appropriate to consider what the judge said at the original sentencing as well as at the resentencing.

Finally, Justice Breyer indicated that the Court was not saying that a sentence modification never requires a more detailed explanation than was provided in this case, and explained that "under different facts and a different record, the district court's use of a barebones form order in response to a motion like petitioner's would be inadequate."

Justice Kennedy, joined by Justices Kagan and Sotomayor, dissented. He explained that "[m]y disagreement with the majority is based on a serious problem—the difficulty for prisoners and appellate courts in ascertaining a district court's reasons for imposing a sentence when the court fails to state those reasons on the record; yet, in the end, my disagreement turns on a small difference, for a remedy is simple and easily attained." His remedy is "a slight expansion of the AO-247 form," "to include just a few more categories covering the factors most often bearing on a trial court's sentencing determination," so that "district judges would have a helpful form that might well reduce the time for consideration of cases—and even if not would help ensure the full consideration which tends to result in uniformity and fairness."

## Page 1590. Add after the discussion of *Peugh v. United States*:

Justice Alito wrote for a unanimous Court in Koons v. United States, 138 S. Ct. 1783 (2018), as it held that five defendants who were sentenced below mandatory minimums because they gave substantial assistance to the government did not qualify for sentence reductions under 18 U.S.C. § 3582(c)(2), which makes defendants eligible if they were sentenced "based on a sentencing range" that was later lowered by the United States Sentencing Commission. Justice Alito reasoned that their sentences were not "based on" their lowered Guidelines ranges but, instead, were "based on" their mandatory minimums and substantial assistance.

In another sentencing case, Justice Kennedy wrote for the Court in Hughes v. United States, 138 S. Ct. 1765 (2018), holding that a defendant may seek relief under § 3582(c)(2) if he entered a plea agreement under Federal Rule of Criminal Procedure 11(c)(1)(C) (Type-C agreement), which permits the defendant and the Government to "agree that a specific sentence or sentencing range is the appropriate disposition of the case," and "binds the court [to the agreed-upon sentence] once [it] accepts the plea agreement." Justice Kennedy noted that in deciding whether to approve the agreement the district court must consider the Sentencing Guidelines and may not accept the agreement unless the sentence is within the applicable Guidelines range, or it is outside that range for justifiable reasons specifically set out.

The government indicted Hughes in 2013 on drug and gun charges for his participation in a conspiracy to distribute methamphetamine. The parties negotiated a Type-C plea agreement pursuant to which Hughes agreed to plead guilty to two of the four charges (conspiracy to distribute methamphetamine and being a felon in possession of a gun) and in exchange the Government agreed to dismiss the other two charges and to refrain from filing an information giving formal notification to the District Court of his prior drug felonies. Hughes would have faced a mandatory life sentence if the government had filed the information. The agreement stipulated that Hughes would receive a sentence of 180 months, but it did not refer to any particular Guidelines range. The district court calculated the guideline range as 188 to 235 months before hearing from Hughes, his mother and his daughter and approving the agreement in light of the sentencing factors set forth in 18 U.S.C. § 3553 (a).

The Sentencing Commission amended the Guidelines less than two months after Hughes' sentencing and reduced the base offense level by two levels for most drug offenses. The Commission later made the amendment retroactive for defendants who, like Hughes, already had been sentenced under the higher offense levels. Under the revised Guidelines Hughes' sentencing range is 151 to 188 months, which is approximately three to four years lower than the range in effect when he was sentenced. Hughes filed a motion for a sentence reduction. The lower courts concluded that he was ineligible, and the Supreme Court reversed.

Justice Kennedy noted that the Guidelines are only advisory and cited *Koons* as an example:

> If the Guidelines range was not "a relevant part of the analytic framework the judge used to determine the sentence or to approve the agreement," * * * then the defendant's sentence was not based on that sentencing range, and relief under § 3582(c)(2) is unavailable. And that is so regardless of whether a defendant pleaded guilty pursuant to a Type-C agreement or whether the agreement itself referred to a Guidelines range. The statutory language points to the reasons for the sentence that the district court imposed, not the reasons for the parties' plea agreement. Still, cases like *Koons* are a narrow exception to the general rule that, in most cases, a defendant's sentence will be "based on" his Guidelines range. In federal sentencing the Guidelines are a district court's starting point, so when the Commission lowers a defendant's Guidelines range the defendant will be eligible for relief under § 3582(c)(2) absent clear demonstration, based on the record as a whole, that the court would have imposed the same sentence regardless of the Guidelines.

Justice Sotomayor concurred. She noted that the Court confronted the same question in Freeman v. United States, 564 U. S. 522 (2011), which ended in a 4–1–4 decision that left lower courts confused as to whether the plurality [opinion by Chief Justice Roberts] or the concurring opinion [of Justice Sotomayor] controlled. She voted with the majority in *Hughes* "to ensure clarity and stability in the law and promote[ ] 'uniformity in sentencing imposed by different federal courts for similar criminal conduct.' "

Chief Justice Roberts, joined by Justices Thomas and Alito, dissented and relied upon his *Freeman* plurality opinion and Justice Sotomayor's *Freeman* concurrence:

> As the Court points out, a district court considering whether to accept a Type-C agreement must consult the Guidelines, as the District Court did here. But "when determining the sentence to impose," the district court may base its decision on "one thing and one thing only—the plea agreement." Freeman, 564 U. S., at 545 (ROBERTS, C. J., dissenting). The Court characterizes this distinction as "artificial," arguing that the district court's ultimate imposition of a sentence often has as much to do with its Guidelines calculation as anything else. But that is not so: With a Type-C agreement, the sentence is set by the parties, not by a judge applying the Guidelines. Far from being "artificial," that distinction is central to what makes a Type-C plea a Type-C plea. "In the (C) agreement context" it is "the binding plea agreement that is the foundation for the term of imprisonment." Freeman, 564 U. S., at 535 (opinion of SOTOMAYOR, J.). "To hold otherwise would be to contravene the very purpose of (C) agreements—to bind the district court and allow the Government and the defendant to determine what sentence he will receive." Id., at 536.

> \* \* \*

> The Court finds new justification for its interpretation in Peugh v. United States, 569 U. S. 530 (2013), and Molina-Martinez v. United States, 578 U. S. ___ (2016). But those cases—which do not concern the language of § 3582(c)(2) or sentencing pursuant to Type-C agreements—do not inform the distinct question at hand. \* \* \*

The Chief Justice observed that "[t]he Government may well be able to limit the frustrating effects of today's decision in the long run \* \* \* by adding a provision to every Type-C agreement in which the defendant agrees to waive any right to seek a sentence reduction following future Guidelines amendments."

# CHAPTER 12

## DOUBLE JEOPARDY

■ ■ ■

### V. MULTIPLE PROSECUTIONS OF CONVICTED DEFENDANTS

**Page 1666. Add the following new section**

### E. WAIVER BY DEFENDANT

#### CURRIER V. VIRGINIA
Supreme Court of the United States, 2018.
138 S. Ct. 2144.

**JUSTICE GORSUCH announced the judgment of the Court and delivered the opinion of the Court with respect to Parts I and II, and an opinion with respect to Part III, in which THE CHIEF JUSTICE, JUSTICE THOMAS, and JUSTICE ALITO join.**

About to face trial, Michael Currier worried the prosecution would introduce prejudicial but probative evidence against him on one count that could infect the jury's deliberations on others. To address the problem, he agreed to sever the charges and hold two trials instead of one. But after the first trial finished, Mr. Currier turned around and argued that proceeding with the second would violate his right against double jeopardy. All of which raises the question: can a defendant who agrees to have the charges against him considered in two trials later successfully argue that the second trial offends the Fifth Amendment's Double Jeopardy Clause?

I

This case began when police dredged up a safe full of guns from a Virginia river. Paul Garrison, the safe's owner, had reported it stolen from his home. Before the theft, Mr. Garrison said, it contained not just the guns but also $71,000 in cash. Now, most of the money was missing. As the investigation unfolded, the police eventually found their way to Mr. Garrison's nephew. Once confronted, the nephew quickly confessed. Along the way, he pointed to Michael Currier as his accomplice. A neighbor also reported that she saw Mr. Currier leave the Garrison home around the time of the crime. On the strength of this evidence, a grand jury indicted Mr. Currier for burglary, grand larceny, and unlawful possession of a firearm by a convicted felon. The last charge followed in light of Mr. Currier's previous convictions for (as it happens) burglary and larceny.

Because the prosecution could introduce evidence of his prior convictions to prove the felon-in-possession charge, and worried that the evidence might prejudice the jury's consideration of the other charges, Mr. Currier and the government agreed to a severance. They asked the court to try the burglary and larceny charges first. Then, they said, the felon-in-possession charge could follow in a second trial. Some jurisdictions routinely refuse requests like this. Instead, they seek to address the risk of prejudice with an instruction directing the jury to consider the defendant's prior convictions only when assessing the felon-in-possession charge. Other jurisdictions allow parties to stipulate to the defendant's past convictions so the particulars of those crimes don't reach the jury's ears. Others take a more protective approach yet and view severance requests with favor. Because Virginia falls into this last group, the trial court granted the parties' joint request in this case.

The promised two trials followed. At the first, the prosecution produced the nephew and the neighbor who testified to Mr. Currier's involvement in the burglary and larceny. But Mr. Currier argued that the nephew lied and the neighbor was unreliable and, in the end, the jury acquitted. Then, before the second trial on the firearm charge could follow, Mr. Currier sought to stop it. Now, he argued, holding a second trial would amount to double jeopardy. Alternatively and at the least, he asked the court to forbid the government from relitigating in the second trial any issue resolved in his favor at the first. So, for example, he said the court should exclude from the new proceeding any evidence about the burglary and larceny. The court replied that it could find nothing in the Double Jeopardy Clause requiring either result so it allowed the second trial to proceed unfettered. In the end, the jury convicted Mr. Currier on the felon-in-possession charge.

Before the Virginia Court of Appeals, Mr. Currier repeated his double jeopardy arguments without success. The court held that the "concern that lies at the core" of the Double Jeopardy Clause—namely, "the avoidance of prosecutorial oppression and overreaching through successive trials"—had no application here because the charges were severed for Mr. Currier's benefit and at his behest. The Virginia Supreme Court summarily affirmed. Because courts have reached conflicting results on the double jeopardy arguments Mr. Currier pressed in this case, we granted certiorari to resolve them.

## II

The Double Jeopardy Clause, applied to the States through the Fourteenth Amendment, provides that no person may be tried more than once "for the same offence." This guarantee recognizes the vast power of the sovereign, the ordeal of a criminal trial, and the injustice our criminal justice system would invite if prosecutors could treat trials as dress rehearsals until they secure the convictions they seek. See Green v. United States, 355 U. S. 187, 188 (1957). At the same time, this Court has said, the Clause was not written or originally understood to pose "an insuperable obstacle to the administration of justice" in cases where "there is no semblance of [these] type[s] of oppressive practices." Wade v. Hunter, 336 U. S. 684, 688–689 (1949).

On which side of the line does our case fall? Mr. Currier suggests this Court's decision in Ashe v. Swenson, 397 U. S. 436 (1970), requires a ruling for him. There, the government accused a defendant of robbing six poker players in a game at a private home. At the first trial, the jury acquitted the defendant of robbing one victim. Then the State sought to try the defendant for robbing a second victim. This Court held the second prosecution violated the Double Jeopardy Clause. To be sure, the Clause speaks of barring successive trials for the same offense. And, to be sure, the State sought to try the defendant for a *different* robbery. But, the Court reasoned, because the first jury necessarily found that the defendant "was not one of the robbers," a second jury could not "rationally" convict the defendant of robbing the second victim without calling into question the earlier acquittal. In these circumstances, the Court indicated, any relitigation of the issue whether the defendant participated as "one of the robbers" would be tantamount to the forbidden relitigation of the same offense resolved at the first trial.

*Ashe*'s suggestion that the relitigation of an issue can sometimes amount to the impermissible relitigation of an offense represented a significant innovation in our jurisprudence. Some have argued that it sits uneasily with this Court's double jeopardy precedent and the Constitution's original meaning. But whatever else may be said about *Ashe*, we have emphasized that its test is a demanding one. *Ashe* forbids a second trial only if to secure a conviction the prosecution must prevail on an issue the jury necessarily resolved in the defendant's favor in the first trial. A second trial "is not precluded simply because it is unlikely—or even very unlikely—that the original jury acquitted without finding the fact in question." To say that the second trial is tantamount to a trial of the same offense as the first and thus forbidden by the Double Jeopardy Clause, we must be able to say that "it would have been *irrational* for the jury" in the first trial to acquit without finding in the defendant's favor on a fact essential to a conviction in the second.

Bearing all that in mind, a critical difference immediately emerges between our case and *Ashe*. Even assuming without deciding that Mr. Currier's second trial qualified as the retrial of the same offense under *Ashe*, he consented to it. Nor does anyone doubt that trying all three charges in one trial would have prevented any possible *Ashe* complaint Mr. Currier might have had.

How do these features affect the double jeopardy calculus? A precedent points the way. In Jeffers v. United States, 432 U. S. 137 (1977), the defendant sought separate trials on each of the counts against him to reduce the possibility of prejudice. The court granted his request. After the jury convicted the defendant in the first trial of a lesser-included offense, he argued that the prosecution could not later try him for a greater offense. In any other circumstance the defendant likely would have had a good argument. Historically, courts have treated greater and lesser-included offenses as the same offense for double jeopardy purposes, so a conviction on one normally precludes a later trial on the other. But, *Jeffers* concluded, it's different when the defendant consents to two trials where one could have done. If a single trial on multiple charges would suffice to avoid a double jeopardy complaint, "there is no violation of the Double Jeopardy Clause when [the defendant] elects to have the . . . offenses tried separately and persuades the trial court to honor his election." 432 U. S., at 152.

What was true in *Jeffers*, we hold, can be no less true here. If a defendant's consent to two trials can overcome concerns lying at the historic core of the Double Jeopardy Clause, so too we think it must overcome a double jeopardy complaint under *Ashe*. Nor does anything in *Jeffers* suggest that the outcome should be different if the first trial yielded an acquittal rather than a conviction when a defendant consents to severance. While we acknowledge that *Ashe*'s protections apply only to trials following acquittals, as a general rule, the Double Jeopardy Clause protects against a second prosecution for the same offense after conviction as well as against a second prosecution for the same offense after acquittal. Because the Clause applies equally in both situations, consent to a second trial should in general have equal effect in both situations.

Holding otherwise would introduce an unwarranted inconsistency not just with *Jeffers* but with other precedents too. In United States v. Dinitz, 424 U. S. 600 (1976), for example, this Court held that a defendant's mistrial motion implicitly invited a second trial and was enough to foreclose any double jeopardy complaint about it. In reaching this holding, the Court expressly rejected "the contention that the permissibility of a retrial depends on a knowing, voluntary, and intelligent waiver" from the defendant. Instead, it explained, none of the "prosecutorial or judicial overreaching" forbidden by the Constitution can be found when a second trial follows thanks to the defendant's motion. In

United States v. Scott, 437 U. S. 82 (1978), this Court likewise held that a defendant's motion effectively invited a retrial of the same offense, and "the Double Jeopardy Clause, which guards against Government oppression, does not relieve a defendant from the consequences of [a] voluntary choice" like that. * * * While relinquishing objections sometimes turns on state or federal procedural rules, these precedents teach that consenting to two trials when one would have avoided a double jeopardy problem precludes any constitutional violation associated with holding a second trial. In these circumstances, our cases hold, the defendant wins a potential benefit and experiences none of the prosecutorial "oppression" the Double Jeopardy Clause exists to prevent.

Nor, again, can we discern a good reason to treat *Ashe* double jeopardy complaints more favorably than traditional ones when a defendant consents to severance.

Against these precedents, Mr. Currier asks us to consider others, especially Harris v. Washington, 404 U. S. 55 (1971) (per curiam) and Turner v. Arkansas, 407 U. S. 366 (1972) (per curiam). But these cases merely applied *Ashe*'s test and concluded that a second trial was impermissible. They did not address the question whether double jeopardy protections apply if the defendant *consents* to a second trial. Meanwhile, as we've seen, *Jeffers*, *Dinitz*, and *Scott* focus on that question directly and make clear that a defendant's consent dispels any specter of double jeopardy abuse that holding two trials might otherwise present. This Court's teachings are consistent and plain: the "Clause, which guards against Government oppression, does not relieve a defendant from the consequences of his voluntary choice." *Scott*, *supra*, at 99.

Mr. Currier replies that he had no real choice but to seek two trials. Without a second trial, he says, evidence of his prior convictions would have tainted the jury's consideration of the burglary and larceny charges. And, he notes, Virginia law guarantees a severance in cases like his unless the defendant and prosecution agree to a single trial. But no one disputes that the Constitution permitted Virginia to try all three charges at once with appropriate cautionary instructions. So this simply isn't a case where the defendant had to give up one constitutional right to secure another. Instead, Mr. Currier faced a lawful choice between two courses of action that each bore potential costs and rationally attractive benefits. It might have been a hard choice. But litigants every day face difficult decisions. Whether it's the defendant who finds himself in the shoes of Jeffers, Dinitz, and Scott and forced to choose between allowing an imperfect trial to proceed or seeking a second that promises its own risks. Or whether it's the defendant who must decide between exercising his right to testify in his own defense or keeping impeachment evidence of past bad acts from the jury. See, *e.g.,* Brown v. United States, 356 U. S. 148, 154–157 (1958). This Court has held repeatedly that difficult strategic choices like these are "not the same as no choice," United States v. Martinez-Salazar, 528 U. S. 304, 315 (2000), and the Constitution "does not . . . forbid requiring" a litigant to make them, McGautha v. California, 402 U. S. 183, 213 (1971).

III

Even if he voluntarily consented to holding the second trial, Mr. Currier argues, that consent did not extend to the relitigation of any issues the first jury resolved in his favor. So, Mr. Currier says, the court should have excluded evidence suggesting he possessed the guns in Mr. Garrison's home, leaving the prosecution to prove that he possessed them only later, maybe down by the river. To support this argument, Mr. Currier points to issue preclusion principles in civil cases and invites us to import them for the first time into the criminal law through the Double Jeopardy Clause. In his view, the Clause should do much more than bar the retrial of the same offense (or crimes tantamount to the same offense under *Ashe*); it should be read now to prevent the parties from retrying any issue or introducing any evidence about a previously tried issue. While the dissent today agrees with us that the trial court committed no double jeopardy violation in holding the second trial, on this alternative argument it sides with Mr. Currier.

We cannot. Even assuming for argument's sake that Mr. Currier's consent to *holding* a second trial didn't more broadly imply consent to the *manner* it was conducted, we must reject his argument on a narrower ground. Just last Term this Court warned that issue preclusion principles should have only "guarded application . . . in criminal cases." Bravo-Fernandez v. United States, 580 U. S. ___, ___(2016) (slip op. at 4). We think that caution remains sound.

Mr. Currier's problems begin with the text of the Double Jeopardy Clause. As we've seen, the Clause speaks not about prohibiting the relitigation of issues or evidence but offenses. Contrast this with the language of the Reexamination Clause. There, the Seventh Amendment says that "[i]n Suits at common law . . . *no fact* tried by a jury, *shall be otherwise re-examined* in any Court of the United States, than according to the rules of the common law." (Emphasis added.) Words in one provision are, of course, often understood "by comparing them with other words and sentences in the same instrument." 1 J. Story, Commentaries on the Constitution of the United States § 400, p. 384 (1833). So it's difficult to ignore that only in the Seventh Amendment—and only for civil suits—can we find anything resembling contemporary issue preclusion doctrine.

What problems the text suggests, the original public understanding of the Fifth Amendment confirms. The Double Jeopardy Clause took its cue from English common law pleas that prevented courts from retrying a criminal defendant previously acquitted or convicted of the crime in question. * * *

* * *

This Court's contemporary double jeopardy cases confirm what the text and history suggest. Under Blockburger v. United States, 284 U. S. 299 (1932), the courts apply today much the same double jeopardy test they did at the founding. To prevent a second trial on a new charge, the defendant must show an identity of statutory elements between the two charges against him; it's not enough that "a substantial overlap [exists] in the proof offered to establish the crimes." Iannelli v. United States, 420 U. S. 770, 785, n. 17 (1975). Of course, *Ashe* later pressed *Blockburger's* boundaries by suggesting that, in narrow circumstances, the retrial of an issue can be considered tantamount to the retrial of an offense. But, as we've seen, even there a court's ultimate focus remains on the practical identity of offenses, and the only available remedy is the traditional double jeopardy bar against the retrial of the same offense—not a bar against the relitigation of issues or evidence. Even at the outer reaches of our double jeopardy jurisprudence, then, this Court has never sought to regulate the retrial of issues or evidence in the name of the Double Jeopardy Clause.

Nor in acknowledging this do we plow any new ground. In Dowling v. United States, 493 U. S. 342 (1990), the defendant faced charges of bank robbery. At trial, the prosecution introduced evidence of the defendant's involvement in an earlier crime, even though the jury in that case had acquitted. Like Mr. Currier, the defendant in *Dowling* argued that the trial court should have barred relitigation of an issue resolved in his favor in an earlier case and therefore excluded evidence of the acquitted offense. But the Court refused the request and in doing so expressly "decline[d] to extend *Ashe* . . . to exclude in all circumstances, as [the defendant] would have it, relevant and probative evidence that is otherwise admissible under the Rules of Evidence simply because it relates to alleged criminal conduct for which a defendant has been acquitted." If a second trial is permissible, the admission of evidence at that trial is governed by normal evidentiary rules—not by the terms of the Double Jeopardy Clause. "So far as merely evidentiary . . . facts are concerned," the Double Jeopardy Clause "is inoperative." Yates v. United States, 354 U. S. 298, 338 (1957).

On its own terms, too, any effort to transplant civil preclusion principles into the Double Jeopardy Clause would quickly meet trouble. While the Clause embodies a kind of "claim preclusion" rule, even this rule bears little in common with its civil counterpart. In civil cases, a claim generally may not be tried if it arises out of the same transaction or common nucleus of operative facts as another already tried. But in a criminal case, *Blockburger* precludes a trial on an offense only if a court has previously heard the same offense as measured by its statutory elements. And this Court has emphatically refused to import into criminal double jeopardy law the civil law's more generous "same transaction" or same criminal "episode" test. See Garrett v. United States, 471 U. S. 773, 790 (1985); see also Ashe, 397 U. S., at 448 (Harlan, J., concurring).

It isn't even clear that civil preclusion principles would help defendants like Mr. Currier. Issue preclusion addresses the effect in a current case of a prior adjudication in *another case*. So it doesn't often have much to say about the preclusive effects of rulings "within the framework of a continuing action." Usually, only the more flexible law of the case doctrine governs the preclusive effect of an earlier decision "within a single action." And that doctrine might counsel against affording conclusive effect to a prior jury verdict on a particular issue when the parties *agreed* to hold a second trial covering much the same terrain at a later stage of the proceedings. Besides, even if issue preclusion is the right doctrine for cases like ours, its application usually depends on an underlying confidence that the result achieved in the initial litigation was substantially correct. As a result, the doctrine does not often bar the relitigation of issues when "[t]he party against whom preclusion is sought could not, as a matter of law, have obtained review of the judgment in the initial action." Restatement (Second) of Judgments § 28. In criminal cases, of course, the government cannot obtain appellate review of acquittals. So a faithful application of civil preclusion principles in our case and others like it might actually militate *against* finding preclusion.

Neither Mr. Currier nor the dissent offers a persuasive reply to these points. They cannot dispute that the text of the Double Jeopardy Clause, which bars a prosecution for the same offense, is inconsistent with an issue preclusion rule that purports to bar a second prosecution involving a different offense. They decline to "engage" with the Clause's history, though the dissent appears to agree that the Clause was not originally understood to include an issue preclusion rule. Neither Mr. Currier nor the dissent seeks to show that, even taken on their own terms, civil issue preclusion principles would apply to cases like this one. Without text, history, or logic to stand on, the dissent leans heavily on a comparison to *Dowling*. In *Dowling*, the dissent emphasizes, the two trials involved different criminal episodes while the two trials here addressed the same set of facts. But *Dowling* did not rest its holding on this feature and the dissent does not explain its relevance. If issue preclusion really did exist in criminal law, why wouldn't it preclude the retrial of *any* previously tried issue, regardless whether that issue stems from the same or a different "criminal episode"?

In the end, Mr. Currier and the dissent must emphasize various policy reasons for adopting a new rule of issue preclusion into the criminal law. They contend that issue preclusion is "needed" to combat the "prosecutorial excesses" that could result from the proliferation of criminal offenses, though we aren't sure what to make of this given the dissent's later claim that "issue preclusion requires no showing of prosecutorial overreaching," In any event, there are risks with the approach Mr. Currier and the dissent propose. Consider, for example, the ironies that grafting civil preclusion principles onto the criminal law could invite. Issue preclusion is sometimes applied offensively against civil defendants who lost on an issue in an earlier case. *Parklane Hosiery Co.* v. *Shore*, 439 U. S. 322, 331–332 (1979). By parallel logic, could we expect the government to invoke the doctrine to bar criminal defendants from relitigating issues decided against them in a prior trial? It's an outcome few defendants would welcome but one some have already promoted. See, *e.g.,* Kennelly, Precluding the Accused: Offensive Collateral Estoppel in Criminal Cases, 80 Va. L. Rev. 1379, 1380–1381, 1416, 1426–1427 (1994); Vestal, Issue Preclusion and Criminal Prosecutions, 65 Iowa L. Rev. 281, 297, 320–321 (1980).

Maybe worse yet, consider the possible effect on severances. Today, some state courts grant severance motions liberally to benefit defendants. But what would happen if this Court unilaterally increased the costs associated with severance in the form of allowing issue preclusion for defendants only? Granting a severance is no small thing. It means a court must expend resources for two trials where the Constitution would have permitted one. Witnesses and victims must endure a more protracted ordeal. States sometimes accept these costs to protect a defendant from potential prejudice. But 20 States appearing before us have warned that some jurisdictions might respond to any decision increasing the costs of severed trials by making them less freely available. Of course, that's only a prediction. But it's a hard if unwanted fact that "[t]oday's elaborate body of procedural rules" can contribute to making "trials expensive [and] rare." W. Stuntz, The Collapse of American Criminal Justice 39 (2011). And it would be a mistake to ignore the possibility that by making severances more costly we might wind up making them rarer too.

The fact is, civil preclusion principles and double jeopardy are different doctrines, with different histories, serving different purposes. Historically, both claim and issue preclusion have sought to "promot[e] judicial economy by preventing needless litigation." That interest may make special sense in civil cases where often only money is at stake. But the Double Jeopardy Clause and the common law principles it built upon govern *criminal* cases and concern more than efficiency. They aim instead, as we've seen, to balance vital interests against abusive prosecutorial practices with consideration to the public's safety. The

Clause's terms and history simply do not contain the rights Mr. Currier seeks.

Nor are we at liberty to rewrite those terms or that history. While the growing number of criminal offenses in our statute books may be cause for concern, no one should expect (or want) judges to revise the Constitution to address every social problem they happen to perceive. The proper authorities, the States and Congress, are empowered to adopt new laws or rules experimenting with issue or claim preclusion in criminal cases if they wish. In fact, some States have already done so. On these matters, the Constitution dictates no answers but entrusts them to a selfgoverning people to resolve.

### JUSTICE KENNEDY, concurring in part.

I join Parts I and II of the Court's opinion, which, in my view, suffice to resolve this case in a full and proper way.

There is a strong public "interest in giving the prosecution one complete opportunity to convict those who have violated its laws." Arizona v. Washington, 434 U. S. 497, 509 (1978). The reason that single opportunity did not occur in one trial here was because both parties consented to sever the possession charge to avoid introducing evidence of petitioner's prior conviction during his trial for burglary and larceny. * * *

* * *

The end result is that when a defendant's voluntary choices lead to a second prosecution he cannot later use the Double Jeopardy Clause, whether thought of as protecting against multiple trials or the relitigation of issues, to forestall that second prosecution. The extent of the Double Jeopardy Clause protections discussed and defined in *Ashe* need not be reexamined here; for, whatever the proper formulation and implementation of those rights are, they can be lost when a defendant agrees to a second prosecution. Of course, this conclusion is premised on the defendant's having a voluntary choice, and a different result might obtain if that premise were absent. Cf. Turner v. Arkansas, 407 U. S. 366, 367 (1972) (*per curiam*) (applying *Ashe* to a second trial where state law prohibited a single trial of the charges at issue).

### JUSTICE GINSBURG, with whom JUSTICE BREYER, JUSTICE SOTOMAYOR, and JUSTICE KAGAN join, dissenting.

* * *

I would hold that Currier's acquiescence in severance of the felon-in-possession charge does not prevent him from raising a plea of issue preclusion based on the jury acquittals of breaking and entering and grand larceny.

I

This Court's decisions "have recognized that the [Double Jeopardy] Clause embodies two vitally important interests." Yeager v. United States, 557 U. S. 110, 117 (2009). The first is the deeply ingrained principle that the State with all its resources and power should not be allowed to make repeated attempts to convict an individual for an alleged offense, thereby subjecting him to embarrassment, expense and ordeal and compelling him to live in a continuing state of anxiety and insecurity, as well as enhancing the possibility that even though innocent he may be found guilty. The second interest the Clause serves is preservation of the "finality of judgments," particularly acquittals * * *.

The Clause effectuates its overall guarantee through multiple protections. Historically, among those protections, the Court has safeguarded the right not to be subject to multiple trials for the "same offense." See Brown v. Ohio, 432 U. S. 161, 165 (1977). That claim-preclusive rule stops the government from litigating the "same offense" or criminal charge in successive prosecutions, regardless of whether the first trial ends in a conviction or an acquittal. To determine whether two offenses are the "same," this Court has held, a court must look to the offenses' elements. Blockburger v. United States, 284 U. S. 299, 304 (1932). If each offense "requires proof of a fact which the other does not," *Blockburger* established, the offenses are discrete and the prosecution of one does not bar later prosecution of the other. If, however, two offenses are greater and lesser included offenses, the government cannot prosecute them successively.

Also shielded by the Double Jeopardy Clause is the issue-preclusive effect of an acquittal. First articulated in Ashe v. Swenson, 397 U. S. 436 (1970), the issue-preclusive aspect of the Double Jeopardy Clause prohibits the government from relitigating issues necessarily resolved in a defendant's favor at an earlier trial presenting factually related offenses. *Ashe* involved the robbery of six poker players by a group of masked men. Missouri tried Ashe first for the robbery of Donald Knight. At trial, proof that Knight was the victim of a robbery was "unassailable"; the sole issue in dispute was whether Ashe was one of the robbers. A jury found Ashe not guilty. Missouri then tried Ashe for robbing a different poker player at the same table. The witnesses at the second trial "were for the most part the same," although their testimony for the prosecution was "substantially stronger" than it was at the first trial. The State also "refined its case" by declining to call a witness whose identification testimony at the first trial had been "conspicuously negative." The second time around, the State secured a conviction.

Although the second prosecution involved a different victim and thus a different "offense," this Court held that the second prosecution violated the Double Jeopardy Clause. A component of that Clause, the Court explained, rests on the principle that "when an issue of ultimate fact has once been determined by a valid and final judgment, that issue cannot again be litigated between the same parties in any future lawsuit." Consequently, "after a jury determined by its verdict that [Ashe] was not one of the robbers," the State could not "constitutionally hale him before a new jury to litigate that issue again."

In concluding that the Double Jeopardy Clause includes issue-preclusion protection for defendants, the Court acknowledged that no prior decision had "squarely held [issue preclusion] to be a constitutional requirement." "Until perhaps a century ago," the Court explained, "few situations arose calling for [issue preclusion's] application." "[A]t common law" and "under early federal criminal statutes, offense categories were relatively few and distinct," and "[a] single course of criminal conduct was likely to yield but a single offense." "[W]ith the advent of specificity in draftsmanship and the extraordinary proliferation of overlapping and related statutory offenses," however, "it became possible for prosecutors to spin out a startlingly numerous series of offenses from a single alleged criminal transaction." With this proliferation, "the potential for unfair and abusive reprosecutions became far more pronounced."

Toward the end of the 19th century, courts increasingly concluded that greater protections than those traditionally afforded under the Double Jeopardy Clause were needed to spare defendants from prosecutorial excesses. Federal courts, cognizant of the increased potential for exposing defendants to multiple charges based on the same criminal episode, borrowed issue-preclusion principles from the civil context to bar relitigation of issues necessarily resolved against the government in a criminal trial. * * * By 1970, when *Ashe* was decided, issue preclusion, "[a]lthough first developed in civil litigation," had become "an established rule of federal criminal law." The question presented in *Ashe* was whether issue preclusion is not just an established rule of federal criminal procedure, but also a rule of constitutional stature. The Court had no hesitation in concluding that it is.

Since *Ashe*, this Court has reaffirmed that issue preclusion ranks with claim preclusion as a Double Jeopardy Clause component. Harris v. Washington, 404 U. S. 55, 56 (1971) (per curiam). Given criminal codes of prolix character, issue preclusion both arms defendants against prosecutorial excesses and preserves the integrity of acquittals * * *.

## II

* * *

The sole issue in dispute at the first trial, Currier maintains, was whether he participated in the break-in and theft. The case was submitted to the jury, which acquitted Currier of both offenses.

* * *

## III

The Court holds that even if Currier could have asserted a double jeopardy issue-preclusion defense in opposition to the second trial, he relinquished that right by acquiescing in severance of the felon-in-possession charge. This holding is not sustainable. A defendant's consent to severance does not waive his right to rely on the issue-preclusive effect of an acquittal.

## A

It bears clarification first that, contra to the Court's presentation, issue preclusion requires no showing of prosecutorial overreaching. * * * This Court so ruled in Harris v. Washington, 404 U. S. 55, and it has subsequently reinforced the point in Turner v. Arkansas, 407 U. S. 366 (1972) (per curiam), and Yeager v. United States, 557 U. S. 110.

In *Harris*, the Washington Supreme Court declined to give an acquittal issue-preclusive effect because there was "no indication of bad faith of the state in deliberately making a 'trial run' in the first prosecution." State v. Harris, 78 Wash. 2d 894, 901, 480 P. 2d 484, 488 (1971). The State Supreme Court further observed that "it was to the advantage of the defendant, and not the state, to separate the trials" because certain evidence was inadmissible in the first trial that would be admissible in the second. This Court reversed and explained that an acquittal has issue-preclusive effect "irrespective of the good faith of the State in bringing successive prosecutions."

In *Turner*, Arkansas prosecutors believed the defendant had robbed and murdered someone. An Arkansas statute required that murder be charged separately, with no other charges appended. After a jury acquitted Turner on the murder charge, the State sought to try him for robbery. Even though state law, not an overzealous prosecutor, dictated the sequential trials, this Court held that the defendant was entitled to assert issue preclusion and found the case "squarely controlled by *Ashe*."

In *Yeager*, the defendant stood trial on numerous factually related offenses. After a jury acquitted on some counts but hung on others, the prosecution sought to retry a number of the hung counts. The defendant argued that issue preclusion should apply in the second trial. In opposition, the prosecution stressed that a retrial "presen[ted] none of the governmental overreaching that double jeopardy is supposed to prevent." Indeed, the prosecution had "attempted to bring all the charges in a single proceeding," and it was seeking a second trial on some charges only "because the jury hung." The Court did not regard as controlling the lack of prosecutorial overreaching. Instead, it emphasized that "[a] jury's verdict of acquittal represents the community's collective judgment regarding all the evidence and arguments presented to it" and that, once rendered, an acquittal's "finality is unassailable."

B

There is in Currier's case no suggestion that he expressly waived a plea of issue preclusion at a second trial, or that he failed to timely assert the plea. Instead, the contention, urged by the prosecution and embraced by this Court, is that Currier surrendered his right to assert the issuepreclusive effect of his first-trial acquittals by consenting to two trials.

This Court "indulge[s] every reasonable presumption against waiver of fundamental constitutional rights." Johnson v. Zerbst, 304 U. S. 458, 464 (1938) (internal quotation marks omitted). It has found "waiver by conduct" only where a defendant has engaged in "conduct inconsistent with the assertion of [the] right." Pierce Oil Corp. v. Phoenix Refining Co., 259 U. S. 125, 129 (1922). * * * Where, however, a defendant takes no action inconsistent with the assertion of a right, the defendant will not be found to have waived the right.

Currier took no action inconsistent with assertion of an issue-preclusion plea. To understand why, one must comprehend just what issue preclusion forecloses. Unlike the right against a second trial for the same offense (claim preclusion), issue preclusion prevents relitigation of a previously rejected theory of criminal liability without necessarily barring a successive trial. Take Ashe, for example. Issue preclusion prevented the prosecution from arguing, at a second trial, that Ashe was one of the robbers who held up the poker players at gunpoint. But if the prosecution sought to prove, instead, that Ashe waited outside during the robbery and then drove the getaway car, issue preclusion would not have barred that trial. Similarly here, the prosecution could not again attempt to prove that Currier participated in the break-in and theft of the safe at the Garrisons' residence. But a second trial could be mounted if the prosecution alleged, for instance, that Currier was present at the river's edge when others showed up to dump the safe in the river, and that Currier helped to empty out and replace the guns contained in the safe.

In short, issue preclusion does not operate, as claim preclusion does, to bar a successive trial altogether. Issue preclusion bars only a subset of possible trials—those in which the prosecution rests its case on a theory of liability a jury earlier rejected. That being so, consenting to a second trial is not inconsistent with—and therefore does not foreclose—a defendant's gaining the issue-preclusive effect of an acquittal.

The Court cites Jeffers v. United States, 432 U. S. 137 (1977), United States v. Dinitz, 424 U. S. 600 (1976), and United States v. Scott, 437 U. S. 82 (1978), as support for a second trial, on the ground that Currier consented to it. Those decisions do not undermine the inviolacy of an acquittal.

In *Jeffers*, the defendant was charged with two offenses, one of which was a lesser included offense of the other. He asked for, and gained, separate trials of the two charges. After *conviction* on the lesser included charge, he argued that a second trial on the remaining charge would violate his double jeopardy right "against multiple prosecutions." A plurality of this Court rejected Jeffers' argument, reasoning that he had waived the relevant right because he was "solely responsible for the successive prosecutions."

*Jeffers* presented a claim-preclusion question. The Court there said not one word about issue preclusion. Nor did the Court address the staying power of an acquittal. It had no occasion to do so, as Jeffers was *convicted* on the first charge. * * *

*Dinitz* and *Scott* are even weaker reeds. In *Dinitz*, the defendant requested, and gained, a mistrial after the trial judge expelled his lead counsel from the courtroom. In *Scott*, the defendant sought and obtained dismissal of two of three counts prior to their submission to the jury. The question in each case was whether the defendant's actions deprived him of the right to be spared from a second trial on the same offenses. Both decisions simply concluded that when a defendant voluntarily seeks to terminate a trial before a substantive ruling on guilt or innocence, the Double Jeopardy Clause is not offended by a second trial. The cases, however, said nothing about the issue-preclusive effect of a prior acquittal at a subsequent trial. * * *

## IV

Venturing beyond JUSTICE KENNEDY's rationale for resolving this case, the plurality would take us back to the days before the Court recognized issue preclusion as a constitutionally grounded component of the Double Jeopardy Clause. * * * I would not engage in that endeavor to restore things past. One decision, however, should be set straight. The plurality asserts that Dowling v. United States, 493 U. S. 342 (1990), established that issue preclusion has no role to play in regulating the issues or evidence presented at a successive trial. *Dowling* did no such thing. The case is tied to Federal Rule of Evidence 404(b), which allows the prosecution to introduce evidence of a defendant's past criminal conduct for described purposes other than to show a defendant's bad character. See Fed. Rule Evid. 404(b)(2). The defendant in *Dowling* was prosecuted for robbing a bank. To bolster its case that Dowling was the perpetrator, the Government sought to introduce evidence that Dowling participated in a home invasion two weeks after the bank robbery. One difficulty for the prosecution: Dowling had been acquitted of the home invasion. Nevertheless, the trial court admitted the evidence, informing the jurors that Dowling had been acquitted of the home-invasion charge and instructing them on the "limited purpose" for which the evidence was introduced.

The Court in *Dowling* "decline[d] to extend *Ashe*" to forbid the prosecution from introducing evidence, under Rule 404(b), of a crime for which the defendant had been acquitted, one involving criminal conduct unrelated to the bank robbery for which Dowling stood trial. The charge for which Dowling was acquitted took place at a different time and involved different property, a different location, and different victims. * * * It surely could not be said that, in the bank robbery trial, Dowling was being tried a second time for the later-occurring home invasion offense. Here, by contrast, the two trials involved the same criminal episode. * * *

Extending *Dowling* from the Evidence Rule 404(b) context in which it was embedded to retrials involving the same course of previously acquitted conduct would undermine issue-preclusion's core tenet. That tenet was well stated by Judge Friendly in *United States* v. *Kramer*, 289 F. 2d 909 (CA2 1961):

> "A defendant who has satisfied one jury that he had no responsibility for a crime ought not be forced to convince another of this [lack of responsibility] . . . . The very nub of [issue preclusion] is to extend *res judicata* beyond those cases where the prior judgment is a complete bar. The Government is free, within limits set by the Fifth Amendment, to charge an acquitted defendant with other crimes claimed to arise from the same or related conduct; but it may not prove the new charge by asserting facts necessarily determined against it on the first trial . . . ." *Id.,* at 915–916 (citation omitted).

So here. The first trial established that Currier did not participate in breaking and entering the Garrisons' residence or in stealing their safe. The government can attempt to prove Currier possessed firearms through a means other than breaking and entering the Garrisons' residence and stealing their safe. But the government should not be permitted to show in the felon-in-possession trial what it failed to show in the first trial, *i.e.,* Currier's participation in the charged breaking and entering and grand larceny, after a full and fair opportunity to do so.

* * *

# CHAPTER 13

## POST-CONVICTION CHALLENGES

■ ■ ■

### II. GROUNDS FOR DIRECT ATTACKS ON A CONVICTION

#### D. THE EFFECT OF AN ERROR ON THE VERDICT

1. Harmless Error

Page 1723. Add the following after the section on *Gonzalez-Lopez*:

##### *Defense Counsel's Conceding Guilt over the Defendant's Objection is a Structural Error: McCoy v. Louisiana*

The defendant in McCoy v. Louisiana, 138 S.Ct. 1500 (2018), was tried for capital murder. All the evidence indicated that he committed the murders. But the defendant steadfastly denied committing the murders, and blamed it all on a far-flung conspiracy against him. He testified to that effect at trial. Trial counsel chose, as a matter of strategy—and over McCoy's strenuous objections—to concede that the defendant did the killings, but to argue that he did not have the requisite mental state to commit murder, given his serious mental and emotional issues. McCoy was convicted of murder and sentenced to death.

The Supreme Court, in an opinion by Justice Ginsburg for six Justices, held that defense counsel has no authority under the Sixth Amendment to concede guilt over the objection of the defendant. That is because the decision whether or not to contest guilt is a matter of personal autonomy and a decision to be made by the client. [The Court's discussion of this point is set out in full in this Supplement, Chapter Ten.]

The Court further found that when defense counsel does make such an argument, it constitutes a structural error, not susceptible to harmless error review. Justice Ginsburg explained the Court's ruling on structural error as follows:

> Because a client's autonomy, not counsel's competence, is in issue, we do not apply our ineffective-assistance-of-counsel jurisprudence to McCoy's claim. To gain redress for attorney

error, a defendant ordinarily must show prejudice. Here, however, the violation of McCoy's protected autonomy right was complete when the court allowed counsel to usurp control of an issue within McCoy's sole prerogative.

Violation of a defendant's Sixth Amendment-secured autonomy ranks as error of the kind our decisions have called "structural"; when present, such an error is not subject to harmless-error review. * * * An error may be ranked structural, we have explained, "if the right at issue is not designed to protect the defendant from erroneous conviction but instead protects some other interest," such as "the fundamental legal principle that a defendant must be allowed to make his own choices about the proper way to protect his own liberty." An error might also count as structural when its effects are too hard to measure, as is true of the right to counsel of choice, or where the error will inevitably signal fundamental unfairness, as we have said of a judge's failure to tell the jury that it may not convict unless it finds the defendant's guilt beyond a reasonable doubt.

Under at least the first two rationales, counsel's admission of a client's guilt over the client's express objection is error structural in kind. Such an admission blocks the defendant's right to make the fundamental choices about his own defense. And the effects of the admission would be immeasurable, because a jury would almost certainly be swayed by a lawyer's concession of his client's guilt. McCoy must therefore be accorded a new trial without any need first to show prejudice.

Justice Alito, joined by Justices Thomas and Gorsuch, dissented.

## 2. Plain Error

### Page 1729. Add after the discussion of *Olano*:

In Rosales-Mireles v. United States, 138 S. Ct. 1897 (2018), Justice Sotomayor wrote for seven justices as the Court held that a miscalculation of a Guidelines sentencing range that has been determined to be plain and to affect a defendant's substantial rights calls for a court of appeals to exercise its discretion under Rule 52(b) to vacate the defendant's sentence in the ordinary case.

Rosales-Mireles pled guilty to illegal reentry into the United States. The Probation Office mistakenly counted a state misdemeanor conviction twice in calculating the Guidelines range, and its presentence report yielded a Guidelines range of 77 to 96 months when the correctly calculated range would have been 70 to 87 months. Rosales-Mireles did not object to the error in the District Court, which relied on the miscalculated Guidelines range to sentence him to 78 months of imprisonment. He challenged the incorrect Guidelines range for the first time on appeal. The Fifth Circuit found that the error was plain and affected Rosales-Mireles' substantial rights but declined to remand the case because he had not established that the error would seriously affect the fairness, integrity, or public reputation of judicial proceedings because neither the error nor the resulting sentence "would shock the conscience."

The opinion sets forth the four prongs that must be satisfied before an error is declared to be plain: (1) the error must not have been intentionally relinquished or abandoned; (2) it must be plain (i.e., clear or obvious; (3) it must have affected the defendant's substantial rights; and (4) the error must seriously affect the fairness, integrity or public reputation of judicial proceedings. The Court's focus was on the fourth prong.

Justice Sotomayor reasoned that (a) that district judges have ultimate responsibility to apply the Guidelines correctly but the Guidelines are sufficiently complex that judges sometimes make mistakes; (b) the Court in *Olano* rejected a rule that would have called for relief only "in those circumstances in which a miscarriage of justice would otherwise result"—i.e., where a defendant is actually innocent, so that the Fifth Circuit's rule was also unduly restrictive; (c) *Molina-Martinez* recognized that "[w]hen a defendant is sentenced under an incorrect Guidelines range—whether or not the defendant's ultimate sentence falls within the correct range—the error itself can, and most often will, be sufficient to show a reasonable probability of a different outcome absent the error"; and (d) "[t[he risk of unnecessary deprivation of liberty particularly undermines the fairness, integrity, or public reputation of judicial proceedings in the context of a plain Guidelines error because of the role the district court plays in calculating the range and the relative ease of correcting the error."

Justice Thomas, joined by Justice Alito, dissented. He agreed with the conclusion that the Fifth Circuit's rule was unduly narrow, but concluded that the Court's broad statement that Guideline errors will ordinarily satisfy the fourth prong of plain-error review contravened precedents establishing that this prong must applied on a case-specific and fact-intensive basis.

# THE FEDERAL RULES OF CRIMINAL PROCEDURE

■ ■ ■

## TITLE I.  APPLICABILITY

### Rule 1.  Scope; Definitions

**(a) Scope.**

**(1)** *In General.* These rules govern the procedure in all criminal proceedings in the United States district courts, the United States courts of appeals, and the Supreme Court of the United States.

**(2)** *State or Local Judicial Officer.* When a rule so states, it applies to a proceeding before a state or local judicial officer.

**(3)** *Territorial Courts.* These rules also govern the procedure in all criminal proceedings in the following courts:

(A)  the district court of Guam;

(B)  the district court for the Northern Mariana Islands, except as otherwise provided by law; and

(C)  the district court of the Virgin Islands, except that the prosecution of offenses in that court must be by indictment or information as otherwise provided by law.

**(4)** *Removed Proceedings.* Although these rules govern all proceedings after removal from a state court, state law governs a dismissal by the prosecution.

**(5)** *Excluded Proceedings.* Proceedings not governed by these rules include:

(A)  the extradition and rendition of a fugitive;

(B)  a civil property forfeiture for violating a federal statute;

(C)  the collection of a fine or penalty;

(D)  a proceeding under a statute governing juvenile delinquency to the extent the procedure is inconsistent with the statute, unless Rule 20(d) provides otherwise;

(E)  a dispute between seamen under 22 U.S.C. §§ 256–258; and

113

(F) a proceeding against a witness in a foreign country under 28 U.S.C. § 1784.

**(b) Definitions**. The following definitions apply to these rules:

**(1)** "Attorney for the government" means:

(A) the Attorney General or an authorized assistant;

(B) a United States attorney or an authorized assistant;

(C) when applicable to cases arising under Guam law, the Guam Attorney General or other person whom Guam law authorizes to act in the matter; and

(D) any other attorney authorized by law to conduct proceedings under these rules as a prosecutor.

**(2)** "Court" means a federal judge performing functions authorized by law.

**(3)** "Federal judge" means:

(A) a justice or judge of the United States as these terms are defined in 28 U.S.C. § 451;

(B) a magistrate judge; and

(C) a judge confirmed by the United States Senate and empowered by statute in any commonwealth, territory, or possession to perform a function to which a particular rule relates.

**(4)** "Judge" means a federal judge or a state or local judicial officer.

**(5)** "Magistrate judge" means a United States magistrate judge as defined in 28 U.S.C. §§ 631–639.

**(6)** "Oath" includes an affirmation.

**(7)** "Organization" is defined in 18 U.S.C. § 18.

**(8)** "Petty offense" is defined in 18 U.S.C. § 19.

**(9)** "State" includes the District of Columbia, and any commonwealth, territory, or possession of the United States.

**(10)** "State or local judicial officer" means:

(A) a state or local officer authorized to act under 18 U.S.C. § 3041; and

(B) a judicial officer empowered by statute in the District of Columbia or in any commonwealth, territory, or possession to perform a function to which a particular rule relates.

**(11)**"Telephone" means any technology for transmitting live electronic voice communication.

**(12)**"Victim" means a "crime victim" as defined in 18 U.S.C. § 3771(e).

**(c) Authority of a Justice or Judge of the United States**. When these rules authorize a magistrate judge to act, any other federal judge may also act.

## Rule 2. Interpretation

These rules are to be interpreted to provide for the just determination of every criminal proceeding, to secure simplicity in procedure and fairness in administration, and to eliminate unjustifiable expense and delay.

## TITLE II.   PRELIMINARY PROCEEDINGS

## Rule 3. The Complaint

The complaint is a written statement of the essential facts constituting the offense charged. Except as provided in Rule 4.1, it must be made under oath before a magistrate judge or, if none is reasonably available, before a state or local judicial officer.

## Rule 4. Arrest Warrant or Summons on a Complaint

**(a) Issuance.** If the complaint or one or more affidavits filed with the complaint establish probable cause to believe that an offense has been committed and that the defendant committed it, the judge must issue an arrest warrant to an officer authorized to execute it. At the request of an attorney for the government, the judge must issue a summons, instead of a warrant, to a person authorized to serve it. A judge may issue more than one warrant or summons on the same complaint. If an individual fails to appear in response to a summons, a judge may, and upon request of an attorney for the government must, issue a warrant. If an organizational defendant fails to appear in response to a summons, a judge may take any action authorized by United States law.

**(b) Form.**

**(1)** *Warrant.* A warrant must:

(A) contain the defendant's name or, if it is unknown, a name or description by which the defendant can be identified with reasonable certainty;

(B) describe the offense charged in the complaint;

(C) command that the defendant be arrested and brought without unnecessary delay before a magistrate judge or, if none is reasonably available, before a state or local judicial officer; and

(D) be signed by a judge.

**(2) *Summons.*** A summons must be in the same form as a warrant except that it must require the defendant to appear before a magistrate judge at a stated time and place.

**(c) Execution or Service, and Return.**

**(1) *By Whom.*** Only a marshal or other authorized officer may execute a warrant. Any person authorized to serve a summons in a federal civil action may serve a summons.

**(2) *Location.*** A warrant may be executed, or a summons served, within the jurisdiction of the United States or anywhere else a federal statute authorizes an arrest. A summons to an organization under Rule 4(c)(3)(D) may also be served at a place not within a judicial district of the United States.

**(3) *Manner.***

(A) A warrant is executed by arresting the defendant. Upon arrest, an officer possessing the original or a duplicate original warrant must show it to the defendant. If the officer does not possess the warrant, the officer must inform the defendant of the warrant's existence and of the offense charged and, at the defendant's request, must show the original or a duplicate original warrant to the defendant as soon as possible.

(B) A summons is served on an individual defendant:

(i) by delivering a copy to the defendant personally; or

(ii) by leaving a copy at the defendant's residence or usual place of abode with a person of suitable age and discretion residing at that location and by mailing a copy to the defendant's last known address.

(C) A summons is served on an organization in a judicial district of the United States by delivering a copy to an officer, to a managing or general agent, or to another agent appointed or legally authorized to receive service of process. If the agent is one authorized by statute and the statute so requires, a copy must also be mailed to the organization.

(D) A summons is served on an organization not within a judicial district of the United States:

(i) by delivering a copy, in a manner authorized by the foreign jurisdiction's law, to a managing or general agent, or to an agent appointed or legally authorized to receive service of process; or

(ii)  by any other means that gives notice, including one that is:

(a)  stipulated by the parties;

(b)  undertaken by a foreign authority in response to a letter rogatory, a letter of request, or a request submitted under an applicable international agreement; or

(c)  permitted by an international agreement.

**(4)  *Return.***

(A)  After executing a warrant, the officer must return it to the judge before whom the defendant is brought in accordance with Rule 5. The officer may do so by reliable electronic means. At the request of an attorney for the government, an unexecuted warrant must be brought back to and canceled by a magistrate judge or, if none is reasonably available, by a state or local judicial officer.

(B)  The person to whom a summons was delivered for service must return it on or before the return day.

(C)  At the request of an attorney for the government, a judge may deliver an unexecuted warrant, an unserved summons, or a copy of the warrant or summons to the marshal or other authorized person for execution or service.

**(d)  Warrant by Telephone or Other Reliable Electronic Means.** In accordance with Rule 4.1, a magistrate judge may issue a warrant or summons based on information communicated by telephone or other reliable electronic means.

## Rule 4.1. Complaint, Warrant, or Summons by Telephone or Other Reliable Electronic Means

**(a)  In General.** A magistrate judge may consider information communicated by telephone or other reliable electronic means when reviewing a complaint or deciding whether to issue a warrant or summons.

**(b)  Procedures.** If a magistrate judge decides to proceed under this rule, the following procedures apply:

**(1)  *Taking Testimony Under Oath.*** The judge must place under oath—and may examine—the applicant and any person on whose testimony the application is based.

**(2)** *Creating a Record of the Testimony and Exhibits.*

(A) *Testimony Limited to Attestation.* If the applicant does no more than attest to the contents of a written affidavit submitted by reliable electronic means, the judge must acknowledge the attestation in writing on the affidavit.

(B) *Additional Testimony or Exhibits.* If the judge considers additional testimony or exhibits, the judge must:

(i) have the testimony recorded verbatim by an electronic recording device, by a court reporter, or in writing;

(ii) have any recording or reporter's notes transcribed, have the transcription certified as accurate, and file it;

(iii) sign any other written record, certify its accuracy, and file it; and

(iv) make sure that the exhibits are filed.

**(3)** *Preparing a Proposed Duplicate Original of a Complaint, Warrant, or Summons.* The applicant must prepare a proposed duplicate original of a complaint, warrant, or summons, and must read or otherwise transmit its contents verbatim to the judge.

**(4)** *Preparing an Original Complaint, Warrant, or Summons.* If the applicant reads the contents of the proposed duplicate original, the judge must enter those contents into an original complaint, warrant, or summons. If the applicant transmits the contents by reliable electronic means, the transmission received by the judge may serve as the original.

**(5)** *Modification.* The judge may modify the complaint, warrant, or summons. The judge must then:

(A) transmit the modified version to the applicant by reliable electronic means; or

(B) file the modified original and direct the applicant to modify the proposed duplicate original accordingly.

**(6)** *Issuance.* To issue the warrant or summons, the judge must:

(A) sign the original documents;

(B) enter the date and time of issuance on the warrant or summons; and

(C) transmit the warrant or summons by reliable electronic means to the applicant or direct the applicant to sign the judge's name and enter the date and time on the duplicate original.

**(c) Suppression Limited.** Absent a finding of bad faith, evidence obtained from a warrant issued under this rule is not subject to suppression on the ground that issuing the warrant in this manner was unreasonable under the circumstances.

## Rule 5. Initial Appearance

**(a) In General.**

**(1) *Appearance Upon an Arrest.***

(A) A person making an arrest within the United States must take the defendant without unnecessary delay before a magistrate judge, or before a state or local judicial officer as Rule 5(c) provides, unless a statute provides otherwise.

(B) A person making an arrest outside the United States must take the defendant without unnecessary delay before a magistrate judge, unless a statute provides otherwise.

**(2) *Exceptions.***

(A) An officer making an arrest under a warrant issued upon a complaint charging solely a violation of 18 U.S.C. § 1073 need not comply with this rule if:

(i) the person arrested is transferred without unnecessary delay to the custody of appropriate state or local authorities in the district of arrest; and

(ii) an attorney for the government moves promptly, in the district where the warrant was issued, to dismiss the complaint.

(B) If a defendant is arrested for violating probation or supervised release, Rule 32.1 applies.

(C) If a defendant is arrested for failing to appear in another district, Rule 40 applies.

**(3) *Appearance Upon a Summons.*** When a defendant appears in response to a summons under Rule 4, a magistrate judge must proceed under Rule 5(d) or (e), as applicable.

**(b) Arrest Without a Warrant.** If a defendant is arrested without a warrant, a complaint meeting Rule 4(a)'s requirement of probable cause must be promptly filed in the district where the offense was allegedly committed.

**(c) Place of Initial Appearance; Transfer to Another District.**

**(1)** *Arrest in the District Where the Offense Was Allegedly Committed.* If the defendant is arrested in the district where the offense was allegedly committed:

(A)  the initial appearance must be in that district; and

(B)  if a magistrate judge is not reasonably available, the initial appearance may be before a state or local judicial officer.

**(2)** *Arrest in a District Other Than Where the Offense Was Allegedly Committed.* If the defendant was arrested in a district other than where the offense was allegedly committed, the initial appearance must be:

(A)  in the district of arrest; or

(B)  in an adjacent district if:

(i)   the appearance can occur more promptly there; or

(ii)  the offense was allegedly committed there and the initial appearance will occur on the day of arrest.

**(3)** *Procedures in a District Other Than Where the Offense Was Allegedly Committed.* If the initial appearance occurs in a district other than where the offense was allegedly committed, the following procedures apply:

(A)  the magistrate judge must inform the defendant about the provisions of Rule 20;

(B)  if the defendant was arrested without a warrant, the district court where the offense was allegedly committed must first issue a warrant before the magistrate judge transfers the defendant to that district;

(C)  the magistrate judge must conduct a preliminary hearing if required by Rule 5.1;

(D)  the magistrate judge must transfer the defendant to the district where the offense was allegedly committed if:

(i)   the government produces the warrant, a certified copy of the warrant, or a reliable electronic form of either; and

(ii)  the judge finds that the defendant is the same person named in the indictment, information, or warrant; and

(E)  when a defendant is transferred and discharged, the clerk must promptly transmit the papers and any bail to the clerk in the district where the offense was allegedly committed.

**(4)** *Procedure for Persons Extradited to the United States.* If the defendant is surrendered to the United States in accordance with a request for the defendant's extradition, the initial appearance must be in the district (or one of the districts) where the offense is charged.

**(d) Procedure in a Felony Case.**

**(1)** *Advice.* If the defendant is charged with a felony, the judge must inform the defendant of the following:

(A) the complaint against the defendant, and any affidavit filed with it;

(B) the defendant's right to retain counsel or to request that counsel be appointed if the defendant cannot obtain counsel;

(C) the circumstances, if any, under which the defendant may secure pretrial release;

(D) any right to a preliminary hearing;

(E) the defendant's right not to make a statement, and that any statement made may be used against the defendant; and

(F) that a defendant who is not a United States citizen may request that an attorney for the government or a federal law enforcement official notify a consular officer from the defendant's country of nationality that the defendant has been arrested—but that even without the defendant's request, a treaty or other international agreement may require consular notification.

**(2)** *Consulting with Counsel.* The judge must allow the defendant reasonable opportunity to consult with counsel.

**(3)** *Detention or Release.* The judge must detain or release the defendant as provided by statute or these rules.

**(4)** *Plea.* A defendant may be asked to plead only under Rule 10.

**(e) Procedure in a Misdemeanor Case.** If the defendant is charged with a misdemeanor only, the judge must inform the defendant in accordance with Rule 58(b)(2).

**(f) Video Teleconferencing.** Video teleconferencing may be used to conduct an appearance under this rule if the defendant consents.

**Rule 5.1. Preliminary Hearing**

**(a) In General.** If a defendant is charged with an offense other than a petty offense, a magistrate judge must conduct a preliminary hearing unless:

(1) the defendant waives the hearing;

(2) the defendant is indicted;

(3) the government files an information under Rule 7(b) charging the defendant with a felony;

(4) the government files an information charging the defendant with a misdemeanor; or

(5) the defendant is charged with a misdemeanor and consents to trial before a magistrate judge.

(b) **Selecting a District.** A defendant arrested in a district other than where the offense was allegedly committed may elect to have the preliminary hearing conducted in the district where the prosecution is pending.

(c) **Scheduling.** The magistrate judge must hold the preliminary hearing within a reasonable time, but no later than 14 days after the initial appearance if the defendant is in custody and no later than 21 days if not in custody.

(d) **Extending the Time.** With the defendant's consent and upon a showing of good cause—taking into account the public interest in the prompt disposition of criminal cases—a magistrate judge may extend the time limits in Rule 5.1(c) one or more times. If the defendant does not consent, the magistrate judge may extend the time limits only on a showing that extraordinary circumstances exist and justice requires the delay.

(e) **Hearing and Finding.** At the preliminary hearing, the defendant may cross-examine adverse witnesses and may introduce evidence but may not object to evidence on the ground that it was unlawfully acquired. If the magistrate judge finds probable cause to believe an offense has been committed and the defendant committed it, the magistrate judge must promptly require the defendant to appear for further proceedings.

(f) **Discharging the Defendant.** If the magistrate judge finds no probable cause to believe an offense has been committed or the defendant committed it, the magistrate judge must dismiss the complaint and discharge the defendant. A discharge does not preclude the government from later prosecuting the defendant for the same offense.

(g) **Recording the Proceedings.** The preliminary hearing must be recorded by a court reporter or by a suitable recording device. A recording of the proceeding may be made available to any party upon request. A copy of the recording and a transcript may be provided to any party upon request and upon any payment required by applicable Judicial Conference regulations.

**(h) Producing a Statement.**

**(1)** *In General.* Rule 26.2(a)–(d) and (f) applies at any hearing under this rule, unless the magistrate judge for good cause rules otherwise in a particular case.

**(2)** *Sanctions for Not Producing a Statement.* If a party disobeys a Rule 26.2 order to deliver a statement to the moving party, the magistrate judge must not consider the testimony of a witness whose statement is withheld.

## TITLE III.   THE GRAND JURY, THE INDICTMENT, AND THE INFORMATION

### Rule 6.  The Grand Jury

**(a) Summoning a Grand Jury.**

**(1)** *In General.* When the public interest so requires, the court must order that one or more grand juries be summoned. A grand jury must have 16 to 23 members, and the court must order that enough legally qualified persons be summoned to meet this requirement.

**(2)** *Alternate Jurors.* When a grand jury is selected, the court may also select alternate jurors. Alternate jurors must have the same qualifications and be selected in the same manner as any other juror. Alternate jurors replace jurors in the same sequence in which the alternates were selected. An alternate juror who replaces a juror is subject to the same challenges, takes the same oath, and has the same authority as the other jurors.

**(b) Objection to the Grand Jury or to a Grand Juror.**

**(1)** *Challenges.* Either the government or a defendant may challenge the grand jury on the ground that it was not lawfully drawn, summoned, or selected, and may challenge an individual juror on the ground that the juror is not legally qualified.

**(2)** *Motion to Dismiss an Indictment.* A party may move to dismiss the indictment based on an objection to the grand jury or on an individual juror's lack of legal qualification, unless the court has previously ruled on the same objection under Rule 6(b)(1). The motion to dismiss is governed by 28 U.S.C. § 1867(e). The court must not dismiss the indictment on the ground that a grand juror was not legally qualified if the record shows that at least 12 qualified jurors concurred in the indictment.

**(c) Foreperson and Deputy Foreperson.** The court will appoint one juror as the foreperson and another as the deputy foreperson. In the foreperson's absence, the deputy foreperson will act as the foreperson.

The foreperson may administer oaths and affirmations and will sign all indictments. The foreperson—or another juror designated by the foreperson—will record the number of jurors concurring in every indictment and will file the record with the clerk, but the record may not be made public unless the court so orders.

**(d) Who May Be Present.**

**(1)** *While the Grand Jury Is in Session.* The following persons may be present while the grand jury is in session: attorneys for the government, the witness being questioned, interpreters when needed, and a court reporter or an operator of a recording device.

**(2)** *During Deliberations and Voting.* No person other than the jurors, and any interpreter needed to assist a hearing-impaired or speech-impaired juror, may be present while the grand jury is deliberating or voting.

**(e) Recording and Disclosing the Proceedings.**

**(1)** *Recording the Proceedings.* Except while the grand jury is deliberating or voting, all proceedings must be recorded by a court reporter or by a suitable recording device. But the validity of a prosecution is not affected by the unintentional failure to make a recording. Unless the court orders otherwise, an attorney for the government will retain control of the recording, the reporter's notes, and any transcript prepared from those notes.

**(2)** *Secrecy.*

(A)  No obligation of secrecy may be imposed on any person except in accordance with Rule 6(e)(2)(B).

(B)  Unless these rules provide otherwise, the following persons must not disclose a matter occurring before the grand jury:

    (i)   a grand juror;

    (ii)  an interpreter;

    (iii) a court reporter;

    (iv)  an operator of a recording device;

    (v)   a person who transcribes recorded testimony;

    (vi)  an attorney for the government; or

    (vii) a person to whom disclosure is made under Rule 6(e)(3)(A)(ii) or (iii).

**(3)** *Exceptions.*

(A) Disclosure of a grand-jury matter—other than the grand jury's deliberations or any grand juror's vote—may be made to:

> (i) an attorney for the government for use in performing that attorney's duty;

> (ii) any government personnel—including those of a state, state subdivision, Indian tribe, or foreign government—that an attorney for the government considers necessary to assist in performing that attorney's duty to enforce federal criminal law; or

> (iii) a person authorized by 18 U.S.C. § 3322.

(B) A person to whom information is disclosed under Rule 6(e)(3)(A)(ii) may use that information only to assist an attorney for the government in performing that attorney's duty to enforce federal criminal law. An attorney for the government must promptly provide the court that impaneled the grand jury with the names of all persons to whom a disclosure has been made, and must certify that the attorney has advised those persons of their obligation of secrecy under this rule.

(C) An attorney for the government may disclose any grand-jury matter to another federal grand jury.

(D) An attorney for the government may disclose any grand-jury matter involving foreign intelligence, counterintelligence (as defined in 50 U.S.C. § 3003), or foreign intelligence information (as defined in Rule 6(e)(3)(D)(iii)) to any federal law enforcement, intelligence, protective, immigration, national defense, or national security official to assist the official receiving the information in the performance of that official's duties. An attorney for the government may also disclose any grand-jury matter involving, within the United States or elsewhere, a threat of attack or other grave hostile acts of a foreign power or its agent, a threat of domestic or international sabotage or terrorism, or clandestine intelligence gathering activities by an intelligence service or network of a foreign power or by its agent, to any appropriate federal, state, state subdivision, Indian tribal, or foreign government official, for the purpose of preventing or responding to such threat or activities.

> (i) Any official who receives information under Rule 6(e)(3)(D) may use the information only as necessary in the conduct of that person's official duties subject to any limitations on the unauthorized disclosure of such

information. Any state, state subdivision, Indian tribal, or foreign government official who receives information under Rule 6(e)(3)(D) may use the information only in a manner consistent with any guidelines issued by the Attorney General and the Director of National Intelligence.

(ii) Within a reasonable time after disclosure is made under Rule 6(e)(3)(D), an attorney for the government must file, under seal, a notice with the court in the district where the grand jury convened stating that such information was disclosed and the departments, agencies, or entities to which the disclosure was made.

(iii) As used in Rule 6(e)(3)(D), the term "foreign intelligence information" means:

(a) information, whether or not it concerns a United States person, that relates to the ability of the United States to protect against—

• actual or potential attack or other grave hostile acts of a foreign power or its agent;

• sabotage or international terrorism by a foreign power or its agent; or

• clandestine intelligence activities by an intelligence service or network of a foreign power or by its agent; or

(b) information, whether or not it concerns a United States person, with respect to a foreign power or foreign territory that relates to—

• the national defense or the security of the United States; or

• the conduct of the foreign affairs of the United States.

(E) The court may authorize disclosure—at a time, in a manner, and subject to any other conditions that it directs—of a grand-jury matter:

(i) preliminarily to or in connection with a judicial proceeding;

(ii) at the request of a defendant who shows that a ground may exist to dismiss the indictment because of a matter that occurred before the grand jury;

(iii) at the request of the government, when sought by a foreign court or prosecutor for use in an official criminal investigation;

(iv) at the request of the government if it shows that the matter may disclose a violation of State, Indian tribal, or foreign criminal law, as long as the disclosure is to an appropriate state, state-subdivision, Indian tribal, or foreign government official for the purpose of enforcing that law; or

(v) at the request of the government if it shows that the matter may disclose a violation of military criminal law under the Uniform Code of Military Justice, as long as the disclosure is to an appropriate military official for the purpose of enforcing that law.

(F) A petition to disclose a grand-jury matter under Rule 6(e)(3)(E)(i) must be filed in the district where the grand jury convened. Unless the hearing is ex parte—as it may be when the government is the petitioner—the petitioner must serve the petition on, and the court must afford a reasonable opportunity to appear and be heard to:

(i) an attorney for the government;

(ii) the parties to the judicial proceeding; and

(iii) any other person whom the court may designate.

(G) If the petition to disclose arises out of a judicial proceeding in another district, the petitioned court must transfer the petition to the other court unless the petitioned court can reasonably determine whether disclosure is proper. If the petitioned court decides to transfer, it must send to the transferee court the material sought to be disclosed, if feasible, and a written evaluation of the need for continued grand-jury secrecy. The transferee court must afford those persons identified in Rule 6(e)(3)(F) a reasonable opportunity to appear and be heard.

**(4)** *Sealed Indictment.* The magistrate judge to whom an indictment is returned may direct that the indictment be kept secret until the defendant is in custody or has been released pending trial. The clerk must then seal the indictment, and no person may disclose the indictment's existence except as necessary to issue or execute a warrant or summons.

**(5)** *Closed Hearing.* Subject to any right to an open hearing in a contempt proceeding, the court must close any hearing to the extent necessary to prevent disclosure of a matter occurring before a grand jury.

**(6)** *Sealed Records.* Records, orders, and subpoenas relating to grand-jury proceedings must be kept under seal to the extent and as long as necessary to prevent the unauthorized disclosure of a matter occurring before a grand jury.

**(7)** *Contempt.* A knowing violation of Rule 6, or of any guidelines jointly issued by the Attorney General and the Director of National Intelligence under Rule 6, may be punished as a contempt of court.

**(f)** **Indictment and Return.** A grand jury may indict only if at least 12 jurors concur. The grand jury—or its foreperson or deputy foreperson—must return the indictment to a magistrate judge in open court. To avoid unnecessary cost or delay, the magistrate judge may take the return by video teleconference from the court where the grand jury sits. If a complaint or information is pending against the defendant and 12 jurors do not concur in the indictment, the foreperson must promptly and in writing report the lack of concurrence to the magistrate judge.

**(g)** **Discharging the Grand Jury.** A grand jury must serve until the court discharges it, but it may serve more than 18 months only if the court, having determined that an extension is in the public interest, extends the grand jury's service. An extension may be granted for no more than 6 months, except as otherwise provided by statute.

**(h)** **Excusing a Juror.** At any time, for good cause, the court may excuse a juror either temporarily or permanently, and if permanently, the court may impanel an alternate juror in place of the excused juror.

**(i)** **"Indian Tribe" Defined.** "Indian tribe" means an Indian tribe recognized by the Secretary of the Interior on a list published in the Federal Register under 25 U.S.C. § 479a–1.

## Rule 7. The Indictment and the Information

**(a)** **When Used.**

**(1)** *Felony.* An offense (other than criminal contempt) must be prosecuted by an indictment if it is punishable:

(A) by death; or

(B) by imprisonment for more than one year.

**(2)** *Misdemeanor.* An offense punishable by imprisonment for one year or less may be prosecuted in accordance with Rule 58(b)(1).

**(b)** **Waiving Indictment.** An offense punishable by imprisonment for more than one year may be prosecuted by information if the defendant—in open court and after being advised of the nature of the charge and of the defendant's rights—waives prosecution by indictment.

**(c) Nature and Contents.**

**(1) *In General.*** The indictment or information must be a plain, concise, and definite written statement of the essential facts constituting the offense charged and must be signed by an attorney for the government. It need not contain a formal introduction or conclusion. A count may incorporate by reference an allegation made in another count. A count may allege that the means by which the defendant committed the offense are unknown or that the defendant committed it by one or more specified means. For each count, the indictment or information must give the official or customary citation of the statute, rule, regulation, or other provision of law that the defendant is alleged to have violated. For purposes of an indictment referred to in section 3282 of title 18, United States Code, for which the identity of the defendant is unknown, it shall be sufficient for the indictment to describe the defendant as an individual whose name is unknown, but who has a particular DNA profile, as that term is defined in section 3282.

**(2) *Citation Error.*** Unless the defendant was misled and thereby prejudiced, neither an error in a citation nor a citation's omission is a ground to dismiss the indictment or information or to reverse a conviction.

**(d) Surplusage.** Upon the defendant's motion, the court may strike surplusage from the indictment or information.

**(e) Amending an Information.** Unless an additional or different offense is charged or a substantial right of the defendant is prejudiced, the court may permit an information to be amended at any time before the verdict or finding.

**(f) Bill of Particulars.** The court may direct the government to file a bill of particulars. The defendant may move for a bill of particulars before or within 14 days after arraignment or at a later time if the court permits. The government may amend a bill of particulars subject to such conditions as justice requires.

## Rule 8. Joinder of Offenses or Defendants

**(a) Joinder of Offenses.** The indictment or information may charge a defendant in separate counts with 2 or more offenses if the offenses charged—whether felonies or misdemeanors or both—are of the same or similar character, or are based on the same act or transaction, or are connected with or constitute parts of a common scheme or plan.

**(b) Joinder of Defendants.** The indictment or information may charge 2 or more defendants if they are alleged to have participated in the same act or transaction, or in the same series of acts or transactions, constituting an offense or offenses. The defendants may be charged in one or more counts together or separately. All defendants need not be charged in each count.

## Rule 9. Arrest Warrant or Summons on an Indictment or Information

**(a) Issuance.** The court must issue a warrant—or at the government's request, a summons—for each defendant named in an indictment or named in an information if one or more affidavits accompanying the information establish probable cause to believe that an offense has been committed and that the defendant committed it. The court may issue more than one warrant or summons for the same defendant. If a defendant fails to appear in response to a summons, the court may, and upon request of an attorney for the government must, issue a warrant. The court must issue the arrest warrant to an officer authorized to execute it or the summons to a person authorized to serve it.

**(b) Form.**

(1) *Warrant.* The warrant must conform to Rule 4(b)(1) except that it must be signed by the clerk and must describe the offense charged in the indictment or information.

(2) *Summons.* The summons must be in the same form as a warrant except that it must require the defendant to appear before the court at a stated time and place.

**(c) Execution or Service; Return; Initial Appearance.**

(1) *Execution or Service.*

(A) The warrant must be executed or the summons served as provided in Rule 4(c)(1), (2), and (3).

(B) The officer executing the warrant must proceed in accordance with Rule 5(a)(1).

(2) *Return.* A warrant or summons must be returned in accordance with Rule 4(c)(4).

(3) *Initial Appearance.* When an arrested or summoned defendant first appears before the court, the judge must proceed under Rule 5.

**(d) Warrant by Telephone or Other Means.** In accordance with Rule 4.1, a magistrate judge may issue an arrest warrant or summons based on information communicated by telephone or other reliable electronic means.

# TITLE IV. ARRAIGNMENT AND PREPARATION FOR TRIAL

## Rule 10. Arraignment

**(a) In General.** An arraignment must be conducted in open court and must consist of:

**(1)** ensuring that the defendant has a copy of the indictment or information;

**(2)** reading the indictment or information to the defendant or stating to the defendant the substance of the charge; and then

**(3)** asking the defendant to plead to the indictment or information.

**(b) Waiving Appearance.** A defendant need not be present for the arraignment if:

**(1)** the defendant has been charged by indictment or misdemeanor information;

**(2)** the defendant, in a written waiver signed by both the defendant and defense counsel, has waived appearance and has affirmed that the defendant received a copy of the indictment or information and that the plea is not guilty; and

**(3)** the court accepts the waiver.

**(c) Video Teleconferencing.** Video teleconferencing may be used to arraign a defendant if the defendant consents.

## Rule 11. Pleas

**(a) Entering a Plea.**

**(1)** *In General.* A defendant may plead not guilty, guilty, or (with the court's consent) nolo contendere.

**(2)** *Conditional Plea.* With the consent of the court and the government, a defendant may enter a conditional plea of guilty or nolo contendere, reserving in writing the right to have an appellate court review an adverse determination of a specified pretrial motion. A defendant who prevails on appeal may then withdraw the plea.

**(3)** *Nolo Contendere Plea.* Before accepting a plea of nolo contendere, the court must consider the parties' views and the public interest in the effective administration of justice.

**(4)** *Failure to Enter a Plea.* If a defendant refuses to enter a plea or if a defendant organization fails to appear, the court must enter a plea of not guilty.

**(b)** **Considering and Accepting a Guilty or Nolo Contendere Plea.**

**(1)** *Advising and Questioning the Defendant.* Before the court accepts a plea of guilty or nolo contendere, the defendant may be placed under oath, and the court must address the defendant personally in open court. During this address, the court must inform the defendant of, and determine that the defendant understands, the following:

(A) the government's right, in a prosecution for perjury or false statement, to use against the defendant any statement that the defendant gives under oath;

(B) the right to plead not guilty, or having already so pleaded, to persist in that plea;

(C) the right to a jury trial;

(D) the right to be represented by counsel—and if necessary have the court appoint counsel—at trial and at every other stage of the proceeding;

(E) the right at trial to confront and cross-examine adverse witnesses, to be protected from compelled self-incrimination, to testify and present evidence, and to compel the attendance of witnesses;

(F) the defendant's waiver of these trial rights if the court accepts a plea of guilty or nolo contendere;

(G) the nature of each charge to which the defendant is pleading;

(H) any maximum possible penalty, including imprisonment, fine, and term of supervised release;

(I) any mandatory minimum penalty;

(J) any applicable forfeiture;

(K) the court's authority to order restitution;

(L) the court's obligation to impose a special assessment;

(M) in determining a sentence, the court's obligation to calculate the applicable sentencing-guideline range and to consider that range, possible departures under the Sentencing Guidelines, and other sentencing factors under 18 U.S.C. § 3553(a);

(N) the terms of any plea-agreement provision waiving the right to appeal or to collaterally attack the sentence; and

(O) that, if convicted, a defendant who is not a United States citizen may be removed from the United States, denied citizenship, and denied admission to the United States in the future.

**(2)** *Ensuring That a Plea Is Voluntary.* Before accepting a plea of guilty or nolo contendere, the court must address the defendant personally in open court and determine that the plea is voluntary and did not result from force, threats, or promises (other than promises in a plea agreement).

**(3)** *Determining the Factual Basis for a Plea.* Before entering judgment on a guilty plea, the court must determine that there is a factual basis for the plea.

**(c) Plea Agreement Procedure.**

**(1)** *In General.* An attorney for the government and the defendant's attorney, or the defendant when proceeding pro se, may discuss and reach a plea agreement. The court must not participate in these discussions. If the defendant pleads guilty or nolo contendere to either a charged offense or a lesser or related offense, the plea agreement may specify that an attorney for the government will:

(A)  not bring, or will move to dismiss, other charges;

(B) recommend, or agree not to oppose the defendant's request, that a particular sentence or sentencing range is appropriate or that a particular provision of the Sentencing Guidelines, or policy statement, or sentencing factor does or does not apply (such a recommendation or request does not bind the court); or

(C)  agree that a specific sentence or sentencing range is the appropriate disposition of the case, or that a particular provision of the Sentencing Guidelines, or policy statement, or sentencing factor does or does not apply (such a recommendation or request binds the court once the court accepts the plea agreement).

**(2)** *Disclosing a Plea Agreement.* The parties must disclose the plea agreement in open court when the plea is offered, unless the court for good cause allows the parties to disclose the plea agreement in camera.

**(3)** *Judicial Consideration of a Plea Agreement.*

(A)  To the extent the plea agreement is of the type specified in Rule 11(c)(1)(A) or (C), the court may accept the agreement, reject it, or defer a decision until the court has reviewed the presentence report.

(B)  To the extent the plea agreement is of the type specified in Rule 11(c)(1)(B), the court must advise the defendant that the defendant has no right to withdraw the plea if the court does not follow the recommendation or request.

**(4)  *Accepting a Plea Agreement.*** If the court accepts the plea agreement, it must inform the defendant that to the extent the plea agreement is of the type specified in Rule 11(c)(1)(A) or (C), the agreed disposition will be included in the judgment.

**(5)  *Rejecting a Plea Agreement.*** If the court rejects a plea agreement containing provisions of the type specified in Rule 11(c)(1)(A) or (C), the court must do the following on the record and in open court (or, for good cause, in camera):

(A)  inform the parties that the court rejects the plea agreement;

(B)  advise the defendant personally that the court is not required to follow the plea agreement and give the defendant an opportunity to withdraw the plea; and

(C)  advise the defendant personally that if the plea is not withdrawn, the court may dispose of the case less favorably toward the defendant than the plea agreement contemplated.

**(d)  Withdrawing a Guilty or Nolo Contendere Plea.** A defendant may withdraw a plea of guilty or nolo contendere:

**(1)**  before the court accepts the plea, for any reason or no reason; or

**(2)**  after the court accepts the plea, but before it imposes sentence if:

(A)  the court rejects a plea agreement under Rule 11(c)(5); or

(B)  the defendant can show a fair and just reason for requesting the withdrawal.

**(e)  Finality of a Guilty or Nolo Contendere Plea.** After the court imposes sentence, the defendant may not withdraw a plea of guilty or nolo contendere, and the plea may be set aside only on direct appeal or collateral attack.

**(f)  Admissibility or Inadmissibility of a Plea, Plea Discussions, and Related Statements.** The admissibility or inadmissibility of a plea, a plea discussion, and any related statement is governed by Federal Rule of Evidence 410.

**(g) Recording the Proceedings.** The proceedings during which the defendant enters a plea must be recorded by a court reporter or by a suitable recording device. If there is a guilty plea or a nolo contendere plea, the record must include the inquiries and advice to the defendant required under Rule 11(b) and (c).

**(h) Harmless Error.** A variance from the requirements of this rule is harmless error if it does not affect substantial rights.

## Rule 12. Pleadings and Pretrial Motions

**(a) Pleadings.** The pleadings in a criminal proceeding are the indictment, the information, and the pleas of not guilty, guilty, and nolo contendere.

**(b) Pretrial Motions.**

**(1)** *In General.* A party may raise by pretrial motion any defense, objection, or request that the court can determine without a trial on the merits. Rule 47 applies to a pretrial motion.

**(2)** *Motions That May Be Made at Any Time.* A motion that the court lacks jurisdiction may be made at any time while the case is pending.

**(3)** *Motions That Must Be Made Before Trial.* The following defenses, objections, and requests must be must be raised by pretrial motion if the basis for the motion is then reasonably available and the motion can be determined without a trial on the merits:

(A) a defect in instituting the prosecution, including

(i)   improper venue;

(ii)  preindictment delay;

(iii) a violation of the constitutional right to a speedy trial;

(iv)  selective or vindictive prosecution; and

(v)   an error in the grand-jury proceeding or preliminary hearing;

(B) a defect in the indictment or information, including;

(i)   joining two or more offense in the same count (duplicity);

(ii)  charging the same offense in more than one count (multiplicity);

(iii) lack of specificity;

(iv)  improper joinder; and

(v)   failure to state an offense;

(C)   suppression of evidence;

(D)   severance of charges or defendants under Rule 14; and

(E)   discovery under Rule 16.

**(4)** *Notice of the Government's Intent to Use Evidence.*

(A) *At the Government's Discretion.* At the arraignment or as soon afterward as practicable, the government may notify the defendant of its intent to use specified evidence at trial in order to afford the defendant an opportunity to object before trial under Rule 12(b)(3)(C).

(B) *At the Defendant's Request.* At the arraignment or as soon afterward as practicable, the defendant may, in order to have an opportunity to move to suppress evidence under Rule 12(b)(3)(C), request notice of the government's intent to use (in its evidence-in-chief at trial) any evidence that the defendant may be entitled to discover under Rule 16.

**(c) Deadline for a Pretrial Motion; Consequences of Not Making a Timely Motion.**

**(1)** *Setting the Deadline.* The court may, at the arraignment or as soon afterward as practicable, set a deadline for the parties to make pretrial motions and may also schedule a motion hearing. If the court does not set one, the deadline is the start of trial.

**(2)** *Extending or Resetting the Deadline.* At any time before trial, the court may extend or reset the deadline for pretrial motions.

**(3)** *Consequences of Not Making a Timely Motion Under Rule 12(b)(3).* If a party does not meet the deadline for making a Rule 12(b)(3) motion, the motion is untimely. But a court may consider the defense, objection, or request if the party shows good cause.

**(d) Ruling on a Motion.** The court must decide every pretrial motion before trial unless it finds good cause to defer a ruling. The court must not defer ruling on a pretrial motion if the deferral will adversely affect a party's right to appeal. When factual issues are involved in deciding a motion, the court must state its essential findings on the record.

**(e) [Reserved.]**

**(f) Recording the Proceedings.** All proceedings at a motion hearing, including any findings of fact and conclusions of law made orally by the court, must be recorded by a court reporter or a suitable recording device.

**(g) Defendant's Continued Custody or Release Status.** If the court grants a motion to dismiss based on a defect in instituting the prosecution, in the indictment, or in the information, it may order the defendant to be released or detained under 18 U.S.C. § 3142 for a specified time until a new indictment or information is filed. This rule does not affect any federal statutory period of limitations.

**(h) Producing Statements at a Suppression Hearing.** Rule 26.2 applies at a suppression hearing under Rule 12(b)(3)(C). At a suppression hearing, a law enforcement officer is considered a government witness.

### Rule 12.1. Notice of an Alibi Defense

**(a) Government's Request for Notice and Defendant's Response.**

**(1)** *Government's Request.* An attorney for the government may request in writing that the defendant notify an attorney for the government of any intended alibi defense. The request must state the time, date, and place of the alleged offense.

**(2)** *Defendant's Response.* Within 14 days after the request, or at some other time the court sets, the defendant must serve written notice on an attorney for the government of any intended alibi defense. The defendant's notice must state:

(A) each specific place where the defendant claims to have been at the time of the alleged offense; and

(B) the name, address, and telephone number of each alibi witness on whom the defendant intends to rely.

**(b) Disclosing Government Witnesses.**

**(1)** *Disclosure.*

(A) *In General.* If the defendant serves a Rule 12.1(a)(2) notice, an attorney for the government must disclose in writing to the defendant or the defendant's attorney:

(i) the name of each witness—and the address and telephone number of each witness other than a victim—that the government intends to rely on to establish that the defendant was present at the scene of the alleged offense; and

(ii) each government rebuttal witness to the defendant's alibi defense.

(B) *Victim's Address and Telephone Number.* If the government intends to rely on a victim's testimony to establish that the defendant was present at the scene of the alleged offense and the defendant establishes a need for the victim's address and telephone number, the court may:

(i)   order the government to provide the information in writing to the defendant or the defendant's attorney; or

(ii) fashion a reasonable procedure that allows preparation of the defense and also protects the victim's interests.

**(2)** *Time to Disclose.* Unless the court directs otherwise, an attorney for the government must give its Rule 12.1(b)(1) disclosure within 14 days after the defendant serves notice of an intended alibi defense under Rule 12.1(a)(2), but no later than 14 days before trial.

**(c)   Continuing Duty to Disclose.**

**(1)** *In General.* Both an attorney for the government and the defendant must promptly disclose in writing to the other party the name of each additional witness—and the address and telephone number of each additional witness other than a victim—if:

(A) the disclosing party learns of the witness before or during trial; and

(B) the witness should have been disclosed under Rule 12.1(a) or (b) if the disclosing party had known of the witness earlier.

**(2)** *Address and Telephone Number of an Additional Victim Witness.* The address and telephone number of an additional victim witness must not be disclosed except as provided in Rule 12.1(b)(1)(B).

**(d)   Exceptions.** For good cause, the court may grant an exception to any requirement of Rule 12.1(a)–(c).

**(e)   Failure to Comply.** If a party fails to comply with this rule, the court may exclude the testimony of any undisclosed witness regarding the defendant's alibi. This rule does not limit the defendant's right to testify.

**(f)   Inadmissibility of Withdrawn Intention.** Evidence of an intention to rely on an alibi defense, later withdrawn, or of a statement made in connection with that intention, is not, in any civil or criminal proceeding, admissible against the person who gave notice of the intention.

**Rule 12.2. Notice of an Insanity Defense; Mental Examination**

**(a)   Notice of an Insanity Defense.** A defendant who intends to assert a defense of insanity at the time of the alleged offense must so notify an attorney for the government in writing within the time provided for filing a pretrial motion, or at any later time the court sets, and file a copy of the notice with the clerk. A defendant who fails to do so cannot rely on an insanity defense. The court may, for good cause, allow the defendant to file the notice late, grant additional trial-preparation time, or make other appropriate orders.

**(b) Notice of Expert Evidence of a Mental Condition.** If a defendant intends to introduce expert evidence relating to a mental disease or defect or any other mental condition of the defendant bearing on either (1) the issue of guilt or (2) the issue of punishment in a capital case, the defendant must—within the time provided for filing a pretrial motion or at any later time the court sets—notify an attorney for the government in writing of this intention and file a copy of the notice with the clerk. The court may, for good cause, allow the defendant to file the notice late, grant the parties additional trial-preparation time, or make other appropriate orders.

**(c) Mental Examination.**

    **(1)** *Authority to Order an Examination; Procedures.*

        (A) The court may order the defendant to submit to a competency examination under 18 U.S.C. § 4241.

        (B) If the defendant provides notice under Rule 12.2(a), the court must, upon the government's motion, order the defendant to be examined under 18 U.S.C. § 4242. If the defendant provides notice under Rule 12.2(b) the court may, upon the government's motion, order the defendant to be examined under procedures ordered by the court.

    **(2)** *Disclosing Results and Reports of Capital Sentencing Examination.* The results and reports of any examination conducted solely under Rule 12.2(c)(1) after notice under Rule 12.2(b)(2) must be sealed and must not be disclosed to any attorney for the government or the defendant unless the defendant is found guilty of one or more capital crimes and the defendant confirms an intent to offer during sentencing proceedings expert evidence on mental condition.

    **(3)** *Disclosing Results and Reports of the Defendant's Expert Examination.* After disclosure under Rule 12.2(c)(2) of the results and reports of the government's examination, the defendant must disclose to the government the results and reports of any examination on mental condition conducted by the defendant's expert about which the defendant intends to introduce expert evidence.

    **(4)** *Inadmissibility of a Defendant's Statements.* No statement made by a defendant in the course of any examination conducted under this rule (whether conducted with or without the defendant's consent), no testimony by the expert based on the statement, and no other fruits of the statement may be admitted into evidence against the defendant in any criminal proceeding except on an issue regarding mental condition on which the defendant:

(A) has introduced evidence of incompetency or evidence requiring notice under Rule 12.2(a) or (b)(1), or

(B) has introduced expert evidence in a capital sentencing proceeding requiring notice under Rule 12.2(b)(2).

**(d) Failure to Comply.**

**(1)** *Failure to Give Notice or to Submit to Examination.* The court may exclude any expert evidence from the defendant on the issue of the defendant's mental disease, mental defect, or any other mental condition bearing on the defendant's guilt or the issue of punishment in a capital case if the defendant fails to:

(A) give notice under Rule 12.2(b); or

(B) submit to an examination when ordered under Rule 12.2(c).

**(2)** *Failure to Disclose.* The court may exclude any expert evidence for which the defendant has failed to comply with the disclosure requirement of Rule 12.2(c)(3).

**(e) Inadmissibility of Withdrawn Intention.** Evidence of an intention as to which notice was given under Rule 12.2(a) or (b), later withdrawn, is not, in any civil or criminal proceeding, admissible against the person who gave notice of the intention.

## Rule 12.3. Notice of a Public-Authority Defense

**(a) Notice of the Defense and Disclosure of Witnesses.**

**(1)** *Notice in General.* If a defendant intends to assert a defense of actual or believed exercise of public authority on behalf of a law enforcement agency or federal intelligence agency at the time of the alleged offense, the defendant must so notify an attorney for the government in writing and must file a copy of the notice with the clerk within the time provided for filing a pretrial motion, or at any later time the court sets. The notice filed with the clerk must be under seal if the notice identifies a federal intelligence agency as the source of public authority.

**(2)** *Contents of Notice.* The notice must contain the following information:

(A) the law enforcement agency or federal intelligence agency involved;

(B) the agency member on whose behalf the defendant claims to have acted; and

(C) the time during which the defendant claims to have acted with public authority.

**(3)** ***Response to the Notice.*** An attorney for the government must serve a written response on the defendant or the defendant's attorney within 14 days after receiving the defendant's notice, but no later than 21 days before trial. The response must admit or deny that the defendant exercised the public authority identified in the defendant's notice.

**(4)** ***Disclosing Witnesses.***

(A) *Government's Request.* An attorney for the government may request in writing that the defendant disclose the name, address, and telephone number of each witness the defendant intends to rely on to establish a public-authority defense. An attorney for the government may serve the request when the government serves its response to the defendant's notice under Rule 12.3(a)(3), or later, but must serve the request no later than 21 days before trial.

(B) *Defendant's Response.* Within 14 days after receiving the government's request, the defendant must serve on an attorney for the government a written statement of the name, address, and telephone number of each witness.

(C) *Government's Reply.* Within 14 days after receiving the defendant's statement, an attorney for the government must serve on the defendant or the defendant's attorney a written statement of the name of each witness—and the address and telephone number of each witness other than a victim—that the government intends to rely on to oppose the defendant's public-authority defense.

(D) *Victim's Address and Telephone Number.* If the government intends to rely on a victim's testimony to oppose the defendant's public-authority defense and the defendant establishes a need for the victim's address and telephone number, the court may:

(i)   order the government to provide the information in writing to the defendant or the defendant's attorney; or

(ii) fashion a reasonable procedure that allows for preparing the defense and also protects the victim's interests.

**(5)** *Additional Time.* The court may, for good cause, allow a party additional time to comply with this rule.

**(b) Continuing Duty to Disclose.**

**(1)** *In General.* Both an attorney for the government and the defendant must promptly disclose in writing to the other party the name of any additional witness—and the address, and telephone number of any additional witness other than a victim—if:

(A) the disclosing party learns of the witness before or during trial; and

(B) the witness should have been disclosed under Rule 12.3(a)(4) if the disclosing party had known of the witness earlier.

**(2)** *Address and Telephone Number of an Additional Victim-Witness.* The address and telephone number of an additional victim-witness must not be disclosed except as provided in Rule 12.3(a)(4)(D).

**(c) Failure to Comply.** If a party fails to comply with this rule, the court may exclude the testimony of any undisclosed witness regarding the public-authority defense. This rule does not limit the defendant's right to testify.

**(d) Protective Procedures Unaffected.** This rule does not limit the court's authority to issue appropriate protective orders or to order that any filings be under seal.

**(e) Inadmissibility of Withdrawn Intention.** Evidence of an intention as to which notice was given under Rule 12.3(a), later withdrawn, is not, in any civil or criminal proceeding, admissible against the person who gave notice of the intention.

## Rule 12.4. Disclosure Statement[a]

### (a) Who Must File.

**(1)** *Nongovernmental       Corporate       Party.*       Any nongovernmental corporate party to a proceeding in a district court must file a statement that identifies any parent corporation and any publicly held corporation that owns 10% or more of its stock or states that there is no such corporation.

**(2)** *Organizational Victim.* If an organization is a victim of the alleged criminal activity, the government must file a statement identifying the victim. If the organizational victim is a corporation, the statement must also disclose the information required by Rule 12.4(a)(1) to the extent it can be obtained through due diligence.

### (b) Time for Filing; Supplemental Filing. A party must:

**(1)** file the Rule 12.4(a) statement upon the defendant's initial appearance; and

**(2)** promptly file a supplemental statement upon any change in the information that the statement requires.

## Rule 13. Joint Trial of Separate Cases

The court may order that separate cases be tried together as though brought in a single indictment or information if all offenses and all defendants could have been joined in a single indictment or information.

---

[a]   Editor's Note: On December 1, 2018, the following changes to Criminal Rule 12.4 will go into effect. New matter is underlined and deleted matter is struck through.

Rule 12.4. Disclosure Statement

(a) Who Must File.

(1) *Nongovernmental Corporate Party.* Any nongovernmental corporate party to a proceeding in a district court must file a statement that identifies any parent corporation and any publicly held corporation that owns 10% or more of its stock or states that there is no such corporation.

(2) *Organizational Victim.* Unless the government shows good cause, it must file a statement identifying any organizational victim of the alleged criminal activity.If an organization is a victim of the alleged criminal activity, the government must file a statement identifying the victim. If the organizational victim is a corporation, the statement must also disclose the information required by Rule 12.4(a)(1) to the extent it can be obtained through due diligence.

(b) Time forto Fileing; SupplementalLater Filing. A party must:

(1) file the Rule 12.4(a) statement within 28 days afterupon the defendant's initial appearance; and

(2) promptly file a latersupplemental statement if any required information changes upon any change in the information that the statement requires.

## Rule 14. Relief from Prejudicial Joinder

**(a) Relief.** If the joinder of offenses or defendants in an indictment, an information, or a consolidation for trial appears to prejudice a defendant or the government, the court may order separate trials of counts, sever the defendants' trials, or provide any other relief that justice requires.

**(b) Defendant's Statements.** Before ruling on a defendant's motion to sever, the court may order an attorney for the government to deliver to the court for in camera inspection any defendant's statement that the government intends to use as evidence.

## Rule 15. Depositions

**(a) When Taken.**

**(1)** *In General.* A party may move that a prospective witness be deposed in order to preserve testimony for trial. The court may grant the motion because of exceptional circumstances and in the interest of justice. If the court orders the deposition to be taken, it may also require the deponent to produce at the deposition any designated material that is not privileged, including any book, paper, document, record, recording, or data.

**(2)** *Detained Material Witness.* A witness who is detained under 18 U.S.C. § 3144 may request to be deposed by filing a written motion and giving notice to the parties. The court may then order that the deposition be taken and may discharge the witness after the witness has signed under oath the deposition transcript.

**(b) Notice.**

**(1)** *In General.* A party seeking to take a deposition must give every other party reasonable written notice of the deposition's date and location. The notice must state the name and address of each deponent. If requested by a party receiving the notice, the court may, for good cause, change the deposition's date or location.

**(2)** *To the Custodial Officer.* A party seeking to take the deposition must also notify the officer who has custody of the defendant of the scheduled date and location.

**(c) Defendant's Presence.**

**(1)** *Defendant in Custody.* Except as authorized by Rule 15(c)(3), the officer who has custody of the defendant must produce the defendant at the deposition and keep the defendant in the witness's presence during the examination, unless the defendant:

(A) waives in writing the right to be present; or

(B) persists in disruptive conduct justifying exclusion after being warned by the court that disruptive conduct will result in the defendant's exclusion.

**(2)** *Defendant Not in Custody.* Except as authorized by Rule 15(c)(3), a defendant who is not in custody has the right upon request to be present at the deposition, subject to any conditions imposed by the court. If the government tenders the defendant's expenses as provided in Rule 15(d) but the defendant still fails to appear, the defendant—absent good cause—waives both the right to appear and any objection to the taking and use of the deposition based on that right.

**(3)** *Taking Depositions Outside the United States Without the Defendant's Presence.* The deposition of a witness who is outside the United States may be taken without the defendant's presence if the court makes case-specific findings of all the following:

(A) the witness's testimony could provide substantial proof of a material fact in a felony prosecution;

(B) there is a substantial likelihood that the witness's attendance at trial cannot be obtained;

(C) the witness's presence for a deposition in the United States cannot be obtained;

(D) the defendant cannot be present because:

(i) the country where the witness is located will not permit the defendant to attend the deposition;

(ii) for an in-custody defendant, secure transportation and continuing custody cannot be assured at the witness's location; or

(iii) for an out-of-custody defendant, no reasonable conditions will assure an appearance at the deposition or at trial or sentencing; and

(E) the defendant can meaningfully participate in the deposition through reasonable means.

**(d) Expenses.** If the deposition was requested by the government, the court may—or if the defendant is unable to bear the deposition expenses, the court must—order the government to pay:

**(1)** any reasonable travel and subsistence expenses of the defendant and the defendant's attorney to attend the deposition; and

**(2)** the costs of the deposition transcript.

**(e) Manner of Taking.** Unless these rules or a court order provides otherwise, a deposition must be taken and filed in the same manner as a deposition in a civil action, except that:

(1) A defendant may not be deposed without that defendant's consent.

(2) The scope and manner of the deposition examination and cross-examination must be the same as would be allowed during trial.

(3) The government must provide to the defendant or the defendant's attorney, for use at the deposition, any statement of the deponent in the government's possession to which the defendant would be entitled at trial.

**(f) Admissibility and Use as Evidence.** An order authorizing a deposition to be taken under this rule does not determine its admissibility. A party may use all or part of a deposition as provided by the Federal Rules of Evidence.

**(g) Objections.** A party objecting to deposition testimony or evidence must state the grounds for the objection during the deposition.

**(h) Depositions by Agreement Permitted.** The parties may by agreement take and use a deposition with the court's consent.

## Rule 16. Discovery and Inspection

**(a) Government's Disclosure.**

**(1) *Information Subject to Disclosure.***

(A) *Defendant's Oral Statement.* Upon a defendant's request, the government must disclose to the defendant the substance of any relevant oral statement made by the defendant, before or after arrest, in response to interrogation by a person the defendant knew was a government agent if the government intends to use the statement at trial.

(B) *Defendant's Written or Recorded Statement.* Upon a defendant's request, the government must disclose to the defendant, and make available for inspection, copying, or photographing, all of the following:

(i) any relevant written or recorded statement by the defendant if:

- the statement is within the government's possession, custody, or control; and

    •    the attorney for the government knows—or through due diligence could know—that the statement exists;

    (ii) the portion of any written record containing the substance of any relevant oral statement made before or after arrest if the defendant made the statement in response to interrogation by a person the defendant knew was a government agent; and

    (iii) the defendant's recorded testimony before a grand jury relating to the charged offense.

    (C) *Organizational Defendant.* Upon a defendant's request, if the defendant is an organization, the government must disclose to the defendant any statement described in Rule 16(a)(1)(A) and (B) if the government contends that the person making the statement:

    (i)   was legally able to bind the defendant regarding the subject of the statement because of that person's position as the defendant's director, officer, employee, or agent; or

    (ii) was personally involved in the alleged conduct constituting the offense and was legally able to bind the defendant regarding that conduct because of that person's position as the defendant's director, officer, employee, or agent.

    (D) *Defendant's Prior Record.* Upon a defendant's request, the government must furnish the defendant with a copy of the defendant's prior criminal record that is within the government's possession, custody, or control if the attorney for the government knows—or through due diligence could know—that the record exists.

    (E) *Documents and Objects.* Upon a defendant's request, the government must permit the defendant to inspect and to copy or photograph books, papers, documents, data, photographs, tangible objects, buildings or places, or copies or portions of any of these items, if the item is within the government's possession, custody, or control and:

    (i)   the item is material to preparing the defense;

    (ii) the government intends to use the item in its case-in-chief at trial; or

    (iii) the item was obtained from or belongs to the defendant.

(F) *Reports of Examinations and Tests.* Upon a defendant's request, the government must permit a defendant to inspect and to copy or photograph the results or reports of any physical or mental examination and of any scientific test or experiment if:

(i) the item is within the government's possession, custody, or control;

(ii) the attorney for the government knows—or through due diligence could know—that the item exists; and

(iii) the item is material to preparing the defense or the government intends to use the item in its case-in-chief at trial.

(G) *Expert Witnesses.* At the defendant's request, the government must give to the defendant a written summary of any testimony that the government intends to use under Rules 702, 703, or 705 of the Federal Rules of Evidence during its case-in-chief at trial. If the government requests discovery under subdivision (b)(1)(C)(ii) and the defendant complies, the government must, at the defendant's request, give to the defendant a written summary of testimony that the government intends to use under Rules 702, 703, or 705 of the Federal Rules of Evidence as evidence at trial on the issue of the defendant's mental condition. The summary provided under this subparagraph must describe the witness's opinions, the bases and reasons for those opinions, and the witness's qualifications.

**(2)** *Information Not Subject to Disclosure.* Except as permitted by Rule 16(a)(1)(A)–(D), (F), and (G), this rule does not authorize the discovery or inspection of reports, memoranda, or other internal government documents made by an attorney for the government or other government agent in connection with investigating or prosecuting the case. Nor does this rule authorize the discovery or inspection of statements made by prospective government witnesses except as provided in 18 U.S.C. § 3500.

**(3)** *Grand Jury Transcripts.* This rule does not apply to the discovery or inspection of a grand jury's recorded proceedings, except as provided in Rules 6, 12(h), 16(a)(1), and 26.2.

**(b) Defendant's Disclosure.**

**(1)** *Information Subject to Disclosure.*

(A) *Documents and Objects.* If a defendant requests disclosure under Rule 16(a)(1)(E) and the government complies, then the defendant must permit the government, upon request, to inspect and to copy or photograph books, papers, documents, data, photographs, tangible objects, buildings or places, or copies or portions of any of these items if:

    (i) the item is within the defendant's possession, custody, or control; and

    (ii) the defendant intends to use the item in the defendant's case-in-chief at trial.

(B) *Reports of Examinations and Tests.* If a defendant requests disclosure under Rule 16(a)(1)(F) and the government complies, the defendant must permit the government, upon request, to inspect and to copy or photograph the results or reports of any physical or mental examination and of any scientific test or experiment if:

    (i) the item is within the defendant's possession, custody, or control; and

    (ii) the defendant intends to use the item in the defendant's case-in-chief at trial, or intends to call the witness who prepared the report and the report relates to the witness's testimony.

(C) *Expert Witnesses.* The defendant must, at the government's request, give to the government a written summary of any testimony that the defendant intends to use under Rules 702, 703, or 705 of the Federal Rules of Evidence as evidence at trial, if—

    (i) the defendant requests disclosure under subdivision (a)(1)(G) and the government complies; or

    (ii) the defendant has given notice under Rule 12.2(b) of an intent to present expert testimony on the defendant's mental condition.

This summary must describe the witness's opinions, the bases and reasons for those opinions, and the witness's qualifications.

**(2) *Information Not Subject to Disclosure.*** Except for scientific or medical reports, Rule 16(b)(1) does not authorize discovery or inspection of:

    (A) reports, memoranda, or other documents made by the defendant, or the defendant's attorney or agent, during the case's investigation or defense; or

    (B) a statement made to the defendant, or the defendant's attorney or agent, by:

        (i) the defendant;

(ii)  a government or defense witness; or

(iii)  a prospective government or defense witness.

**(c)  Continuing  Duty  to  Disclose.** A  party  who  discovers additional  evidence  or  material  before  or  during  trial  must  promptly disclose its existence to the other party or the court if:

(1)  the evidence or material is subject to discovery or inspection under this rule; and

(2)  the other party previously requested, or the court ordered, its production.

**(d)  Regulating Discovery.**

(1)  *Protective  and  Modifying  Orders.* At  any  time  the  court may, for good cause, deny, restrict, or defer discovery or inspection, or grant other appropriate relief. The court may permit a party to show good cause by a written statement that the court will inspect ex parte. If relief is granted, the court must preserve the entire text of the party's statement under seal.

(2)  *Failure to Comply.* If a party fails to comply with this rule, the court may:

(A)  order that party to permit the discovery or inspection; specify its time, place, and manner; and prescribe other just terms and conditions;

(B)  grant a continuance;

(C)  prohibit that party from introducing the undisclosed evidence; or

(D)  enter  any  other  order  that  is  just  under  the circumstances.

## Rule 17. Subpoena

**(a)  Content.** A subpoena must state the court's name and the title of the proceeding, include the seal of the court, and command the witness to attend and testify at the time and place the subpoena specifies. The clerk  must  issue  a  blank  subpoena—signed  and  sealed—to  the  party requesting it, and that party must fill in the blanks before the subpoena is served.

**(b)  Defendant  Unable  to  Pay.** Upon  a  defendant's  ex  parte application, the court must order that a subpoena be issued for a named witness if the defendant shows an inability to pay the witness's fees and the necessity of the witness's presence for an adequate defense. If the court orders a subpoena to be issued, the process costs and witness fees will be paid in the same manner as those paid for witnesses the government subpoenas.

**(c) Producing Documents and Objects.**

**(1)** *In General.* A subpoena may order the witness to produce any books, papers, documents, data, or other objects the subpoena designates. The court may direct the witness to produce the designated items in court before trial or before they are to be offered in evidence. When the items arrive, the court may permit the parties and their attorneys to inspect all or part of them.

**(2)** *Quashing or Modifying the Subpoena.* On motion made promptly, the court may quash or modify the subpoena if compliance would be unreasonable or oppressive.

**(3)** *Subpoena for Personal or Confidential Information About a Victim.* After a complaint, indictment, or information is filed, a subpoena requiring the production of personal or confidential information about a victim may be served on a third party only by court order. Before entering the order and unless there are exceptional circumstances, the court must require giving notice to the victim so that the victim can move to quash or modify the subpoena or otherwise object.

**(d) Service.** A marshal, a deputy marshal, or any nonparty who is at least 18 years old may serve a subpoena. The server must deliver a copy of the subpoena to the witness and must tender to the witness one day's witness-attendance fee and the legal mileage allowance. The server need not tender the attendance fee or mileage allowance when the United States, a federal officer, or a federal agency has requested the subpoena.

**(e) Place of Service.**

**(1)** *In the United States.* A subpoena requiring a witness to attend a hearing or trial may be served at any place within the United States.

**(2)** *In a Foreign Country.* If the witness is in a foreign country, 28 U.S.C. § 1783 governs the subpoena's service.

**(f) Issuing a Deposition Subpoena.**

**(1)** *Issuance.* A court order to take a deposition authorizes the clerk in the district where the deposition is to be taken to issue a subpoena for any witness named or described in the order.

**(2)** *Place.* After considering the convenience of the witness and the parties, the court may order—and the subpoena may require— the witness to appear anywhere the court designates.

**(g) Contempt.** The court (other than a magistrate judge) may hold in contempt a witness who, without adequate excuse, disobeys a subpoena issued by a federal court in that district. A magistrate judge may hold in contempt a witness who, without adequate excuse, disobeys a subpoena issued by that magistrate judge as provided in 28 U.S.C. § 636(e).

**(h) Information Not Subject to a Subpoena.** No party may subpoena a statement of a witness or of a prospective witness under this rule. Rule 26.2 governs the production of the statement.

## Rule 17.1. Pretrial Conference

On its own, or on a party's motion, the court may hold one or more pretrial conferences to promote a fair and expeditious trial. When a conference ends, the court must prepare and file a memorandum of any matters agreed to during the conference. The government may not use any statement made during the conference by the defendant or the defendant's attorney unless it is in writing and is signed by the defendant and the defendant's attorney.

## TITLE V.   VENUE

## Rule 18. Place of Prosecution and Trial

Unless a statute or these rules permit otherwise, the government must prosecute an offense in a district where the offense was committed. The court must set the place of trial within the district with due regard for the convenience of the defendant, any victim, and the witnesses, and the prompt administration of justice.

## Rule 19. [Reserved]

## Rule 20. Transfer for Plea and Sentence

**(a) Consent to Transfer.** A prosecution may be transferred from the district where the indictment or information is pending, or from which a warrant on a complaint has been issued, to the district where the defendant is arrested, held, or present if:

> **(1)** the defendant states in writing a wish to plead guilty or nolo contendere and to waive trial in the district where the indictment, information, or complaint is pending, consents in writing to the court's disposing of the case in the transferee district, and files the statement in the transferee district; and

> **(2)** the United States attorneys in both districts approve the transfer in writing.

**(b) Clerk's Duties.** After receiving the defendant's statement and the required approvals, the clerk where the indictment, information, or complaint is pending must send the file, or a certified copy, to the clerk in the transferee district.

**(c) Effect of a Not Guilty Plea.** If the defendant pleads not guilty after the case has been transferred under Rule 20(a), the clerk must return the papers to the court where the prosecution began, and that court must restore the proceeding to its docket. The defendant's statement that the defendant wished to plead guilty or nolo contendere is not, in any civil or criminal proceeding, admissible against the defendant.

**(d) Juveniles.**

**(1)** *Consent to Transfer.* A juvenile, as defined in 18 U.S.C. § 5031, may be proceeded against as a juvenile delinquent in the district where the juvenile is arrested, held, or present if:

(A) the alleged offense that occurred in the other district is not punishable by death or life imprisonment;

(B) an attorney has advised the juvenile;

(C) the court has informed the juvenile of the juvenile's rights—including the right to be returned to the district where the offense allegedly occurred—and the consequences of waiving those rights;

(D) the juvenile, after receiving the court's information about rights, consents in writing to be proceeded against in the transferee district, and files the consent in the transferee district;

(E) the United States attorneys for both districts approve the transfer in writing; and

(F) the transferee court approves the transfer.

**(2)** *Clerk's Duties.* After receiving the juvenile's written consent and the required approvals, the clerk where the indictment, information, or complaint is pending or where the alleged offense occurred must send the file, or a certified copy, to the clerk in the transferee district.

## Rule 21. Transfer for Trial

**(a) For Prejudice.** Upon the defendant's motion, the court must transfer the proceeding against that defendant to another district if the court is satisfied that so great a prejudice against the defendant exists in the transferring district that the defendant cannot obtain a fair and impartial trial there.

**(b) For Convenience.** Upon the defendant's motion, the court may transfer the proceeding, or one or more counts, against that defendant to another district for the convenience of the parties, any victim, and the witnesses, and in the interest of justice.

**(c) Proceedings on Transfer.** When the court orders a transfer, the clerk must send to the transferee district the file, or a certified copy, and any bail taken. The prosecution will then continue in the transferee district.

**(d) Time to File a Motion to Transfer.** A motion to transfer may be made at or before arraignment or at any other time the court or these rules prescribe.

## Rule 22. [Transferred]

## TITLE VI.   TRIAL

### Rule 23. Jury or Nonjury Trial

**(a) Jury Trial.** If the defendant is entitled to a jury trial, the trial must be by jury unless:

    **(1)** the defendant waives a jury trial in writing;

    **(2)** the government consents; and

    **(3)** the court approves.

**(b) Jury Size.**

    **(1)** *In General.* A jury consists of 12 persons unless this rule provides otherwise.

    **(2)** *Stipulation for a Smaller Jury.* At any time before the verdict, the parties may, with the court's approval, stipulate in writing that:

        (A) the jury may consist of fewer than 12 persons; or

        (B) a jury of fewer than 12 persons may return a verdict if the court finds it necessary to excuse a juror for good cause after the trial begins.

    **(3)** *Court Order for a Jury of 11.* After the jury has retired to deliberate, the court may permit a jury of 11 persons to return a verdict, even without a stipulation by the parties, if the court finds good cause to excuse a juror.

**(c) Nonjury Trial.** In a case tried without a jury, the court must find the defendant guilty or not guilty. If a party requests before the finding of guilty or not guilty, the court must state its specific findings of fact in open court or in a written decision or opinion.

**Rule 24. Trial Jurors**

  **(a) Examination.**

   **(1)** *In General.* The court may examine prospective jurors or may permit the attorneys for the parties to do so.

   **(2)** *Court Examination.* If the court examines the jurors, it must permit the attorneys for the parties to:

      (A) ask further questions that the court considers proper; or

      (B) submit further questions that the court may ask if it considers them proper.

  **(b) Peremptory Challenges.** Each side is entitled to the number of peremptory challenges to prospective jurors specified below. The court may allow additional peremptory challenges to multiple defendants, and may allow the defendants to exercise those challenges separately or jointly.

   **(1)** *Capital Case.* Each side has 20 peremptory challenges when the government seeks the death penalty.

   **(2)** *Other Felony Case.* The government has 6 peremptory challenges and the defendant or defendants jointly have 10 peremptory challenges when the defendant is charged with a crime punishable by imprisonment of more than one year.

   **(3)** *Misdemeanor Case.* Each side has 3 peremptory challenges when the defendant is charged with a crime punishable by fine, imprisonment of one year or less, or both.

  **(c) Alternate Jurors.**

   **(1)** *In General.* The court may impanel up to 6 alternate jurors to replace any jurors who are unable to perform or who are disqualified from performing their duties.

   **(2)** *Procedure.*

      (A) Alternate jurors must have the same qualifications and be selected and sworn in the same manner as any other juror.

      (B) Alternate jurors replace jurors in the same sequence in which the alternates were selected. An alternate juror who replaces a juror has the same authority as the other jurors.

   **(3)** *Retaining Alternate Jurors.* The court may retain alternate jurors after the jury retires to deliberate. The court must ensure that a retained alternate does not discuss the case with anyone until that alternate replaces a juror or is discharged. If an alternate replaces a juror after deliberations have begun, the court must instruct the jury to begin its deliberations anew.

**(4)** *Peremptory Challenges.* Each side is entitled to the number of additional peremptory challenges to prospective alternate jurors specified below. These additional challenges may be used only to remove alternate jurors.

(A) *One or Two Alternates.* One additional peremptory challenge is permitted when one or two alternates are impaneled.

(B) *Three or Four Alternates.* Two additional peremptory challenges are permitted when three or four alternates are impaneled.

(C) *Five or Six Alternates.* Three additional peremptory challenges are permitted when five or six alternates are impaneled.

### Rule 25. Judge's Disability

**(a) During Trial.** Any judge regularly sitting in or assigned to the court may complete a jury trial if:

**(1)** the judge before whom the trial began cannot proceed because of death, sickness, or other disability; and

**(2)** the judge completing the trial certifies familiarity with the trial record.

**(b) After a Verdict or Finding of Guilty.**

**(1)** *In General.* After a verdict or finding of guilty, any judge regularly sitting in or assigned to a court may complete the court's duties if the judge who presided at trial cannot perform those duties because of absence, death, sickness, or other disability.

**(2)** *Granting a New Trial.* The successor judge may grant a new trial if satisfied that:

(A) a judge other than the one who presided at the trial cannot perform the post-trial duties; or

(B) a new trial is necessary for some other reason.

### Rule 26. Taking Testimony

In every trial the testimony of witnesses must be taken in open court, unless otherwise provided by a statute or by rules adopted under 28 U.S.C. §§ 2072–2077.

## Rule 26.1. Foreign Law Determination

A party intending to raise an issue of foreign law must provide the court and all parties with reasonable written notice. Issues of foreign law are questions of law, but in deciding such issues a court may consider any relevant material or source—including testimony—without regard to the Federal Rules of Evidence.

## Rule 26.2. Producing a Witness's Statement

**(a) Motion to Produce.** After a witness other than the defendant has testified on direct examination, the court, on motion of a party who did not call the witness, must order an attorney for the government or the defendant and the defendant's attorney to produce, for the examination and use of the moving party, any statement of the witness that is in their possession and that relates to the subject matter of the witness's testimony.

**(b) Producing the Entire Statement.** If the entire statement relates to the subject matter of the witness's testimony, the court must order that the statement be delivered to the moving party.

**(c) Producing a Redacted Statement.** If the party who called the witness claims that the statement contains information that is privileged or does not relate to the subject matter of the witness's testimony, the court must inspect the statement in camera. After excising any privileged or unrelated portions, the court must order delivery of the redacted statement to the moving party. If the defendant objects to an excision, the court must preserve the entire statement with the excised portion indicated, under seal, as part of the record.

**(d) Recess to Examine a Statement.** The court may recess the proceedings to allow time for a party to examine the statement and prepare for its use.

**(e) Sanction for Failure to Produce or Deliver a Statement.** If the party who called the witness disobeys an order to produce or deliver a statement, the court must strike the witness's testimony from the record. If an attorney for the government disobeys the order, the court must declare a mistrial if justice so requires.

**(f) "Statement" Defined.** As used in this rule, a witness's "statement" means:

(1) a written statement that the witness makes and signs, or otherwise adopts or approves;

(2) a substantially verbatim, contemporaneously recorded recital of the witness's oral statement that is contained in any recording or any transcription of a recording; or

**(3)** the witness's statement to a grand jury, however taken or recorded, or a transcription of such a statement.

**(g) Scope.** This rule applies at trial, at a suppression hearing under Rule 12, and to the extent specified in the following rules:

**(1)** Rule 5.1(h) (preliminary hearing);

**(2)** Rule 32(i)(2) (sentencing);

**(3)** Rule 32.1(e) (hearing to revoke or modify probation or supervised release);

**(4)** Rule 46(j) (detention hearing); and

**(5)** Rule 8 of the Rules Governing Proceedings under 28 U.S.C. § 2255.

## Rule 26.3. Mistrial

Before ordering a mistrial, the court must give each defendant and the government an opportunity to comment on the propriety of the order, to state whether that party consents or objects, and to suggest alternatives.

## Rule 27. Proving an Official Record

A party may prove an official record, an entry in such a record, or the lack of a record or entry in the same manner as in a civil action.

## Rule 28. Interpreters

The court may select, appoint, and set the reasonable compensation for an interpreter, including an interpreter for the victim. The compensation must be paid from funds provided by law or by the government, as the court may direct.

## Rule 29. Motion for a Judgment of Acquittal

**(a) Before Submission to the Jury.** After the government closes its evidence or after the close of all the evidence, the court on the defendant's motion must enter a judgment of acquittal of any offense for which the evidence is insufficient to sustain a conviction. The court may on its own consider whether the evidence is insufficient to sustain a conviction. If the court denies a motion for a judgment of acquittal at the close of the government's evidence, the defendant may offer evidence without having reserved the right to do so.

**(b) Reserving Decision.** The court may reserve decision on the motion, proceed with the trial (where the motion is made before the close of all the evidence), submit the case to the jury, and decide the motion either before the jury returns a verdict or after it returns a verdict of guilty or is discharged without having returned a verdict. If the court reserves decision, it must decide the motion on the basis of the evidence at the time the ruling was reserved.

**(c)  After Jury Verdict or Discharge.**

**(1)  *Time for a Motion.*** A defendant may move for a judgment of acquittal, or renew such a motion, within 14 days after a guilty verdict or after the court discharges the jury, whichever is later.

**(2)  *Ruling on the Motion.*** If the jury has returned a guilty verdict, the court may set aside the verdict and enter an acquittal. If the jury has failed to return a verdict, the court may enter a judgment of acquittal.

**(3)  *No Prior Motion Required.*** A defendant is not required to move for a judgment of acquittal before the court submits the case to the jury as a prerequisite for making such a motion after jury discharge.

**(d)  Conditional Ruling on a Motion for a New Trial.**

**(1)  *Motion for a New Trial.*** If the court enters a judgment of acquittal after a guilty verdict, the court must also conditionally determine whether any motion for a new trial should be granted if the judgment of acquittal is later vacated or reversed. The court must specify the reasons for that determination.

**(2)  *Finality.*** The court's order conditionally granting a motion for a new trial does not affect the finality of the judgment of acquittal.

**(3)  *Appeal.***

(A)  *Grant of a Motion for a New Trial.* If the court conditionally grants a motion for a new trial and an appellate court later reverses the judgment of acquittal, the trial court must proceed with the new trial unless the appellate court orders otherwise.

(B)  *Denial of a Motion for a New* Trial. If the court conditionally denies a motion for a new trial, an appellee may assert that the denial was erroneous. If the appellate court later reverses the judgment of acquittal, the trial court must proceed as the appellate court directs.

## Rule 29.1. Closing Argument

Closing arguments proceed in the following order:

**(a)** the government argues;

**(b)** the defense argues; and

**(c)** the government rebuts.

## Rule 30. Jury Instructions

**(a) In General.** Any party may request in writing that the court instruct the jury on the law as specified in the request. The request must be made at the close of the evidence or at any earlier time that the court reasonably sets. When the request is made, the requesting party must furnish a copy to every other party.

**(b) Ruling on a Request.** The court must inform the parties before closing arguments how it intends to rule on the requested instructions.

**(c) Time for Giving Instructions.** The court may instruct the jury before or after the arguments are completed, or at both times.

**(d) Objections to Instructions.** A party who objects to any portion of the instructions or to a failure to give a requested instruction must inform the court of the specific objection and the grounds for the objection before the jury retires to deliberate. An opportunity must be given to object out of the jury's hearing and, on request, out of the jury's presence. Failure to object in accordance with this rule precludes appellate review, except as permitted under Rule 52(b).

## Rule 31. Jury Verdict

**(a) Return.** The jury must return its verdict to a judge in open court. The verdict must be unanimous.

**(b) Partial Verdicts, Mistrial, and Retrial.**

**(1)** *Multiple Defendants.* If there are multiple defendants, the jury may return a verdict at any time during its deliberations as to any defendant about whom it has agreed.

**(2)** *Multiple Counts.* If the jury cannot agree on all counts as to any defendant, the jury may return a verdict on those counts on which it has agreed.

**(3)** *Mistrial and Retrial.* If the jury cannot agree on a verdict on one or more counts, the court may declare a mistrial on those counts. The government may retry any defendant on any count on which the jury could not agree.

**(c) Lesser Offense or Attempt.** A defendant may be found guilty of any of the following:

**(1)** an offense necessarily included in the offense charged;

**(2)** an attempt to commit the offense charged; or

**(3)** an attempt to commit an offense necessarily included in the offense charged, if the attempt is an offense in its own right.

**(d) Jury Poll.** After a verdict is returned but before the jury is discharged, the court must on a party's request, or may on its own, poll the jurors individually. If the poll reveals a lack of unanimity, the court may direct the jury to deliberate further or may declare a mistrial and discharge the jury.

## TITLE VII. POST-CONVICTION PROCEDURES

### Rule 32. Sentencing and Judgment

**(a) [Reserved.]**

**(b) Time of Sentencing.**

**(1)** *In General.* The court must impose sentence without unnecessary delay.

**(2)** *Changing Time Limits.* The court may, for good cause, change any time limits prescribed in this rule.

**(c) Presentence Investigation.**

**(1)** *Required Investigation.*

(A) *In General.* The probation officer must conduct a presentence investigation and submit a report to the court before it imposes sentence unless:

(i) 18 U.S.C. § 3593(c) or another statute requires otherwise; or

(ii) the court finds that the information in the record enables it to meaningfully exercise its sentencing authority under 18 U.S.C. § 3553, and the court explains its finding on the record.

(B) *Restitution.* If the law permits restitution, the probation officer must conduct an investigation and submit a report that contains sufficient information for the court to order restitution.

**(2)** *Interviewing the Defendant.* The probation officer who interviews a defendant as part of a presentence investigation must, on request, give the defendant's attorney notice and a reasonable opportunity to attend the interview.

**(d) Presentence Report.**

**(1)** *Applying the Advisory Sentencing Guidelines.* The presentence report must:

(A) identify all applicable guidelines and policy statements of the Sentencing Commission;

(B) calculate the defendant's offense level and criminal history category;

(C) state the resulting sentencing range and kinds of sentences available;

(D) identify any factor relevant to:

(i) the appropriate kind of sentence, or

(ii) the appropriate sentence within the applicable sentencing range; and

(E) identify any basis for departing from the applicable sentencing range.

**(2)** *Additional Information.* The presentence report must also contain the following:

(A) the defendant's history and characteristics, including:

(i) any prior criminal record;

(ii) the defendant's financial condition; and

(iii) any circumstances affecting the defendant's behavior that may be helpful in imposing sentence or in correctional treatment;

(B) information that assesses any financial, social, psychological, and medical impact on any victim;

(C) when appropriate, the nature and extent of nonprison programs and resources available to the defendant;

(D) when the law provides for restitution, information sufficient for a restitution order;

(E) if the court orders a study under 18 U.S.C. § 3552(b), any resulting report and recommendation;

(F) a statement of whether the government seeks forfeiture under Rule 32.2 and any other law; and

(G) any other information that the court requires, including information relevant to the factors under 18 U.S.C. § 3553(a).

**(3)** *Exclusions.* The presentence report must exclude the following:

(A) any diagnoses that, if disclosed, might seriously disrupt a rehabilitation program;

(B) any sources of information obtained upon a promise of confidentiality; and

(C) any other information that, if disclosed, might result in physical or other harm to the defendant or others.

**(e) Disclosing the Report and Recommendation.**

**(1)** *Time to Disclose.* Unless the defendant has consented in writing, the probation officer must not submit a presentence report to the court or disclose its contents to anyone until the defendant has pleaded guilty or nolo contendere, or has been found guilty.

**(2)** *Minimum Required Notice.* The probation officer must give the presentence report to the defendant, the defendant's attorney, and an attorney for the government at least 35 days before sentencing unless the defendant waives this minimum period.

**(3)** *Sentence Recommendation.* By local rule or by order in a case, the court may direct the probation officer not to disclose to anyone other than the court the officer's recommendation on the sentence.

**(f) Objecting to the Report.**

**(1)** *Time to Object.* Within 14 days after receiving the presentence report, the parties must state in writing any objections, including objections to material information, sentencing guideline ranges, and policy statements contained in or omitted from the report.

**(2)** *Serving Objections.* An objecting party must provide a copy of its objections to the opposing party and to the probation officer.

**(3)** *Action on Objections.* After receiving objections, the probation officer may meet with the parties to discuss the objections. The probation officer may then investigate further and revise the presentence report as appropriate.

**(g) Submitting the Report.** At least 7 days before sentencing, the probation officer must submit to the court and to the parties the presentence report and an addendum containing any unresolved objections, the grounds for those objections, and the probation officer's comments on them.

**(h) Notice of Possible Departure from Sentencing Guidelines.** Before the court may depart from the applicable sentencing range on a ground not identified for departure either in the presentence report or in a party's prehearing submission, the court must give the parties reasonable notice that it is contemplating such a departure. The notice must specify any ground on which the court is contemplating a departure.

**(i) Sentencing.**

   **(1)** *In General.* At sentencing, the court:

   (A) must verify that the defendant and the defendant's attorney have read and discussed the presentence report and any addendum to the report;

   (B) must give to the defendant and an attorney for the government a written summary of—or summarize in camera— any information excluded from the presentence report under Rule 32(d)(3) on which the court will rely in sentencing, and give them a reasonable opportunity to comment on that information;

   (C) must allow the parties' attorneys to comment on the probation officer's determinations and other matters relating to an appropriate sentence; and

   (D) may, for good cause, allow a party to make a new objection at any time before sentence is imposed.

   **(2)** *Introducing Evidence; Producing a Statement.* The court may permit the parties to introduce evidence on the objections. If a witness testifies at sentencing, Rule 26.2(a)–(d) and (f) applies. If a party fails to comply with a Rule 26.2 order to produce a witness's statement, the court must not consider that witness's testimony.

   **(3)** *Court Determinations.* At sentencing, the court:

   (A) may accept any undisputed portion of the presentence report as a finding of fact;

   (B) must—for any disputed portion of the presentence report or other controverted matter—rule on the dispute or determine that a ruling is unnecessary either because the matter will not affect sentencing, or because the court will not consider the matter in sentencing; and

   (C) must append a copy of the court's determinations under this rule to any copy of the presentence report made available to the Bureau of Prisons.

   **(4)** *Opportunity to Speak.*

   (A) *By a Party.* Before imposing sentence, the court must:

(i)   provide the defendant's attorney an opportunity to speak on the defendant's behalf;

(ii)   address the defendant personally in order to permit the defendant to speak or present any information to mitigate the sentence; and

(iii) provide an attorney for the government an opportunity to speak equivalent to that of the defendant's attorney.

(B)   *By a Victim.* Before imposing sentence, the court must address any victim of the crime who is present at sentencing and must permit the victim to be reasonably heard.

(C)   *In Camera Proceedings.* Upon a party's motion and for good cause, the court may hear in camera any statement made under Rule 32(i)(4).

**(j)   Defendant's Right to Appeal.**

**(1)   *Advice of a Right to Appeal.***

(A)   *Appealing a Conviction.* If the defendant pleaded not guilty and was convicted, after sentencing the court must advise the defendant of the right to appeal the conviction.

(B)   *Appealing a Sentence.* After sentencing—regardless of the defendant's plea—the court must advise the defendant of any right to appeal the sentence.

(C)   *Appeal Costs.* The court must advise a defendant who is unable to pay appeal costs of the right to ask for permission to appeal in forma pauperis.

**(2)   *Clerk's Filing of Notice.*** If the defendant so requests, the clerk must immediately prepare and file a notice of appeal on the defendant's behalf.

**(k)   Judgment.**

**(1)   *In General.*** In the judgment of conviction, the court must set forth the plea, the jury verdict or the court's findings, the adjudication, and the sentence. If the defendant is found not guilty or is otherwise entitled to be discharged, the court must so order. The judge must sign the judgment, and the clerk must enter it.

**(2)   *Criminal Forfeiture.*** Forfeiture procedures are governed by Rule 32.2.

**Rule 32.1. Revoking or Modifying Probation or Supervised Release**

**(a) Initial Appearance.**

**(1)** *Person In Custody.* A person held in custody for violating probation or supervised release must be taken without unnecessary delay before a magistrate judge.

(A) If the person is held in custody in the district where an alleged violation occurred, the initial appearance must be in that district.

(B) If the person is held in custody in a district other than where an alleged violation occurred, the initial appearance must be in that district, or in an adjacent district if the appearance can occur more promptly there.

**(2)** *Upon a Summons.* When a person appears in response to a summons for violating probation or supervised release, a magistrate judge must proceed under this rule.

**(3)** *Advice.* The judge must inform the person of the following:

(A) the alleged violation of probation or supervised release;

(B) the person's right to retain counsel or to request that counsel be appointed if the person cannot obtain counsel; and

(C) the person's right, if held in custody, to a preliminary hearing under Rule 32.1(b)(1).

**(4)** *Appearance in the District With Jurisdiction.* If the person is arrested or appears in the district that has jurisdiction to conduct a revocation hearing—either originally or by transfer of jurisdiction—the court must proceed under Rule 32.1(b)–(e).

**(5)** *Appearance in a District Lacking Jurisdiction.* If the person is arrested or appears in a district that does not have jurisdiction to conduct a revocation hearing, the magistrate judge must:

(A) if the alleged violation occurred in the district of arrest, conduct a preliminary hearing under Rule 32.1(b) and either:

(i) transfer the person to the district that has jurisdiction, if the judge finds probable cause to believe that a violation occurred; or

(ii) dismiss the proceedings and so notify the court that has jurisdiction, if the judge finds no probable cause to believe that a violation occurred; or

(B) if the alleged violation did not occur in the district of arrest, transfer the person to the district that has jurisdiction if:

(i) the government produces certified copies of the judgment, warrant, and warrant application, or produces copies of those certified documents by reliable electronic means; and

(ii) the judge finds that the person is the same person named in the warrant.

**(6)** *Release or Detention.* The magistrate judge may release or detain the person under 18 U.S.C. § 3143(a)(1) pending further proceedings. The burden of establishing by clear and convincing evidence that the person will not flee or pose a danger to any other person or to the community rests with the person.

**(b) Revocation.**

**(1)** *Preliminary Hearing.*

(A) *In General.* If a person is in custody for violating a condition of probation or supervised release, a magistrate judge must promptly conduct a hearing to determine whether there is probable cause to believe that a violation occurred. The person may waive the hearing.

(B) *Requirements.* The hearing must be recorded by a court reporter or by a suitable recording device. The judge must give the person:

(i) notice of the hearing and its purpose, the alleged violation, and the person's right to retain counsel or to request that counsel be appointed if the person cannot obtain counsel;

(ii) an opportunity to appear at the hearing and present evidence; and

(iii) upon request, an opportunity to question any adverse witness, unless the judge determines that the interest of justice does not require the witness to appear.

(C) *Referral.* If the judge finds probable cause, the judge must conduct a revocation hearing. If the judge does not find probable cause, the judge must dismiss the proceeding.

**(2)** *Revocation Hearing.* Unless waived by the person, the court must hold the revocation hearing within a reasonable time in the district having jurisdiction. The person is entitled to:

(A) written notice of the alleged violation;

(B) disclosure of the evidence against the person;

(C) an opportunity to appear, present evidence, and question any adverse witness unless the court determines that the interest of justice does not require the witness to appear;

(D) notice of the person's right to retain counsel or to request that counsel be appointed if the person cannot obtain counsel; and

(E) an opportunity to make a statement and present any information in mitigation.

**(c) Modification.**

**(1) *In General.*** Before modifying the conditions of probation or supervised release, the court must hold a hearing, at which the person has the right to counsel and an opportunity to make a statement and present any information in mitigation.

**(2) *Exceptions.*** A hearing is not required if:

(A) the person waives the hearing; or

(B) the relief sought is favorable to the person and does not extend the term of probation or of supervised release; and

(C) an attorney for the government has received notice of the relief sought, has had a reasonable opportunity to object, and has not done so.

**(d) Disposition of the Case.** The court's disposition of the case is governed by 18 U.S.C. § 3563 and § 3565 (probation) and § 3583 (supervised release).

**(e) Producing a Statement.** Rule 26.2(a)–(d) and (f) applies at a hearing under this rule. If a party fails to comply with a Rule 26.2 order to produce a witness's statement, the court must not consider that witness's testimony.

## Rule 32.2. Criminal Forfeiture

**(a) Notice to the Defendant.** A court must not enter a judgment of forfeiture in a criminal proceeding unless the indictment or information contains notice to the defendant that the government will seek the forfeiture of property as part of any sentence in accordance with the applicable statute. The notice should not be designated as a count of the indictment or information. The indictment or information need not identify the property subject to forfeiture or specify the amount of any forfeiture money judgment that the government seeks.

**(b) Entering a Preliminary Order of Forfeiture.**

**(1) *Forfeiture Phase of the Trial.***

(A) *Forfeiture Determinations.* As soon as practical after a verdict or finding of guilty, or after a plea of guilty or nolo contendere is accepted, on any count in an indictment or information regarding which criminal forfeiture is sought, the court must determine what property is subject to forfeiture under the applicable statute. If the government seeks forfeiture of specific property, the court must determine whether the government has established the requisite nexus between the property and the offense. If the government seeks a personal money judgment, the court must determine the amount of money that the defendant will be ordered to pay.

(B) *Evidence and Hearing.* The court's determination may be based on evidence already in the record, including any written plea agreement, and on any additional evidence or information submitted by the parties and accepted by the court as relevant and reliable. If the forfeiture is contested, on either party's request the court must conduct a hearing after the verdict or finding of guilty.

**(2) *Preliminary Order.***

(A) *Contents of a Specific Order.* If the court finds that property is subject to forfeiture, it must promptly enter a preliminary order of forfeiture setting forth the amount of any money judgment, directing the forfeiture of specific property, and directing the forfeiture of any substitute property if the government has met the statutory criteria. The court must enter the order without regard to any third party's interest in the property. Determining whether a third party has such an interest must be deferred until any third party files a claim in an ancillary proceeding under Rule 32.2(c).

(B) *Timing.* Unless doing so is impractical, the court must enter the preliminary order sufficiently in advance of sentencing to allow the parties to suggest revisions or modifications before the order becomes final as to the defendant under Rule 32.2(b)(4).

(C) *General Order.* If, before sentencing, the court cannot identify all the specific property subject to forfeiture or calculate the total amount of the money judgment, the court may enter a forfeiture order that:

    (i)  lists any identified property;

    (ii)  describes other property in general terms; and

(iii) states that the order will be amended under Rule 32.2(e)(1) when additional specific property is identified or the amount of the money judgment has been calculated.

**(3)** *Seizing Property.* The entry of a preliminary order of forfeiture authorizes the Attorney General (or a designee) to seize the specific property subject to forfeiture; to conduct any discovery the court considers proper in identifying, locating, or disposing of the property; and to commence proceedings that comply with any statutes governing third-party rights. The court may include in the order of forfeiture conditions reasonably necessary to preserve the property's value pending any appeal.

**(4)** *Sentence and Judgment.*

(A) *When Final.* At sentencing—or at any time before sentencing if the defendant consents—the preliminary forfeiture order becomes final as to the defendant. If the order directs the defendant to forfeit specific property, it remains preliminary as to third parties until the ancillary proceeding is concluded under Rule 32.2(c).

(B) *Notice and Inclusion in the Judgment.* The court must include the forfeiture when orally announcing the sentence or must otherwise ensure that the defendant knows of the forfeiture at sentencing. The court must also include the forfeiture order, directly or by reference, in the judgment, but the court's failure to do so may be corrected at any time under Rule 36.

(C) *Time to Appeal.* The time for the defendant or the government to file an appeal from the forfeiture order, or from the court's failure to enter an order, begins to run when judgment is entered. If the court later amends or declines to amend a forfeiture order to include additional property under Rule 32.2(e), the defendant or the government may file an appeal regarding that property under Federal Rule of Appellate Procedure 4(b). The time for that appeal runs from the date when the order granting or denying the amendment becomes final.

**(5)** *Jury Determination.*

(A) *Retaining the Jury.* In any case tried before a jury, if the indictment or information states that the government is seeking forfeiture, the court must determine before the jury begins deliberating whether either party requests that the jury be retained to determine the forfeitability of specific property if it returns a guilty verdict.

(B) *Special Verdict Form.* If a party timely requests to have the jury determine forfeiture, the government must submit a proposed Special Verdict Form listing each property subject to forfeiture and asking the jury to determine whether the government has established the requisite nexus between the property and the offense committed by the defendant.

**(6)** *Notice of the Forfeiture Order.*

(A) *Publishing and Sending Notice.* If the court orders the forfeiture of specific property, the government must publish notice of the order and send notice to any person who reasonably appears to be a potential claimant with standing to contest the forfeiture in the ancillary proceeding.

(B) *Content of the Notice.* The notice must describe the forfeited property, state the times under the applicable statute when a petition contesting the forfeiture must be filed, and state the name and contact information for the government attorney to be served with the petition.

(C) *Means of Publication; Exceptions to Publication Requirement.* Publication must take place as described in Supplemental Rule G(4)(a)(iii) of the Federal Rules of Civil Procedure, and may be by any means described in Supplemental Rule G(4)(a)(iv). Publication is unnecessary if any exception in Supplemental Rule G(4)(a)(i) applies.

(D) *Means of Sending the Notice.* The notice may be sent in accordance with Supplemental Rules G(4)(b)(iii)–(v) of the Federal Rules of Civil Procedure.

**(7)** *Interlocutory Sale.* At any time before entry of a final forfeiture order, the court, in accordance with Supplemental Rule G(7) of the Federal Rules of Civil Procedure, may order the interlocutory sale of property alleged to be forfeitable.

**(c) Ancillary Proceeding; Entering a Final Order of Forfeiture.**

**(1)** *In General.* If, as prescribed by statute, a third party files a petition asserting an interest in the property to be forfeited, the court must conduct an ancillary proceeding, but no ancillary proceeding is required to the extent that the forfeiture consists of a money judgment.

(A) In the ancillary proceeding, the court may, on motion, dismiss the petition for lack of standing, for failure to state a claim, or for any other lawful reason. For purposes of the motion, the facts set forth in the petition are assumed to be true.

(B) After disposing of any motion filed under Rule 32.2(c)(1)(A) and before conducting a hearing on the petition, the court may permit the parties to conduct discovery in accordance with the Federal Rules of Civil Procedure if the court determines that discovery is necessary or desirable to resolve factual issues. When discovery ends, a party may move for summary judgment under Federal Rule of Civil Procedure 56.

**(2)** *Entering a Final Order.* When the ancillary proceeding ends, the court must enter a final order of forfeiture by amending the preliminary order as necessary to account for any third-party rights. If no third party files a timely petition, the preliminary order becomes the final order of forfeiture if the court finds that the defendant (or any combination of defendants convicted in the case) had an interest in the property that is forfeitable under the applicable statute. The defendant may not object to the entry of the final order on the ground that the property belongs, in whole or in part, to a codefendant or third party; nor may a third party object to the final order on the ground that the third party had an interest in the property.

**(3)** *Multiple Petitions.* If multiple third-party petitions are filed in the same case, an order dismissing or granting one petition is not appealable until rulings are made on all the petitions, unless the court determines that there is no just reason for delay.

**(4)** *Ancillary Proceeding Not Part of Sentencing.* An ancillary proceeding is not part of sentencing.

**(d) Stay Pending Appeal.** If a defendant appeals from a conviction or an order of forfeiture, the court may stay the order of forfeiture on terms appropriate to ensure that the property remains available pending appellate review. A stay does not delay the ancillary proceeding or the determination of a third party's rights or interests. If the court rules in favor of any third party while an appeal is pending, the court may amend the order of forfeiture but must not transfer any property interest to a third party until the decision on appeal becomes final, unless the defendant consents in writing or on the record.

**(e) Subsequently Located Property; Substitute Property.**

**(1)** *In General.* On the government's motion, the court may at any time enter an order of forfeiture or amend an existing order of forfeiture to include property that:

(A) is subject to forfeiture under an existing order of forfeiture but was located and identified after that order was entered; or

(B) is substitute property that qualifies for forfeiture under an applicable statute.

**(2)** *Procedure.* If the government shows that the property is subject to forfeiture under Rule 32.2(e)(1), the court must:

(A) enter an order forfeiting that property, or amend an existing preliminary or final order to include it; and

(B) if a third party files a petition claiming an interest in the property, conduct an ancillary proceeding under Rule 32.2(c).

**(3)** *Jury Trial Limited.* There is no right to a jury trial under Rule 32.2(e).

## Rule 33. New Trial

**(a) Defendant's Motion.** Upon the defendant's motion, the court may vacate any judgment and grant a new trial if the interest of justice so requires. If the case was tried without a jury, the court may take additional testimony and enter a new judgment.

**(b) Time to File.**

**(1)** *Newly Discovered Evidence.* Any motion for a new trial grounded on newly discovered evidence must be filed within 3 years after the verdict or finding of guilty. If an appeal is pending, the court may not grant a motion for a new trial until the appellate court remands the case.

**(2)** *Other Grounds.* Any motion for a new trial grounded on any reason other than newly discovered evidence must be filed within 14 days after the verdict or finding of guilty.

## Rule 34. Arresting Judgment

**(a) In General.** Upon the defendant's motion or on its own, the court must arrest judgment if the court does not have jurisdiction of the charged offense.

**(b) Time to File.** The defendant must move to arrest judgment within 14 days after the court accepts a verdict or finding of guilty, or after a plea of guilty or nolo contendere.

## Rule 35. Correcting or Reducing a Sentence

**(a) Correcting Clear Error.** Within 14 days after sentencing, the court may correct a sentence that resulted from arithmetical, technical, or other clear error.

**(b)  Reducing a Sentence for Substantial Assistance.**

**(1)  *In General.*** Upon the government's motion made within one year of sentencing, the court may reduce a sentence if the defendant, after sentencing, provided substantial assistance in investigating or prosecuting another person.

**(2)  *Later Motion.*** Upon the government's motion made more than one year after sentencing, the court may reduce a sentence if the defendant's substantial assistance involved:

(A)  information not known to the defendant until one year or more after sentencing;

(B)  information provided by the defendant to the government within one year of sentencing, but which did not become useful to the government until more than one year after sentencing; or

(C)  information the usefulness of which could not reasonably have been anticipated by the defendant until more than one year after sentencing and which was promptly provided to the government after its usefulness was reasonably apparent to the defendant.

**(3)  *Evaluating Substantial Assistance.*** In evaluating whether the defendant has provided substantial assistance, the court may consider the defendant's presentence assistance.

**(4)  *Below Statutory Minimum.*** When acting under Rule 35(b), the court may reduce the sentence to a level below the minimum sentence established by statute.

**(c)  "Sentencing" Defined.** As used in this rule, "sentencing" means the oral announcement of the sentence.

## Rule 36. Clerical Error

After giving any notice it considers appropriate, the court may at any time correct a clerical error in a judgment, order, or other part of the record, or correct an error in the record arising from oversight or omission.

## Rule 37. Ruling on a Motion for Relief That Is Barred by a Pending Appeal

**(a)  Relief Pending Appeal.** If a timely motion is made for relief that the court lacks authority to grant because of an appeal that has been docketed and is pending, the court may:

(1)  defer considering the motion;

**(2)**  deny the motion; or

**(3)**  state either that it would grant the motion if the court of appeals remands for that purpose or that the motion raises a substantial issue.

**(b) Notice to the Court of Appeals.** The movant must promptly notify the circuit clerk under Federal Rule of Appellate Procedure 12.1 if the district court states that it would grant the motion or that the motion raises a substantial issue.

**(c) Remand.** The district court may decide the motion if the court of appeals remands for that purpose.

## Rule 38. Staying a Sentence or a Disability

**(a) Death Sentence.** The court must stay a death sentence if the defendant appeals the conviction or sentence.

**(b) Imprisonment.**

**(1) *Stay Granted.*** If the defendant is released pending appeal, the court must stay a sentence of imprisonment.

**(2) *Stay Denied; Place of Confinement.*** If the defendant is not released pending appeal, the court may recommend to the Attorney General that the defendant be confined near the place of the trial or appeal for a period reasonably necessary to permit the defendant to assist in preparing the appeal.

**(c) Fine.** If the defendant appeals, the district court, or the court of appeals under Federal Rule of Appellate Procedure 8, may stay a sentence to pay a fine or a fine and costs. The court may stay the sentence on any terms considered appropriate and may require the defendant to:

**(1)**  deposit all or part of the fine and costs into the district court's registry pending appeal;

**(2)**  post a bond to pay the fine and costs; or

**(3)**  submit to an examination concerning the defendant's assets and, if appropriate, order the defendant to refrain from dissipating assets.

**(d) Probation.** If the defendant appeals, the court may stay a sentence of probation. The court must set the terms of any stay.

**(e) Restitution and Notice to Victims.**

**(1) *In General.*** If the defendant appeals, the district court, or the court of appeals under Federal Rule of Appellate Procedure 8, may stay—on any terms considered appropriate—any sentence providing for restitution under 18 U.S.C. § 3556 or notice under 18 U.S.C. § 3555.

**(2)** *Ensuring Compliance.* The court may issue any order reasonably necessary to ensure compliance with a restitution order or a notice order after disposition of an appeal, including:

(A) a restraining order;

(B) an injunction;

(C) an order requiring the defendant to deposit all or part of any monetary restitution into the district court's registry; or

(D) an order requiring the defendant to post a bond.

**(f) Forfeiture.** A stay of a forfeiture order is governed by Rule 32.2(d).

**(g) Disability.** If the defendant's conviction or sentence creates a civil or employment disability under federal law, the district court, or the court of appeals under Federal Rule of Appellate Procedure 8, may stay the disability pending appeal on any terms considered appropriate. The court may issue any order reasonably necessary to protect the interest represented by the disability pending appeal, including a restraining order or an injunction.

## Rule 39. [Reserved]

# TITLE VIII.   SUPPLEMENTARY AND SPECIAL PROCEEDINGS

## Rule 40. Arrest for Failing to Appear in Another District or for Violating Conditions of Release Set in Another District

**(a) In General.** A person must be taken without unnecessary delay before a magistrate judge in the district of arrest if the person has been arrested under a warrant issued in another district for:

(i) failing to appear as required by the terms of that person's release under 18 U.S.C. §§ 3141–3156 or by a subpoena; or

(ii) violating conditions of release set in another district.

**(b) Proceedings.** The judge must proceed under Rule 5(c)(3) as applicable.

**(c) Release or Detention Order.** The judge may modify any previous release or detention order issued in another district, but must state in writing the reasons for doing so.

**(d) Video Teleconferencing.** Video teleconferencing may be used to conduct an appearance under this rule if the defendant consents.

## Rule 41. Search and Seizure

**(a) Scope and Definitions.**

**(1) *Scope.*** This rule does not modify any statute regulating search or seizure, or the issuance and execution of a search warrant in special circumstances.

**(2) *Definitions.*** The following definitions apply under this rule:

(A) "Property" includes documents, books, papers, any other tangible objects, and information.

(B) "Daytime" means the hours between 6:00 a.m. and 10:00 p.m. according to local time.

(C) "Federal law enforcement officer" means a government agent (other than an attorney for the government) who is engaged in enforcing the criminal laws and is within any category of officers authorized by the Attorney General to request a search warrant.

(D) "Domestic terrorism" and "international terrorism" have the meanings set out in 18 U.S.C. § 2331.

(E) "Tracking device" has the meaning set out in 18 U.S.C. § 3117(b).

**(b) Venue for a Warrant Application.** At the request of a federal law enforcement officer or an attorney for the government:

**(1)** a magistrate judge with authority in the district—or if none is reasonably available, a judge of a state court of record in the district—has authority to issue a warrant to search for and seize a person or property located within the district;

**(2)** a magistrate judge with authority in the district has authority to issue a warrant for a person or property outside the district if the person or property is located within the district when the warrant is issued but might move or be moved outside the district before the warrant is executed;

**(3)** a magistrate judge—in an investigation of domestic terrorism or international terrorism—with authority in any district in which activities related to the terrorism may have occurred has authority to issue a warrant for a person or property within or outside that district;

**(4)** a magistrate judge with authority in the district has authority to issue a warrant to install within the district a tracking device; the warrant may authorize use of the device to track the movement of a person or property located within the district, outside the district, or both; and

**(5)** a magistrate judge having authority in any district where activities related to the crime may have occurred, or in the District of Columbia, may issue a warrant for property that is located outside the jurisdiction of any state or district, but within any of the following:

    (A) a United States territory, possession, or commonwealth;

    (B) the premises—no matter who owns them—of a United States diplomatic or consular mission in a foreign state, including any appurtenant building, part of a building, or land used for the mission's purposes; or

    (C) a residence and any appurtenant land owned or leased by the United States and used by United States personnel assigned to a United States diplomatic or consular mission in a foreign state.

**(6)** a magistrate judge with authority in any district where activities related to a crime may have occurred has authority to issue a warrant to use remote access to search electronic storage media and to seize or copy electronically stored information located within or outside that district if:

    (A) the district where the media or information is located has been concealed through technological means; or

    (B) in an investigation of a violation of 18 U.S.C. § 1030(a)(5), the media are protected computers that have been damaged without authorization and are located in five or more districts.

**(c) Persons or Property Subject to Search or Seizure.** A warrant may be issued for any of the following:

    **(1)** evidence of a crime;

    **(2)** contraband, fruits of crime, or other items illegally possessed;

    **(3)** property designed for use, intended for use, or used in committing a crime; or

    **(4)** a person to be arrested or a person who is unlawfully restrained.

**(d) Obtaining a Warrant.**

**(1)** *In General.* After receiving an affidavit or other information, a magistrate judge—or if authorized by Rule 41(b), a judge of a state court of record—must issue the warrant if there is probable cause to search for and seize a person or property or to install and use a tracking device.

**(2)** *Requesting a Warrant in the Presence of a Judge.*

(A) *Warrant on an Affidavit.* When a federal law enforcement officer or an attorney for the government presents an affidavit in support of a warrant, the judge may require the affiant to appear personally and may examine under oath the affiant and any witness the affiant produces.

(B) *Warrant on Sworn Testimony.* The judge may wholly or partially dispense with a written affidavit and base a warrant on sworn testimony if doing so is reasonable under the circumstances.

(C) *Recording Testimony.* Testimony taken in support of a warrant must be recorded by a court reporter or by a suitable recording device, and the judge must file the transcript or recording with the clerk, along with any affidavit.

**(3)** *Requesting a Warrant by Telephonic or Other Reliable Electronic Means.* In accordance with Rule 4.1, a magistrate judge may issue a warrant based on information communicated by telephone or other reliable electronic means.

**(e) Issuing the Warrant.**

**(1)** *In General.* The magistrate judge or a judge of a state court of record must issue the warrant to an officer authorized to execute it.

**(2)** *Contents of the Warrant.*

(A) *Warrant to Search for and Seize a Person or Property.* Except for a tracking-device warrant, the warrant must identify the person or property to be searched, identify any person or property to be seized, and designate the magistrate judge to whom it must be returned. The warrant must command the officer to:

(i) execute the warrant within a specified time no longer than 14 days;

(ii) execute the warrant during the daytime, unless the judge for good cause expressly authorizes execution at another time; and

(iii) return the warrant to the magistrate judge designated in the warrant.

(B) *Warrant Seeking Electronically Stored Information.* A warrant under Rule 41(e)(2)(A) may authorize the seizure of electronic storage media or the seizure or copying of electronically stored information. Unless otherwise specified, the warrant authorizes a later review of the media or information consistent with the warrant. The time for executing the warrant in Rule 41(e)(2)(A) and (f)(1)(A) refers to the seizure or on-site copying of the media or information, and not to any later off-site copying or review.

(C) *Warrant for a Tracking Device.* A tracking-device warrant must identify the person or property to be tracked, designate the magistrate judge to whom it must be returned, and specify a reasonable length of time that the device may be used. The time must not exceed 45 days from the date the warrant was issued. The court may, for good cause, grant one or more extensions for a reasonable period not to exceed 45 days each. The warrant must command the officer to:

(i) complete any installation authorized by the warrant within a specified time no longer than 10 days;

(ii) perform any installation authorized by the warrant during the daytime, unless the judge for good cause expressly authorizes installation at another time; and

(iii) return the warrant to the judge designated in the warrant.

**(f) Executing and Returning the Warrant.**

**(1) *Warrant to Search for and Seize a Person or Property.***

(A) *Noting the Time.* The officer executing the warrant must enter on it the exact date and time it was executed.

(B) *Inventory.* An officer present during the execution of the warrant must prepare and verify an inventory of any property seized. The officer must do so in the presence of another officer and the person from whom, or from whose premises, the property was taken. If either one is not present, the officer must prepare and verify the inventory in the presence of at least one other credible person. In a case involving the seizure of electronic storage media or the seizure or copying of electronically stored information, the inventory may be limited to describing the physical storage media that were seized or copied. The officer may retain a copy of the electronically stored information that was seized or copied.

(C) *Receipt.* The officer executing the warrant must give a copy of the warrant and a receipt for the property taken to the person from whom, or from whose premises, the property was taken or leave a copy of the warrant and receipt at the place where the officer took the property. For a warrant to use remote access to search electronic storage media and seize or copy electronically stored information, the officer must make reasonable efforts to serve a copy of the warrant and receipt on the person whose property was searched or who possessed the information that was seized or copied. Service may be accomplished by any means, including electronic means, reasonably calculated to reach that person.

(D) *Return.* The officer executing the warrant must promptly return it—together with a copy of the inventory—to the magistrate judge designated on the warrant. The officer may do so by reliable electronic means. The judge must, on request, give a copy of the inventory to the person from whom, or from whose premises, the property was taken and to the applicant for the warrant.

**(2) *Warrant for a Tracking Device.***

(A) *Noting the Time.* The officer executing a tracking-device warrant must enter on it the exact date and time the device was installed and the period during which it was used.

(B) *Return.* Within 10 days after the use of the tracking device has ended, the officer executing the warrant must return it to the judge designated in the warrant. The officer may do so by reliable electronic means.

(C) *Service.* Within 10 days after the use of the tracking device has ended, the officer executing a tracking-device warrant must serve a copy of the warrant on the person who was tracked or whose property was tracked. Service may be accomplished by delivering a copy to the person who, or whose property, was tracked; or by leaving a copy at the person's residence or usual place of abode with an individual of suitable age and discretion who resides at that location and by mailing a copy to the person's last known address. Upon request of the government, the judge may delay notice as provided in Rule 41(f)(3).

**(3) *Delayed Notice.*** Upon the government's request, a magistrate judge—or if authorized by Rule 41(b), a judge of a state court of record—may delay any notice required by this rule if the delay is authorized by statute.

**(g) Motion to Return Property.** A person aggrieved by an unlawful search and seizure of property or by the deprivation of property may move for the property's return. The motion must be filed in the district where the property was seized. The court must receive evidence on any factual issue necessary to decide the motion. If it grants the motion, the court must return the property to the movant, but may impose reasonable conditions to protect access to the property and its use in later proceedings.

**(h) Motion to Suppress.** A defendant may move to suppress evidence in the court where the trial will occur, as Rule 12 provides.

**(i) Forwarding Papers to the Clerk.** The magistrate judge to whom the warrant is returned must attach to the warrant a copy of the return, of the inventory, and of all other related papers and must deliver them to the clerk in the district where the property was seized.

## Rule 42. Criminal Contempt

**(a) Disposition After Notice.** Any person who commits criminal contempt may be punished for that contempt after prosecution on notice.

**(1)** *Notice.* The court must give the person notice in open court, in an order to show cause, or in an arrest order. The notice must:

(A) state the time and place of the trial;

(B) allow the defendant a reasonable time to prepare a defense; and

(C) state the essential facts constituting the charged criminal contempt and describe it as such.

**(2)** *Appointing a Prosecutor.* The court must request that the contempt be prosecuted by an attorney for the government, unless the interest of justice requires the appointment of another attorney. If the government declines the request, the court must appoint another attorney to prosecute the contempt.

**(3)** *Trial and Disposition.* A person being prosecuted for criminal contempt is entitled to a jury trial in any case in which federal law so provides and must be released or detained as Rule 46 provides. If the criminal contempt involves disrespect toward or criticism of a judge, that judge is disqualified from presiding at the contempt trial or hearing unless the defendant consents. Upon a finding or verdict of guilty, the court must impose the punishment.

**(b) Summary Disposition.** Notwithstanding any other provision of these rules, the court (other than a magistrate judge) may summarily punish a person who commits criminal contempt in its presence if the judge saw or heard the contemptuous conduct and so certifies; a magistrate judge may summarily punish a person as provided in 28 U.S.C. § 636(e). The contempt order must recite the facts, be signed by the judge, and be filed with the clerk.

## TITLE IX.   GENERAL PROVISIONS

### Rule 43. Defendant's Presence

**(a) When Required.** Unless this rule, Rule 5, or Rule 10 provides otherwise, the defendant must be present at:

    **(1)**  the initial appearance, the initial arraignment, and the plea;

    **(2)**  every trial stage, including jury impanelment and the return of the verdict; and

    **(3)**  sentencing.

**(b) When Not Required.** A defendant need not be present under any of the following circumstances:

    **(1)** *Organizational Defendant.* The defendant is an organization represented by counsel who is present.

    **(2)** *Misdemeanor Offense.* The offense is punishable by fine or by imprisonment for not more than one year, or both, and with the defendant's written consent, the court permits arraignment, plea, trial, and sentencing to occur by video teleconferencing or in the defendant's absence.

    **(3)** *Conference or Hearing on a Legal Question.* The proceeding involves only a conference or hearing on a question of law.

    **(4)** *Sentence Correction.* The proceeding involves the correction or reduction of sentence under Rule 35 or 18 U.S.C. § 3582(c).

**(c) Waiving Continued Presence.**

    **(1)** *In General.* A defendant who was initially present at trial, or who had pleaded guilty or nolo contendere, waives the right to be present under the following circumstances:

        **(A)**  when the defendant is voluntarily absent after the trial has begun, regardless of whether the court informed the defendant of an obligation to remain during trial;

        **(B)**  in a noncapital case, when the defendant is voluntarily absent during sentencing; or

(C) when the court warns the defendant that it will remove the defendant from the courtroom for disruptive behavior, but the defendant persists in conduct that justifies removal from the courtroom.

**(2) *Waiver's Effect.*** If the defendant waives the right to be present, the trial may proceed to completion, including the verdict's return and sentencing, during the defendant's absence.

### Rule 44. Right to and Appointment of Counsel

**(a) Right to Appointed Counsel.** A defendant who is unable to obtain counsel is entitled to have counsel appointed to represent the defendant at every stage of the proceeding from initial appearance through appeal, unless the defendant waives this right.

**(b) Appointment Procedure.** Federal law and local court rules govern the procedure for implementing the right to counsel.

**(c) Inquiry Into Joint Representation.**

**(1) *Joint Representation.*** Joint representation occurs when:

(A) two or more defendants have been charged jointly under Rule 8(b) or have been joined for trial under Rule 13; and

(B) the defendants are represented by the same counsel, or counsel who are associated in law practice.

**(2) *Court's Responsibilities in Cases of Joint Representation.*** The court must promptly inquire about the propriety of joint representation and must personally advise each defendant of the right to the effective assistance of counsel, including separate representation. Unless there is good cause to believe that no conflict of interest is likely to arise, the court must take appropriate measures to protect each defendant's right to counsel.

### Rule 45. Computing and Extending Time

**(a) Computing Time.** The following rules apply in computing any time period specified in these rules, in any local rule or court order, or in any statute that does not specify a method of computing time.

**(1) *Period Stated in Days or a Longer Unit.*** When the period is stated in days or a longer unit of time:

(A) exclude the day of the event that triggers the period;

(B) count every day, including intermediate Saturdays, Sundays, and legal holidays; and

(C) include the last day of the period, but if the last day is a Saturday, Sunday, or legal holiday, the period continues to run until the end of the next day that is not a Saturday, Sunday, or legal holiday.

**(2) *Period Stated in Hours.*** When the period is stated in hours:

(A) begin counting immediately on the occurrence of the event that triggers the period;

(B) count every hour, including hours during intermediate Saturdays, Sundays, and legal holidays; and

(C) if the period would end on a Saturday, Sunday, or legal holiday, the period continues to run until the same time on the next day that is not a Saturday, Sunday, or legal holiday.

**(3) *Inaccessibility of the Clerk's Office.*** Unless the court orders otherwise, if the clerk's office is inaccessible:

(A) on the last day for filing under Rule 45(a)(1), then the time for filing is extended to the first accessible day that is not a Saturday, Sunday, or legal holiday; or

(B) during the last hour for filing under Rule 45(a)(2), then the time for filing is extended to the same time on the first accessible day that is not a Saturday, Sunday, or legal holiday.

**(4) *"Last Day" Defined.*** Unless a different time is set by a statute, local rule, or court order, the last day ends:

(A) for electronic filing, at midnight in the court's time zone; and

(B) for filing by other means, when the clerk's office is scheduled to close.

**(5) *"Next Day" Defined.*** The "next day" is determined by continuing to count forward when the period is measured after an event and backward when measured before an event.

**(6) *"Legal Holiday" Defined.*** "Legal holiday" means:

(A) the day set aside by statute for observing New Year's Day, Martin Luther King Jr.'s Birthday, Washington's Birthday, Memorial Day, Independence Day, Labor Day, Columbus Day, Veterans' Day, Thanksgiving Day, or Christmas Day;

(B) any day declared a holiday by the President or Congress; and

(C) for periods that are measured after an event, any other day declared a holiday by the state where the district court is located.

**(b) Extending Time.**

**(1)** *In General.* When an act must or may be done within a specified period, the court on its own may extend the time, or for good cause may do so on a party's motion made:

(A) before the originally prescribed or previously extended time expires; or

(B) after the time expires if the party failed to act because of excusable neglect.

**(2)** *Exception.* The court may not extend the time to take any action under Rule 35, except as stated in that rule.

**(c) Additional Time After Certain Kinds of Service.** Whenever a party must or may act within a specified time after being served and service is made under Federal Rule of Civil Procedure 5(b)(2)(C) (mailing), (D) (leaving with the clerk), or (F) (other means consented to), 3 days are added after the period would otherwise expire under subdivision (a).[b]

## Rule 46. Release from Custody; Supervising Detention

**(a) Before Trial.** The provisions of 18 U.S.C. §§ 3142 and 3144 govern pretrial release.

**(b) During Trial.** A person released before trial continues on release during trial under the same terms and conditions. But the court may order different terms and conditions or terminate the release if necessary to ensure that the person will be present during trial or that the person's conduct will not obstruct the orderly and expeditious progress of the trial.

**(c) Pending Sentencing or Appeal.** The provisions of 18 U.S.C. § 3143 govern release pending sentencing or appeal. The burden of establishing that the defendant will not flee or pose a danger to any other person or to the community rests with the defendant.

---

[b] Editor's Note: On December 1, 2018, the following changes to Criminal Rule 45(c) will go into effect. New material is underlined and deleted material is struck through.

(c) Additional Time After Certain Kinds of Service. Whenever a party must or may act within a specified time after being served and service is made under ~~Federal~~ Rule ~~of Civil Procedure~~ 49(a)(4)(C), (D), and (E)~~5(b)(2)(C) (mailing), (D) (leaving with the clerk), or (F) (other means consented to)~~, 3 days are added after the period would otherwise expire under subdivision (a).

**(d) Pending Hearing on a Violation of Probation or Supervised Release.** Rule 32.1(a)(6) governs release pending a hearing on a violation of probation or supervised release.

**(e) Surety.** The court must not approve a bond unless any surety appears to be qualified. Every surety, except a legally approved corporate surety, must demonstrate by affidavit that its assets are adequate. The court may require the affidavit to describe the following:

**(1)** the property that the surety proposes to use as security;

**(2)** any encumbrance on that property;

**(3)** the number and amount of any other undischarged bonds and bail undertakings the surety has issued; and

**(4)** any other liability of the surety.

**(f) Bail Forfeiture.**

**(1)** *Declaration.* The court must declare the bail forfeited if a condition of the bond is breached.

**(2)** *Setting Aside.* The court may set aside in whole or in part a bail forfeiture upon any condition the court may impose if:

(A) the surety later surrenders into custody the person released on the surety's appearance bond; or

(B) it appears that justice does not require bail forfeiture.

**(3)** *Enforcement.*

(A) *Default Judgment and Execution.* If it does not set aside a bail forfeiture, the court must, upon the government's motion, enter a default judgment.

(B) *Jurisdiction and Service.* By entering into a bond, each surety submits to the district court's jurisdiction and irrevocably appoints the district clerk as its agent to receive service of any filings affecting its liability.

(C) *Motion to Enforce.* The court may, upon the government's motion, enforce the surety's liability without an independent action. The government must serve any motion, and notice as the court prescribes, on the district clerk. If so served, the clerk must promptly mail a copy to the surety at its last known address.

**(4)** *Remission.* After entering a judgment under Rule 46(f)(3), the court may remit in whole or in part the judgment under the same conditions specified in Rule 46(f)(2).

**(g) Exoneration.** The court must exonerate the surety and release any bail when a bond condition has been satisfied or when the court has set aside or remitted the forfeiture. The court must exonerate a surety who deposits cash in the amount of the bond or timely surrenders the defendant into custody.

**(h) Supervising Detention Pending Trial.**

**(1) *In General.*** To eliminate unnecessary detention, the court must supervise the detention within the district of any defendants awaiting trial and of any persons held as material witnesses.

**(2) *Reports.*** An attorney for the government must report biweekly to the court, listing each material witness held in custody for more than 10 days pending indictment, arraignment, or trial. For each material witness listed in the report, an attorney for the government must state why the witness should not be released with or without a deposition being taken under Rule 15(a).

**(i) Forfeiture of Property.** The court may dispose of a charged offense by ordering the forfeiture of 18 U.S.C. § 3142(c)(1)(B)(xi) property under 18 U.S.C. § 3146(d), if a fine in the amount of the property's value would be an appropriate sentence for the charged offense.

**(j) Producing a Statement.**

**(1) *In General.*** Rule 26.2(a)–(d) and (f) applies at a detention hearing under 18 U.S.C. § 3142, unless the court for good cause rules otherwise.

**(2) *Sanctions for Not Producing a Statement.*** If a party disobeys a Rule 26.2 order to produce a witness's statement, the court must not consider that witness's testimony at the detention hearing.

**Rule 47. Motions and Supporting Affidavits**

**(a) In General.** A party applying to the court for an order must do so by motion.

**(b) Form and Content of a Motion.** A motion—except when made during a trial or hearing—must be in writing, unless the court permits the party to make the motion by other means. A motion must state the grounds on which it is based and the relief or order sought. A motion may be supported by affidavit.

**(c) Timing of a Motion.** A party must serve a written motion—other than one that the court may hear ex parte—and any hearing notice at least 7 days before the hearing date, unless a rule or court order sets a different period. For good cause, the court may set a different period upon ex parte application.

**(d) Affidavit Supporting a Motion.** The moving party must serve any supporting affidavit with the motion. A responding party must serve any opposing affidavit at least one day before the hearing, unless the court permits later service.

## Rule 48. Dismissal

**(a) By the Government.** The government may, with leave of court, dismiss an indictment, information, or complaint. The government may not dismiss the prosecution during trial without the defendant's consent.

**(b) By the Court.** The court may dismiss an indictment, information, or complaint if unnecessary delay occurs in:

> **(1)** presenting a charge to a grand jury;
>
> **(2)** filing an information against a defendant; or
>
> **(3)** bringing a defendant to trial.

## Rule 49. Serving and Filing Papers[c]

---

[c]  Editor's Note: On December 1, 2018, the following changes to Criminal Rule 49 will go into effect. New material is underlined and deleted material is struck through:
**Rule 49. Serving and Filing Papers**
(a) Service on a Party.
     (1) *What isWhen Required.* A party must serve on every other partyEach of the following must be served on every party: any written motion (other than one to be heard ex parte), written notice, designation of the record on appeal, or similar paper.
(b) How Made. Service must be made in the manner provided for a civil action.
     (2) *Serving a Party's Attorney.* Unless the court orders otherwise, Wwhen these rules or a court order requires or permits service on a party represented by an attorney, service must be made on the attorney instead of the party, unless the court orders otherwise.
     (3) *Service by Electronic Means.*
          (A) *Using the Court's Electronic-Filing System.* A party represented by an attorney may serve a paper on a registered user by filing it with the court's electronic-filing system. A party not represented by an attorney may do so only if allowed by court order or local rule. Service is complete upon filing, but is not effective if the serving party learns that it did not reach the person to be served.
          (B) *Using Other Electronic Means.* A paper may be served by any other electronic means that the person consented to in writing. Service is complete upon transmission, but is not effective if the serving party learns that it did not reach the person to be served.
     (4) *Service by Nonelectronic Means.* A paper may be served by:
          (A) handing it to the person;
          (B) leaving it:
               (i)  at the person's office with a clerk or other person in charge or, if no one is in charge, in a conspicuous place in the office; or
               (ii)  if the person has no office or the office is closed, at the person's dwelling or usual place of abode with someone of suitable age and discretion who resides there;
          (C) mailing it to the person's last known address—in which event service is complete upon mailing;
          (D) leaving it with the court clerk if the person has no known address; or

**(a) When Required.** A party must serve on every other party any written motion (other than one to be heard ex parte), written notice, designation of the record on appeal, or similar paper.

-----------------------------------

(E) delivering it by any other means that the person consented to in writing—in which event service is complete when the person making service delivers it to the agency designated to make delivery.

**(b) Filing.**

**(1) *When Required; Certificate of Service.*** Any paper that is required to be served must be filed no later than a reasonable time after service. No certificate of service is required when a paper is served by filing it with the court's electronic-filing system. When a paper is served by other means, a certificate of service must be filed with it or within a reasonable time after service or filing.

**(2) Means of Filing.**

(A) *Electronically.* A paper is filed electronically by filing it with the court's electronic-filing system. A filing made through a person's electronic-filing account and authorized by that person, together with the person's name on a signature block, constitutes the person's signature. A paper filed electronically is written or in writing under these rules.

(B) *Nonelectronically.* A paper not filed electronically is filed by delivering it:

(i)    to the clerk; or

(ii)    to a judge who agrees to accept it for filing, and who must then note the filing date on the paper and promptly send it to the clerk.

**(3) Means Used by Represented and Unrepresented Parties.**

(A) *Represented Party.* A party represented by an attorney must file electronically, unless nonelectronic filing is allowed by the court for good cause or is allowed or required by local rule.

(B) *Unrepresented Party.* A party not represented by an attorney must file nonelectronically, unless allowed to file electronically by court order or local rule.

**(4) *Signature.*** Every written motion and other paper must be signed by at least one attorney of record in the attorney's name—or by a person filing a paper if the person is not represented by an attorney. The paper must state the signer's address, e-mail address, and telephone number. Unless a rule or statute specifically states otherwise, a pleading need not be verified or accompanied by an affidavit. The court must strike an unsigned paper unless the omission is promptly corrected after being called to the attorney's or person's attention.

**(5) *Acceptance by the Clerk.*** The clerk must not refuse to file a paper solely because it is not in the form prescribed by these rules or by a local rule or practice.

**(c)   Service and Filing by Nonparties.** A nonparty may serve and file a paper only if doing so is required or permitted by law. A nonparty must serve every party as required by Rule 49(a), but may use the court's electronic-filing system only if allowed by court order or local rule.

~~(e)~~(d) **Notice of a Court Order.** When the court issues an order on any post-arraignment motion, the clerk must ~~provide notice in a manner provided for in a civil action~~serve notice of the entry on each party as required by Rule 49(a). A party also may serve notice of the entry by the same means. Except as Federal Rule of Appellate Procedure 4(b) provides otherwise, the clerk's failure to give notice does not affect the time to appeal, or relieve—or authorize the court to relieve—a party's failure to appeal within the allowed time.

~~(d)   Filing. A party must file with the court a copy of any paper the party is required to serve. A paper must be filed in a manner provided for in a civil action.~~

~~(e)   Electronic Service and Filing. A court may, by local rule, allow papers to be filed, signed, or verified by electronic means that are consistent with any technical standards established by the Judicial Conference of the United States. A local rule may require electronic filing only if reasonable exceptions are allowed. A paper filed electronically in compliance with a local rule is written or in writing under these rules.~~

**(b)  How Made.** Service must be made in the manner provided for a civil action. When these rules or a court order requires or permits service on a party represented by an attorney, service must be made on the attorney instead of the party, unless the court orders otherwise.

**(c)  Notice of a Court Order.** When the court issues an order on any post-arraignment motion, the clerk must provide notice in a manner provided for in a civil action. Except as Federal Rule of Appellate Procedure 4(b) provides otherwise, the clerk's failure to give notice does not affect the time to appeal, or relieve—or authorize the court to relieve—a party's failure to appeal within the allowed time.

**(d)  Filing.** A party must file with the court a copy of any paper the party is required to serve. A paper must be filed in a manner provided for in a civil action.

**(e)  Electronic Service and Filing.** A court may, by local rule, allow papers to be filed, signed, or verified by electronic means that are consistent with any technical standards established by the Judicial Conference of the United States. A local rule may require electronic filing only if reasonable exceptions are allowed. A paper filed electronically in compliance with a local rule is written or in writing under these rules.

## Rule 49.1. Privacy Protection for Filings Made with the Court

**(a)  Redacted Filings.** Unless the court orders otherwise, in an electronic or paper filing with the court that contains an individual's social-security number, taxpayer-identification number, or birth date, the name of an individual known to be a minor, a financial-account number, or the home address of an individual, a party or nonparty making the filing may include only:

**(1)**  the last four digits of the social-security number and taxpayer-identification number;

**(2)**  the year of the individual's birth;

**(3)**  the minor's initials;

**(4)**  the last four digits of the financial-account number; and

**(5)**  the city and state of the home address.

**(b)  Exemptions from the Redaction Requirement.** The redaction requirement does not apply to the following:

**(1)**  a financial-account number or real property address that identifies the property allegedly subject to forfeiture in a forfeiture proceeding;

**(2)**  the record of an administrative or agency proceeding;

**(3)** the official record of a state-court proceeding;

**(4)** the record of a court or tribunal, if that record was not subject to the redaction requirement when originally filed;

**(5)** a filing covered by Rule 49.1(d);

**(6)** a pro se filing in an action brought under 28 U.S.C. §§ 2241, 2254, or 2255;

**(7)** a court filing that is related to a criminal matter or investigation and that is prepared before the filing of a criminal charge or is not filed as part of any docketed criminal case;

**(8)** an arrest or search warrant; and

**(9)** a charging document and an affidavit filed in support of any charging document.

**(c) Immigration Cases.** A filing in an action brought under 28 U.S.C. § 2241 that relates to the petitioner's immigration rights is governed by Federal Rule of Civil Procedure 5.2.

**(d) Filings Made Under Seal.** The court may order that a filing be made under seal without redaction. The court may later unseal the filing or order the person who made the filing to file a redacted version for the public record.

**(e) Protective Orders.** For good cause, the court may by order in a case:

**(1)** require redaction of additional information; or

**(2)** limit or prohibit a nonparty's remote electronic access to a document filed with the court.

**(f) Option for Additional Unredacted Filing Under Seal.** A person making a redacted filing may also file an unredacted copy under seal. The court must retain the unredacted copy as part of the record.

**(g) Option for Filing a Reference List.** A filing that contains redacted information may be filed together with a reference list that identifies each item of redacted information and specifies an appropriate identifier that uniquely corresponds to each item listed. The list must be filed under seal and may be amended as of right. Any reference in the case to a listed identifier will be construed to refer to the corresponding item of information.

**(h) Waiver of Protection of Identifiers.** A person waives the protection of Rule 49.1(a) as to the person's own information by filing it without redaction and not under seal.

## Rule 50. Prompt Disposition

Scheduling preference must be given to criminal proceedings as far as practicable.

## Rule 51. Preserving Claimed Error

**(a) Exceptions Unnecessary.** Exceptions to rulings or orders of the court are unnecessary.

**(b) Preserving a Claim of Error.** A party may preserve a claim of error by informing the court—when the court ruling or order is made or sought—of the action the party wishes the court to take, or the party's objection to the court's action and the grounds for that objection. If a party does not have an opportunity to object to a ruling or order, the absence of an objection does not later prejudice that party. A ruling or order that admits or excludes evidence is governed by Federal Rule of Evidence 103.

## Rule 52. Harmless and Plain Error

**(a) Harmless Error.** Any error, defect, irregularity, or variance that does not affect substantial rights must be disregarded.

**(b) Plain Error.** A plain error that affects substantial rights may be considered even though it was not brought to the court's attention.

## Rule 53. Courtroom Photographing and Broadcasting Prohibited

Except as otherwise provided by a statute or these rules, the court must not permit the taking of photographs in the courtroom during judicial proceedings or the broadcasting of judicial proceedings from the courtroom.

## Rule 54. [Transferred]

**[Editor's Note: In the 2002 restyling of the Criminal Rules, all of Rule 54 was transferred to Rule 1.]**

## Rule 55. Records

The clerk of the district court must keep records of criminal proceedings in the form prescribed by the Director of the Administrative Office of the United States courts. The clerk must enter in the records every court order or judgment and the date of entry.

## Rule 56. When Court is Open

**(a) In General.** A district court is considered always open for any filing, and for issuing and returning process, making a motion, or entering an order.

**(b) Office Hours.** The clerk's office—with the clerk or a deputy in attendance—must be open during business hours on all days except Saturdays, Sundays, and legal holidays.

**(c) Special Hours.** A court may provide by local rule or order that its clerk's office will be open for specified hours on Saturdays or legal holidays other than those set aside by statute for observing New Year's Day, Martin Luther King, Jr.'s Birthday, Washington's Birthday, Memorial Day, Independence Day, Labor Day, Columbus Day, Veterans' Day, Thanksgiving Day, and Christmas Day.

## Rule 57. District Court Rules

**(a) In General.**

**(1)** *Adopting Local Rules.* Each district court acting by a majority of its district judges may, after giving appropriate public notice and an opportunity to comment, make and amend rules governing its practice. A local rule must be consistent with—but not duplicative of—federal statutes and rules adopted under 28 U.S.C. § 2072 and must conform to any uniform numbering system prescribed by the Judicial Conference of the United States.

**(2)** *Limiting Enforcement.* A local rule imposing a requirement of form must not be enforced in a manner that causes a party to lose rights because of an unintentional failure to comply with the requirement.

**(b) Procedure When There Is No Controlling Law.** A judge may regulate practice in any manner consistent with federal law, these rules, and the local rules of the district. No sanction or other disadvantage may be imposed for noncompliance with any requirement not in federal law, federal rules, or the local district rules unless the alleged violator was furnished with actual notice of the requirement before the noncompliance.

**(c) Effective Date and Notice.** A local rule adopted under this rule takes effect on the date specified by the district court and remains in effect unless amended by the district court or abrogated by the judicial council of the circuit in which the district is located. Copies of local rules and their amendments, when promulgated, must be furnished to the judicial council and the Administrative Office of the United States Courts and must be made available to the public.

### Rule 58. Petty Offenses and Other Misdemeanors

**(a) Scope.**

**(1) *In General.*** These rules apply in petty offense and other misdemeanor cases and on appeal to a district judge in a case tried by a magistrate judge, unless this rule provides otherwise.

**(2) *Petty Offense Case Without Imprisonment.*** In a case involving a petty offense for which no sentence of imprisonment will be imposed, the court may follow any provision of these rules that is not inconsistent with this rule and that the court considers appropriate.

**(3) *Definition.*** As used in this rule, the term "petty offense for which no sentence of imprisonment will be imposed" means a petty offense for which the court determines that, in the event of conviction, no sentence of imprisonment will be imposed.

**(b) Pretrial Procedure.**

**(1) *Charging Document.*** The trial of a misdemeanor may proceed on an indictment, information, or complaint. The trial of a petty offense may also proceed on a citation or violation notice.

**(2) *Initial Appearance.*** At the defendant's initial appearance on a petty offense or other misdemeanor charge, the magistrate judge must inform the defendant of the following:

(A)  the charge, and the minimum and maximum penalties, including imprisonment, fines, any special assessment under 18 U.S.C. § 3013, and restitution under 18 U.S.C. § 3556;

(B)  the right to retain counsel;

(C)  the right to request the appointment of counsel if the defendant is unable to retain counsel—unless the charge is a petty offense for which the appointment of counsel is not required;

(D)  the defendant's right not to make a statement, and that any statement made may be used against the defendant;

(E)  the right to trial, judgment, and sentencing before a district judge—unless:

(i)   the charge is a petty offense; or

(ii)  the defendant consents to trial, judgment, and sentencing before a magistrate judge;

(F)  the right to a jury trial before either a magistrate judge or a district judge—unless the charge is a petty offense;

(G) any right to a preliminary hearing under Rule 5.1, and the general circumstances, if any, under which the defendant may secure pretrial release; and

(H) that a defendant who is not a United States citizen may request that an attorney for the government or a federal law enforcement official notify a consular officer from the defendant's country of nationality that the defendant has been arrested—but that even without the defendant's request, a treaty or other international agreement may require consular notification.

**(3)** *Arraignment.*

(A) *Plea Before a Magistrate Judge.* A magistrate judge may take the defendant's plea in a petty offense case. In every other misdemeanor case, a magistrate judge may take the plea only if the defendant consents either in writing or on the record to be tried before a magistrate judge and specifically waives trial before a district judge. The defendant may plead not guilty, guilty, or (with the consent of the magistrate judge) nolo contendere.

(B) *Failure to Consent.* Except in a petty offense case, the magistrate judge must order a defendant who does not consent to trial before a magistrate judge to appear before a district judge for further proceedings.

**(c) Additional Procedures in Certain Petty Offense Cases.** The following procedures also apply in a case involving a petty offense for which no sentence of imprisonment will be imposed:

**(1)** *Guilty or Nolo Contendere Plea.* The court must not accept a guilty or nolo contendere plea unless satisfied that the defendant understands the nature of the charge and the maximum possible penalty.

**(2)** *Waiving Venue.*

(A) *Conditions of Waiving Venue.* If a defendant is arrested, held, or present in a district different from the one where the indictment, information, complaint, citation, or violation notice is pending, the defendant may state in writing a desire to plead guilty or nolo contendere; to waive venue and trial in the district where the proceeding is pending; and to consent to the court's disposing of the case in the district where the defendant was arrested, is held, or is present.

(B) *Effect of Waiving Venue.* Unless the defendant later pleads not guilty, the prosecution will proceed in the district where the defendant was arrested, is held, or is present. The district clerk must notify the clerk in the original district of the defendant's waiver of venue. The defendant's statement of a desire to plead guilty or nolo contendere is not admissible against the defendant.

**(3)** *Sentencing.* The court must give the defendant an opportunity to be heard in mitigation and then proceed immediately to sentencing. The court may, however, postpone sentencing to allow the probation service to investigate or to permit either party to submit additional information.

**(4)** *Notice of a Right to Appeal.* After imposing sentence in a case tried on a not-guilty plea, the court must advise the defendant of a right to appeal the conviction and of any right to appeal the sentence. If the defendant was convicted on a plea of guilty or nolo contendere, the court must advise the defendant of any right to appeal the sentence.

**(d) Paying a Fixed Sum in Lieu of Appearance.**

**(1)** *In General.* If the court has a local rule governing forfeiture of collateral, the court may accept a fixed-sum payment in lieu of the defendant's appearance and end the case, but the fixed sum may not exceed the maximum fine allowed by law.

**(2)** *Notice to Appear.* If the defendant fails to pay a fixed sum, request a hearing, or appear in response to a citation or violation notice, the district clerk or a magistrate judge may issue a notice for the defendant to appear before the court on a date certain. The notice may give the defendant an additional opportunity to pay a fixed sum in lieu of appearance. The district clerk must serve the notice on the defendant by mailing a copy to the defendant's last known address.

**(3)** *Summons or Warrant.* Upon an indictment, or upon a showing by one of the other charging documents specified in Rule 58(b)(1) of probable cause to believe that an offense has been committed and that the defendant has committed it, the court may issue an arrest warrant or, if no warrant is requested by an attorney for the government, a summons. The showing of probable cause must be made under oath or under penalty of perjury, but the affiant need not appear before the court. If the defendant fails to appear before the court in response to a summons, the court may summarily issue a warrant for the defendant's arrest.

**(e) Recording the Proceedings.** The court must record any proceedings under this rule by using a court reporter or a suitable recording device.

**(f) New Trial.** Rule 33 applies to a motion for a new trial.

**(g) Appeal.**

**(1)** *From a District Judge's Order or Judgment.* The Federal Rules of Appellate Procedure govern an appeal from a district judge's order or a judgment of conviction or sentence.

**(2)** *From a Magistrate Judge's Order or Judgment.*

(A) *Interlocutory Appeal.* Either party may appeal an order of a magistrate judge to a district judge within 14 days of its entry if a district judge's order could similarly be appealed. The party appealing must file a notice with the clerk specifying the order being appealed and must serve a copy on the adverse party.

(B) *Appeal from a Conviction or Sentence.* A defendant may appeal a magistrate judge's judgment of conviction or sentence to a district judge within 14 days of its entry. To appeal, the defendant must file a notice with the clerk specifying the judgment being appealed and must serve a copy on an attorney for the government.

(C) *Record.* The record consists of the original papers and exhibits in the case; any transcript, tape, or other recording of the proceedings; and a certified copy of the docket entries. For purposes of the appeal, a copy of the record of the proceedings must be made available to a defendant who establishes by affidavit an inability to pay or give security for the record. The Director of the Administrative Office of the United States Courts must pay for those copies.

(D) *Scope of Appeal.* The defendant is not entitled to a trial de novo by a district judge. The scope of the appeal is the same as in an appeal to the court of appeals from a judgment entered by a district judge.

**(3)** *Stay of Execution and Release Pending Appeal.* Rule 38 applies to a stay of a judgment of conviction or sentence. The court may release the defendant pending appeal under the law relating to release pending appeal from a district court to a court of appeals.

## Rule 59. Matters Before a Magistrate Judge

**(a) Nondispositive Matters.** A district judge may refer to a magistrate judge for determination any matter that does not dispose of a charge or defense. The magistrate judge must promptly conduct the required proceedings and, when appropriate, enter on the record an oral or written order stating the determination. A party may serve and file objections to the order within 14 days after being served with a copy of a written order or after the oral order is stated on the record, or at some other time the court sets. The district judge must consider timely objections and modify or set aside any part of the order that is contrary to law or clearly erroneous. Failure to object in accordance with this rule waives a party's right to review.

**(b) Dispositive Matters.**

**(1)** *Referral to Magistrate Judge.* A district judge may refer to a magistrate judge for recommendation a defendant's motion to dismiss or quash an indictment or information, a motion to suppress evidence, or any matter that may dispose of a charge or defense. The magistrate judge must promptly conduct the required proceedings. A record must be made of any evidentiary proceeding and of any other proceeding if the magistrate judge considers it necessary. The magistrate judge must enter on the record a recommendation for disposing of the matter, including any proposed findings of fact. The clerk must immediately serve copies on all parties.

**(2)** *Objections to Findings and Recommendations.* Within 14 days after being served with a copy of the recommended disposition, or at some other time the court sets, a party may serve and file specific written objections to the proposed findings and recommendations. Unless the district judge directs otherwise, the objecting party must promptly arrange for transcribing the record, or whatever portions of it the parties agree to or the magistrate judge considers sufficient. Failure to object in accordance with this rule waives a party's right to review.

**(3)** *De Novo Review of Recommendations.* The district judge must consider de novo any objection to the magistrate judge's recommendation. The district judge may accept, reject, or modify the recommendation, receive further evidence, or resubmit the matter to the magistrate judge with instructions.

**Rule 60. Victim's Rights**

**(a) In General.**

**(1)** *Notice of a Proceeding.* The government must use its best efforts to give the victim reasonable, accurate, and timely notice of any public court proceeding involving the crime.

**(2)** *Attending the Proceeding.* The court must not exclude a victim from a public court proceeding involving the crime, unless the court determines by clear and convincing evidence that the victim's testimony would be materially altered if the victim heard other testimony at that proceeding. In determining whether to exclude a victim, the court must make every effort to permit the fullest attendance possible by the victim and must consider reasonable alternatives to exclusion. The reasons for any exclusion must be clearly stated on the record.

**(3)** ***Right to Be Heard on Release, a Plea, or Sentencing.*** The court must permit a victim to be reasonably heard at any public proceeding in the district court concerning release, plea, or sentencing involving the crime.

**(b) Enforcement and Limitations.**

**(1)** ***Time for Deciding a Motion.*** The court must promptly decide any motion asserting a victim's rights described in these rules.

**(2)** ***Who May Assert the Rights.*** A victim's rights described in these rules may be asserted by the victim, the victim's lawful representative, the attorney for the government, or any other person as authorized by 18 U.S.C. § 3771(d) and (e).

**(3)** ***Multiple Victims.*** If the court finds that the number of victims makes it impracticable to accord all of them their rights described in these rules, the court must fashion a reasonable procedure that gives effect to these rights without unduly complicating or prolonging the proceedings.

**(4)** ***Where Rights May Be Asserted.*** A victim's rights described in these rules must be asserted in the district where a defendant is being prosecuted for the crime.

**(5)** ***Limitations on Relief.*** A victim may move to reopen a plea or sentence only if:

(A) the victim asked to be heard before or during the proceeding at issue, and the request was denied;

(B) the victim petitions the court of appeals for a writ of mandamus within 10 days after the denial, and the writ is granted; and

(C) in the case of a plea, the accused has not pleaded to the highest offense charged.

**(6)** ***No New Trial.*** A failure to afford a victim any right described in these rules is not grounds for a new trial.

## Rule 61. Title

These rules may be known and cited as the Federal Rules of Criminal Procedure.